(005

Love Brian

Travels with Farley

Travels *with* *Farley*

CLAIRE MOWAT

KEY PORTER BOOKS

Library and Archives Canada Cataloguing in Publication

Mowat, Claire
  Travels with Farley : a memoir / Claire Mowat.

ISBN 1-55263-714-X

1. Mowat, Claire. 2. Mowat, Farley, 1921–. 3. Authors' spouses—Canada—Biography. 4. Authors, Canadian (English)—20th century—Biography. I. Title.

PS8576.O985Z474 2005   C813'.54   C2005-902647

The publisher gratefully acknowledges the support of the Canada Council for the Arts and the Ontario Arts Council for its publishing program. We acknowledge the support of the Government of Ontario through the Ontario Media Development Corporation's Ontario Book Initiative.

We acknowledge the financial support of the Government of Canada through the Book Publishing Industry Development Program (BPIDP) for our publishing activities.

Key Porter Books Limited
Six Adelaide Street East, Tenth Floor
Toronto, Ontario
Canada M5C 1H6

www.keyporter.com

Text design: Peter Maher
Map: John Lightoot
Electronic formatting: Jean Lightfoot Peters

Printed and bound in Canada

05 06 07 08 09 5 4 3 2 1

This book is dedicated to
the memory of
JACK MCCLELLAND, 1922–2004
and
PETER DAVISON, 1928–2004

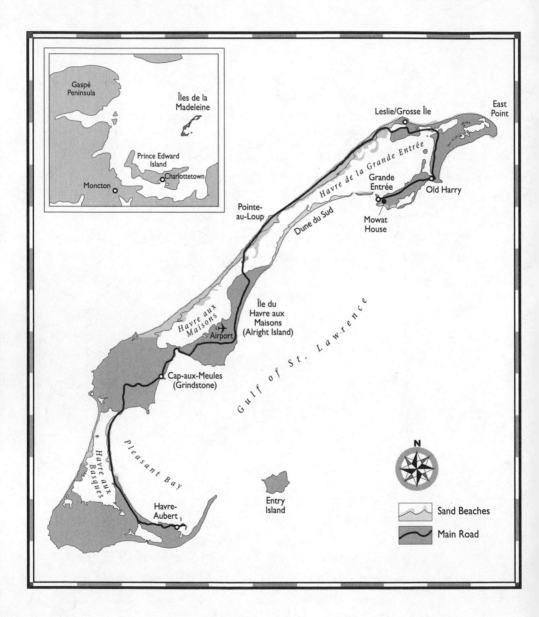

Chapter One

ON A BRIGHT DAY IN MAY, 1969, the Dart Herald airplane departing from Charlottetown for the Magdalens was only half full. Most of the passengers were speaking quietly to one another in French. Across the aisle, a grey-haired woman was trying to amuse a fidgeting child with a brace on one of her skinny legs—in English. They must surely live in the Magdalen Islands, I thought to myself. Why else would they be on this flight? Perhaps they had gone to some mainland city to see a doctor. Why were any of these people heading out that morning to a speck of land in the middle of the Gulf of St. Lawrence? I knew why we were there—to make a film for the CBC. I passed the time guessing about the circumstances of the others.

It wasn't a long flight. After half an hour we could see a string of green islands linked by long ribbons of white sand floating in the dark blue water. From the air it resembled a tropical atoll, as if we had flown south instead of north and could expect to see palm trees when we landed. Whenever we flew anywhere together Farley always sat in the seat by the window, while I preferred the aisle. He relished looking down on the world from a great height. I didn't. I liked to view the planet with my feet planted firmly on the ground.

As we left the plane and stepped onto the tarmac, I spotted a tiny terminal building in the midst of what looked like an untended pasture. The terminal was no bigger than a suburban living room and was jammed with noisy people whose voices drowned out a muffled departure announcement, in French, coming from a scratchy sound system.

We shoved our way through the babbling crowd to retrieve our luggage, and I called to Farley over the din. "Where on earth is everyone going?"

He looked around. "God knows! They can't all be flying out. The plane only holds a couple of dozen. Maybe they're here just for the fun of it...to see who's arrived and who's leaving."

Ten people boarded the plane for the return flight to Charlottetown and as soon as it had taken off, the crowd straggled outside to their parked vehicles and drove away. The show was over. We felt abandoned beside an airstrip with nothing in sight but distant sand dunes. The fellow who sold tickets had closed his wicket and disappeared. The only person still in the building was a taxi driver, who looked at us hopefully. Farley nodded at him and we soon found ourselves in the back seat of his battered old Chevy. I told him, in French, that we were looking for a good hotel.

As we rolled along a two-lane highway I stared out the window at this unfamiliar landscape and pondered the unexpected turn of events that had brought us here. Two months earlier I had been a patient in the Port Hope and District Hospital in eastern Ontario. I was still haunted by the memory of the doctor standing at the foot of my bed in the grey dawn of a cold Saturday in March.

"If you could have held on for a couple more weeks…the baby would have had a chance."

I knew what he was telling me. He had been up most of the night tending to me and to the boy who had lived for only an hour. I knew my baby had died. However drugged and delirious I had been, I had known it was too early to give birth. The baby had been far too small and there had been no cry, no sound at all, only the voices of the nurses trying to be kind to me.

Farley and I had been living in Port Hope, an hour's drive east of Toronto, for a little over a year. Our first five years together had been spent in Burgeo, an outport on the southwest coast of Newfoundland. When we reluctantly accepted that we would, for a variety of reasons, have to move back to the world we thought we had left behind, we had chosen the pretty and rather old-fashioned town of Port Hope, mainly because Farley's mother lived there. We had visited her many times, and we found the town to be a reasonable compromise between our rustic outport life and the hustle and bustle of Toronto, the centre of Canadian publishing.

I was lucky, I reflected, that this disaster had happened to me in the Port Hope hospital. I was lucky that modern medicine existed. My mother's mother had died at the age of thirty-five from complications following childbirth. I was still alive, after two operations to stop the bleeding.

In the days that followed Farley did his best to cheer me. When he came to visit he told me about the antics of our two dogs, Albert and Victoria, which was better than talking about how sorry our mothers, relatives, friends, and neighbours were to hear what had happened.

"Remember Gerry, from CBC television?" he asked the day before I was to leave the hospital. "He wants me to write the script for a documentary they plan to do about lobster fishing on the East Coast."

"And do you want to do it?" I asked.

"I might give it a try...if you come with me, that is. I'd have to do a search for a suitable location...a couple of months from now."

Farley was doing his best to distract me with the prospect of a journey. We both loved the East Coast of Canada, although at that moment I didn't want to consider going anywhere. I also knew I had to get on with my life, no matter what fate had befallen me.

"I was considering the Magdalen Islands," he went on. "Remember how you said you wanted to see what they were like?"

"The Magdalen Islands," I repeated, trying to muster some enthusiasm. "Sure. That could be interesting."

And so it was that, two months later, I found myself in the back of a taxi, barrelling along a narrow highway to the nearest town in the Magdalens. Our taxi driver was a short, heavyset man with a wide mustache and a garrulous personality. He spoke English with a French accent. When we told him this was our first visit to these islands he was eager to tell us that he had been born and raised here, although he had worked away for twenty years in a mine in Noranda in northwestern Quebec. He never planned to leave again. He owned his own home in a local community called Fatima. His wife was very happy to be back. Four of his children were living here, and he hoped that the daughter who had left to work in Montreal would one day return. He wanted us to know he was driving us to the best hotel in Les Îles de la Madeleine. It housed the best restaurant on the islands. We were certain to be content there, he promised. When he let us off, he wished us good luck.

Although it had no Scots affinity, the hotel was called The Aberdeen. It was a two-storey wooden building with the decor of a budget-priced motel anywhere in Canada. We checked in, left our luggage in our no-frills bedroom, and headed downstairs to the basement for lunch in "the best restaurant on the islands." As we later discovered it was, in 1969, the *only* one.

We dined on unremarkable cheeseburgers and *patates frites*. When I scanned the dessert menu I found a choice of Jell-O, *crème glacée*, *tarte-aux-pommes*, and a mysterious item called *beigne-aux-miel*.

"Eet ees a leetle cake weet 'oney," our waitress explained when I inquired as to what it was. She was a shy teenager whose English was about as good as my French. I ordered this cake, which I assumed to be some kind of Quebec delicacy. On arrival it turned out to be a doughnut with a honey glaze, manufactured in Montreal and now several days old.

When the waitress departed Farley started to laugh and so did I. "So much for exotic French cuisine," he chuckled.

"Never mind," I said as I munched my stale doughnut. "I learned a new word today." None of the French courses I had taken had included the word for doughnut.

After lunch we set out to explore the islands. There were no car-rental agencies, but Farley discovered he could hire a car, of sorts, from a nearby service station. The ancient Ford sedan was coated in dust, the engine ran reluctantly and needed a new muffler, but this rattling vehicle would have to do. The attendant didn't inspire us with confidence when he asked to be paid in cash in advance. He didn't bother to look at Farley's driver's licence. After all, there was no possibility of driving off into the sunset, never to be seen again.

This slender archipelago was much larger than we had imagined. On a map of Canada it looks like a tiny apostrophe lost in the immensity of the Gulf of St. Lawrence, but the distance from Havre-Aubert in the southwest to Grande Entrée in the northeast is over fifty miles. In 1969 a narrow road, most of it gravel, connected about twenty settlements. One island stood apart in lonely isolation. That was Entry Island, about two miles east from Havre-Aubert. It was home to about two hundred English-speaking people and could only be reached by boat.

With just one main road we hardly needed a map to find our way, but I like to follow maps. We had brought a nautical chart of the Gulf with us, one of Farley's large collection of charts of all of Canada's eastern shores, and a Texaco road map of the Maritimes. The town where we were staying was Grindstone, on both of our maps, though the name on the post office was Cap-aux-Meules. We were soon to discover that at least half of the villages and islands had two names: one English and one French.

East of the airport the few miles of paved road came to an end and we were driving on gravel. This was a road less travelled and we encountered only a few other vehicles as we drove northeast along the barrier dunes that connect most of the islands. On one side of the road was the pounding surf of the Gulf, while on the other lay the calmer waters of a great lagoon. There were no trees. A fringe of beach grass provided the only touch of green. If it hadn't been for the regiment of telephone poles bearing a single cable marching into the distance, we might have felt we were driving on a desert island.

Eventually we came to the small island of Pointe-au-Loup, an outcropping of red sandstone jutting out of the dunes and home to about a dozen families.

"Someone must have seen a wolf here one time," I surmised, *loup* being the French word for wolf.

"Out here in the middle of the Gulf? Not bloody likely," Farley snorted. "Sea wolf is my guess. That's the old name for the grey seal, and these islands are made for them."

A few miles further on, we stopped the car beside the barachois—the broad saltwater lagoon on our right. It looked like a perfect place for seals. Farley scanned it through his binoculars. A great blue heron, as motionless as a garden ornament, stood near us in shallow water.

"What a spectacle," I whispered, not wanting to disturb that prehistoric-looking bird. "Can't you just see this place in a film? I can picture some solitary figure wandering along this lonely shore...."

"Catching lobsters with his bare hands," Farley quipped.

"Of course not. He has a boat and traps for that. I'm thinking of something like a love interest...maybe a broken heart...."

"Two cormorants. Two Arctic terns. One great blue," Farley recited as he mentally tallied his observations. Once a bird watcher always a bird watcher, I concluded, having lived with this one for several years.

There were no seals to be seen so we drove on to the community called Grosse Île—on the map. The name on the post office was Leslie and the mailboxes we drove past bore names such as Goodwin, MacLean, and Turnbull. A shop sign identified Keating's Canteen. Another sign stated Creighton Richards, General Merchant. It looked as if we were back among our own.

But why did this place have both a French name and an English name, when all the surnames appeared to be English? Who were the people who lived here, and were there any lobster fishermen among them? There were many questions. I suggested we return to the Leslie post office and make enquiries.

A solemn lady behind the counter told us, in English, that several men in the community owned lobster boats. "But," she added, "there's no harbour to haul out in here. You got to go to Old Harry for that."

Old Harry, which appeared not to have an alternate name, was a few miles further east. We drove toward it past a high cape that rose dramatically from the flat, sandy landscape. Then we encountered road construction and our first traffic: two lumbering gravel trucks followed by a small, British-made, 1950s Prefect, a car that by then was almost obsolete on the mainland.

They all stopped in front of us. The truck drivers were calling back and forth in French but the driver of the Prefect, a sad-looking, sandy-haired man, spoke to us in English.

"This here's the end of the Magdalen Island highway," he grumbled. "They bin workin' on it two years now, if you can call it working. Quebec government's never in a hurry to finish anything for us in the English end of the islands."

Twenty minutes later we drove on, through clouds of dust, into Old Harry, a settlement of a dozen or so houses. There was no real harbour, just a point of land slightly protected by a rough stone pier, but open to the great sweep of ocean to the east and north. Boats had to be hauled up on a slipway if they were to survive. We watched while a fisherman, standing in his bobbing trap boat, attached a line to the bow from a motor-driven windlass on shore. The windlass operator shifted into gear and the heavy vessel was slowly hauled up a wooden ramp and then secured above the high-tide level. As soon as it was secured another boat was quickly hauled. In half an hour we watched seven lobster boats stowed safely ashore until tomorrow morning.

We lingered to watch two men loading heavy wooden crates full of live lobsters into the back of a truck. After he had closed the windlass down for the day Farley spoke to the man who operated it.

"Good catch?"

"Pretty good."

"Where do all the lobsters end up after they leave here?"

"Overseas."

"Really? Where?"

"France. Fly them out to Moncton tonight. After that to Montreal. Then over to Paris. Get there sometime tomorrow."

"They must cost a bundle by the time they reach Paris," Farley speculated.

"Guess so," the winch man replied. He appeared to have no interest in the long journey of the lobsters, and no interest in us either.

We sat on a grassy hill and watched the fishermen leave. The last pair, in a dilapidated truck, nodded a wordless greeting as they drove on past.

"All those lobsters make me hungry," I complained. "I wonder could we find some place around here to eat."

"Not likely there's a restaurant. But we might find a store," Farley said. We drove on through the rest of the village. Old Harry was a smaller version of Leslie/Grosse Île. The houses were set well apart from one another, leaving room for a garden, perhaps a hen house or a cow. There was a one-room school and a small, picturesque Anglican Church with an adjoining cemetery. There was only one very small store. It bore a sign advertising Robin Hood flour and the name of the proprietor: Ethel Kincaid.

We stepped inside to find the few shelves crowded with canned goods and packaged food. A chest freezer filled one corner. There was a counter behind which stood a tall, frowning woman we took to be Ethel.

"I close at five. For an hour," was her greeting.

That gave us seven minutes to select what we wanted, pay for it, and leave. I chose a Coffee Crisp chocolate bar and a bag of peanuts. I also bought a postcard bearing a photograph of the Old Harry slipway. Farley bought a Sweet Marie bar—and proceeded to eat it right there, before he had paid for it. Ethel kept an eye on him.

"You live here, I suppose," he asked, trying to start a conversation.

"Yep," was all she had to offer.

"How long has your family been here then?"

She stared at him as if no one had ever dared ask that question before.

"I mean...where did the Kincaids come from?"

"I been here all my life. My parents too."

"And your grandparents as well, I suppose?"

"Them too," she snapped, obviously annoyed that two strangers were prying into something that was none of their business. I switched the conversation to the nice weather that day, but even that didn't improve her mood.

We had paid for our purchases and headed for the door before she relented. "If it's history yer lookin' fer, you talk to Kenny Cook. Drive on a bit and you'll see a lane going off on your right. His house is down there. He'd be home now. Fishin's over fer today."

We found the house easily and were met at the door by Kenny himself, a good-looking if rather scrawny man with thick, wavy, brown hair.

"Seen yas down by the harbour," he said in a welcoming tone as if he had been expecting us. "Come in, come in."

Kenny lived in a partly finished, one-storey house with his wife and seven children. The youngest was a toddler and the oldest a girl of seventeen. His wife and some of the older children had gone to Grindstone that day to see the dentist, and had yet to return. The younger children and a number of their friends filled the house, along with mounds of unsorted laundry and various building materials destined to become part of their home-in-progress.

Kenny turned out to be a gold mine of information. A lobster fisherman, he was also an amateur historian with an abiding interest in his birthplace and in the generations who had preceded him. He had been away, serving in the Canadian Navy for fourteen years before returning to settle down in Old Harry with his burgeoning family. Being stationed in England with the Navy had given him the opportunity to visit the British Museum in London. While his Navy buddies were savouring the pleasures of British pubs and soccer games, Kenny had spent countless hours poring over ancient maps and ships' logs and sailors' diaries. Any document the librarians could find that mentioned the Magdalen Islands had been of interest to him. He was proud of the fact that he was the only person among the Magdalens' English population to have ever undertaken this kind of research, although he told us he had a friend in the French community, a Roman Catholic priest, who was also exploring local history.

"Father Landry and me aren't altogether agreed about all the facts. There's the matter of who settled here first, the English or the French. Some claim it was the French but I believe the English were here just as far back. My great-grandfather and his brother settled here early in the nineteenth century and both married local women of English, Protestant stock who had been here as far back as the French.

"People didn't keep records then like they do now. Where you come from didn't matter as much as finding a way to survive. These islands had good pasture for cows, plenty of wild berries, and lots of fish and seals. Going way back, the main source of money was walrus. Nowadays it's lobsters. Was always a pretty good living to be had here. Still is."

"It seems to me these islands should have belonged to PEI," I suggested. "It's the nearest other part of Canada. There are so many similarities—the red soil, the beaches..."

"Well, at one time these islands were claimed by Newfoundland. Then along came the Quebec Act—that was 1744—which stated these islands belonged to Quebec, and so they have been ever since," Kenny declared authoritatively.

"Funny how things turn out," he continued. "It was the English running things back in those days, mostly people from those thirteen colonies that hadn't rebelled yet. That crowd were out to make as much money as they could. That's where Captain Coffin came into the picture. He was a Boston merchant. This here is Coffin Island, don't forget."

I had noted the name on the map and wondered about its gloomy overtones. It sounded like the sort of name that pirates might have chosen. But no, it had been named after a man.

"The old blackguard," Kenny muttered. "Liked to name things after himself."

"Were there native people here before the French and the English?" I asked.

"I don't believe any Indians lived here in olden times. Winters would have been too hard. There were never any big animals to hunt—no moose, no deer, no rabbits. And you can't fish in the winter because of the ice in the

Gulf. All the same, there must have been natives here from time to time because I've found some of their stone tools. Maybe their canoes got blown here accidentally. Later on, of course, white men brought them here for labour, but they never stayed on. They're gone, along with the walrus."

Farley was intrigued by the reference to walrus. Like most of us, he thought of them as arctic creatures.

"There're no walrus in the Gulf now," Farley said.

Kenny shook his head. "They're long gone. Even my grandfather never saw one. We find walrus skulls and teeth on the beaches after a big storm. Most every family around here has some tusks or teeth on a shelf somewhere. We used to go lookin' for them when we were youngsters."

"So just where did your people come from, Kenny?" I asked cautiously.

"Noel Shore, Nova Scotia—on my father's side."

"Is that in Cape Breton?" I had read in a tourist brochure that the English-speaking people in the Magdalens came from Cape Breton Island.

"No. Noel Shore is on the Bay of Fundy. Some people here trace their roots to Cape Breton: McDonalds, McQuaids, Rankins. But the English here came from a lot of places. There's the Richards, descended from a Welsh sailor cast away over a hundred years ago. Then there's the Keatings, shipwrecked on a passage from Ireland. A good many people were shipwrecked here. Then there's my mother's people, the Takers. They're originally from Finland."

"Finland?" Farley asked, surprised.

"What happened was there was another shipwreck and this one fellow, my other great-grandfather, was rescued. Some said he was Russian and others said he was Finnish. Either way, he just stayed here and married a local girl like a lot of others."

"A community of castaways."

"They all came by ship, for sure. Didn't have Eastern Provincial Airlines those days," Kenny smiled.

It's hard to imagine a time when shipwreck survivors simply stayed where they came ashore and lived out the rest of their lives there. Yet the map of the world is dotted with places where people did exactly that. In a world without passports or visas or birth certificates, you could start life over anywhere. You didn't have to be shipwrecked. Countless sailors deserted their ships in places that had better prospects than those they had left behind.

Kenny's narrative had a ring of Robinson Crusoe about it, a tale I might have expected to hear in the Caribbean or the South Pacific, but not from someone on an island in the cold ocean that washes the shores of eastern Canada.

The intriguing past of this place made it all the more appealing as the subject of a documentary film. I could almost hear the reels spinning in Farley's head.

Kenny was enthusiastic about the film idea and told us about a house for rent in Old Harry. "You folks could stay there. If it's pictures of the lobster fishery you're after, there's plenty to be had right here in Old Harry."

The availability of a furnished house for rent was a stroke of luck. Rural Canada was not dotted with bed-and-breakfast accommodations as it is now. The house—it was really more of a cottage—was not far from Kenny's place. It had belonged to an elderly woman who had recently died and was now the property of her daughter, Rhoda, and Rhoda's husband, Wesley.

Rhoda Turner answered the door to our knock. She spoke in a hushed voice because her husband was taking a nap. He always did at the end of the day's work, she said. He was sixty years old now and the work was taking its toll on him.

She was a cheerful little woman with prematurely white hair and a ready smile. We were the first people to enquire about renting her late mother's house. She told us she hadn't been sure what to do about it. Neighbours had suggested it might be a way to earn a little money in the summer but she had been skeptical. Few people visited Old Harry and any who did seldom stayed more than a few hours. "Nothing much to interest anyone around here," she apologized.

The frame cottage was only a stone's throw from Rhoda's own house. It was probably seventy or eighty years old with a large, bright kitchen and an old-fashioned pantry where china, cutlery, and pots and pans were kept. The rest of the house consisted of a tiny living room and one middle-sized bedroom. A smaller second bedroom had been converted into a two-piece bathroom. From the kitchen we could see the ocean and were within walking distance of the harbour.

"We'll take it," Farley said. He explained that we would be back in a couple of weeks and would stay for a month, assuming the CBC agreed with his choice of location. We paid Rhoda a deposit on the rent. She looked as pleased at the prospect as we were.

Farley was a good choice to write a script about lobster fishing. He had, at that point, written fifteen books. His early work was focused on the Arctic but much of his writing over the previous decade had centred on Canada's Atlantic region. *The Grey Seas Under*, *The Serpent's Coil*, *Westviking*, *This Rock within the Sea*, and his new book, which was to be published later that year, *The Boat Who Wouldn't Float*. They were stories, both comic and tragic, that described the lives of people who ventured out to sea in pursuit of food, wealth, new land, or, in his own case, for the sheer adventure of it all.

Chapter Two

THE CBC PRODUCERS AGREED that the Magdalen Islands would be a suitable location for the film and in June we flew back. The cold, bright days of May had been replaced by a warmer, damper season of fog and rain. We rented yet another dusty, rattling, ten-year-old car and arrived at Rhoda's doorstep to obtain the key to our house. Along with the key, Rhoda presented us with a freshly baked jelly roll and a jar of homemade strawberry jam.

"There's milk in the pantry and tea bags as well, so you'll be all set for the morning," she offered thoughtfully.

This was like coming home to a welcoming family, though Rhoda hardly knew us. In the days ahead she couldn't do enough for us. Whatever we needed, she provided: a clothesline, a mop, some bread pans. Since there was no bathtub or shower in our house, we were invited to use the tub in Rhoda and Wesley's house whenever we liked.

I could hardly believe our good fortune. Over the years Farley and I had all too often stayed in places lacking the amenities most urbanites think they cannot live without. Outdoor privies, shared bathrooms, summer cottages in the winter, no electricity—such had frequently been our lot. By comparison, this cozy little house was luxury.

We settled in quickly. I bought groceries at the small shop run by grumpy Ethel, then I baked two loaves of bread. I set up my portable typewriter on the Formica coffee table so I could type manuscripts or anything else that would help with the film. I loved being involved in whatever Farley was doing. I had had a career—a reasonably well paid one in advertising in Toronto—but I had never been as happy as the day I left it behind forever to become Farley's wife and helpmate. For four years I had spent every working day in a windowless office at a job I didn't like. Would I have wished to return to that when I could be sharing an adventure in a remote place called Old Harry? Not bloody likely.

A CBC film crew arrived the day after we did. In those days it took a lot more manpower to make a film than it does now. A director, cameraman, assistant cameraman, sound technician, and assistant sound man came with a load of heavy, bulky equipment. The crew had booked into the charmless Aberdeen Hotel in Grindstone. This arrangement suited us all. They were entitled to hotel accommodation while on an assignment even if, in this case, it involved a long drive to the site. Farley and I were glad to have our evenings to ourselves, time during which we hoped to get to know our neighbours and get a better understanding of the lives of those who lived in this small village.

"Allo, Farley Mowat!" came a hearty greeting as we were clearing away our supper dishes a few days after our arrival. At our door stood a smiling, short, dark-haired man accompanied by Kenny Cook, who explained, "This here's Father Landry."

"Good evening, Father," Farley greeted him.

"Call me Frédéric," he insisted. "I 'eard you were 'ere to make a film so I know immediately I want to meet this man," he beamed.

We sat down around the kitchen table and Farley offered everyone a drink, which led to a convivial evening.

Forty-year-old Frédéric Landry had been born and raised on the islands. He had studied for the priesthood in Moncton, served briefly as a missionary in Panama, and then returned to Les Îles de la Madeleine to become a parish priest. There were seven parishes on the islands and the priests in charge of all of them were native-born Madelinôts, he told us proudly.

However, church matters were far from Frédéric's mind that evening. He wanted to tell us about the history of these islands—his favourite topic. He told us he intended to establish a museum and had applied for a grant from a federal development fund. For years he had been collecting butter churns, oil lamps, china basins, sealers' clubs, old medicine bottles, photographs, whale bones, and walrus teeth—artifacts that people had relegated to attics, cellars, and sheds. Some of his most cherished items had come from shipwrecks, including anchors, ships' lamps, and old wine bottles. He even had some painted cabin doors that had washed ashore and been incorporated into people's homes.

One of the hundred or more known shipwrecks particularly interested him. In 1847 a sailing vessel named the *Miracle* was blown ashore near East Point. The ship was transporting Irish immigrants to Montreal and, during a ferocious storm, broke up on the shoals only a few miles from where we were staying. The vessel was smashed to pieces on the sandbars and the miracle of the wreck of the *Miracle* is that anyone at all survived.

Many were drowned but, with help from the local people, a few managed to struggle ashore. Several orphaned children were adopted by local families. Since they were Irish Roman Catholics, it was French Catholic families who took them in. These children kept their original surnames but they grew up speaking French, which is why there were people in the local French community with last names such as Delaney, Doyle, or Langford but whose first names might be Alcide, Mireille, Thérèse, or Louis-Philippe.

Kenny and Frédéric had long wanted the memory of this shipwreck to be memorialized. They had come this evening to suggest that Farley might incorporate this tragic event into the film script he was writing.

Farley wasn't sure. It wasn't directly connected to his theme, which was the day-to-day lives of the lobstermen. However, the loss of the *Miracle* was a singularly dramatic part of local history and a tale of a shipwreck can always liven up a story or a film.

Over several drinks of rum the three men contrived a scene that Farley figured would fit into the plot. Father Landry would hold a memorial service for those who died in that shipwreck and he would do so far out on the desolate dunes of East Point, near the place where the ship had been driven ashore. He would invite people from the nearby Catholic parishes. Kenny offered to work with his brother, a carpenter, to build a large wooden cross that would be erected on the shore. I volunteered to paint the ship's name and the date of the disaster on the cross.

"We'd better invite Mr. Hitch too," Kenny added.

"'Oo is Mr. 'Itch?" asked Frédéric.

"Our new minister. The Anglican minister."

"Of course. As many people as possible," Frédéric cried grandly, lifting his arms as if he were giving a benediction.

So our evening ended in a mood of ecumenical camaraderie. And I had experienced something new. I had made friends with a Roman Catholic priest. I had even called him by his first name.

In my earlier years I could never have imagined such a thing. Growing up in Toronto we Protestant children were frequently mystified and sometimes infuriated by the Roman Catholic Church. The Loyal Orange Order, a fervently anti-Catholic fraternal organization that had crossed the ocean from Ireland with Protestant immigrants to Canada, had a pervasive influence on the way we regarded Catholics. My own parents were not bigots and would never have joined the Orange Lodge but, as liberal in outlook as they believed they were, they nevertheless blamed the power of the Catholic Church for such things as the fact that it was so difficult for Canadians to obtain a divorce or get information about birth control. They also believed the Roman Church was keeping Quebec in a state of suppression and superstition. Our Protestant folklore included a lot of biased information about Catholics and no doubt the Catholics got an equal dose of misinformation about us.

By 1969 things had changed markedly. Vatican II, in the early 1960s, had relieved the Roman Church of some of its medieval baggage. The Quiet Revolution in Quebec had catapulted that province out of the eighteenth century and into the twentieth. And a Quebec Catholic who was also the Minister of Justice for Canada had, in 1968, broadened the grounds for divorce and freed thousands of people from remaining deadlocked in bad marriages. His name was Pierre Trudeau.

Now I had made friends with a priest named Frédéric, who preferred to wear a plaid shirt and chinos rather than his black suit and clerical collar.

A few days later we had a visit from the Anglican minister. He had been a resident of the islands only a little longer than we had. A tall, thin, quiet man in his thirties from Montreal, he had recently been ordained and recently married. He and his bride lived in the rectory, a new bungalow on Grosse Île. Like us, the Reverend Alan Hitch was in the process of discovering where he was. He conducted services in the church in Grosse Île, the largest of his three parishes, on alternate Sunday mornings; in the Old Harry church on alternate Sunday afternoons; and every second week he tried to reach Entry Island and hold a service for those isolated people.

Entry Island, the one island community that was not linked to the others by road, intrigued me because it was so difficult to reach. High winds often made navigation impossible.

"What happens in winter? How will you get out there?" I asked.

"They tell me there is open water until about Christmas. After that I hope to get there by snowmobile if the ice freezes hard enough."

We told him about our plan to raise a big cross to commemorate the wreck of the *Miracle*. He said he would be glad to take part as a representative of the English community.

Two weeks later, on a hot July afternoon under a cloudless sky, a crowd of fifty or sixty people trudged for nearly an hour through sand and stiff dune grass to the spot chosen for the raising of the cross. We were led by the two clergymen and followed by a horde of children. The ponderous cross, nearly twenty feet high, was hauled by an old tractor and finally manhandled into a deep hole atop the highest dune. Our CBC cameras rolled as the heavy wooden symbol was manoeuvred into place.

A westerly breeze whipped away most of the words of the priests. On such a perfect day I found it hard to imagine the fierce gale that had driven the *Miracle* ashore here and drowned most of her passengers and crew. Many were buried in these dunes and the winter winds sometimes exhumed them.

After the ceremony Farley and I hiked slowly back to Old Harry. East Point—several thousand acres of sand dunes dotted with small ponds ringed in wild irises —was a wildly beautiful place. In the autumn the ponds were stopovers for thousands of ducks and geese. As we wandered along I kept searching for a walrus tooth or a fragment of whalebone, but none turned up. Most of what I found was debris left by hunters. There were shotgun casings, thousands of them, everywhere we looked.

"Is there a game warden here?" I wondered.

"If so it appears he doesn't give much of a damn—which is too bad. This place should be a wildlife sanctuary. Or a national park."

The filming of our documentary went along smoothly enough. While the fishermen were not exactly overjoyed to have the camera crew hanging around, neither were they antagonistic. There was no overt display of friendliness. We were tolerated outsiders and that was all. The only real friends we made were Kenny and his family, including his brother, Lloyd; Rhoda (but not Wesley); and Father Frédéric Landry.

The two-month-long lobster season was at its end when our crew finished shooting. When we asked the fishermen if they had had a successful season they were always vague in their reply. I finally realized it was a prying question, like asking someone how much money they made. Those eight weeks of fishing provided almost all their earned income for the year. Some years were better than others. Whatever the outcome, Unemployment Insurance from the federal government sustained them and their families through the lean months.

During our final week the bright weather that had blessed us throughout most of the filming changed. The horizon turned to a menacing shade of slate grey and an ominous wind blew from the east. That evening it began to look like shipwreck weather.

Despite the gathering storm we were wistful at the thought of leaving this remarkable place. Farley decided to take a walk along the beach while I prepared supper. We were dining once more on lobster—the cheapest and most available food. We had discovered something few people beyond these shores have a chance to find out: you can get mighty sick and tired of eating lobster day after day. Lobster Newberg, lobster bisque, lobster sandwiches, lobster salad—eventually it began to taste repugnant, too heavy, and too rich.

Farley got back to the house just before a torrential rain began. He opened our last bottle of Algerian red, the budget-priced favourite in Quebec liquor stores at the time. As we sipped wine from juice glasses he told me he felt something had gone wrong that morning when our crew was doing some final shoots. Farley has a sixth sense about moods and undercurrents and while he couldn't describe exactly what it was he knew that something didn't feel right. He asked Kenny about it but Kenny just shrugged.

"Maybe we've just been here too long," I surmised. "Almost a month of intruding into these people's lives. I imagine most of them will be glad to see us go."

Farley nodded. "I hope that's all it is."

Suddenly the power went off. Electricity in the Magdalens, generated by diesel engines, was erratic. It often vanished for short or longer periods for no reason that we knew of, usually in the afternoons. At night it was a real nuisance.

I normally keep candles for such emergencies but I hadn't bothered to buy any here. Suddenly we were in the dark with only a pocket flashlight to help us find our way about.

"I know what," I said brightly. "Ethel's store is open until nine. I'll slip down there and see if she has any candles."

Dashing through the pelting rain, I got there about two minutes before closing time. Ethel didn't sell candles, she told me flatly. But she did know where "Aunt Mary" (the former owner of our rented house) had kept her kerosene lamp—on the top shelf of the cupboard in the bathroom. I ran back, grateful that there were few secrets in Old Harry. The lamp was exactly where Ethel had said it was.

I'd only been home a few minutes when Kenny appeared at our door, soaking wet and looking grave.

"You were right, Farley boy," he said through tight lips. "There's been trouble. They got Lloyd. Beat him up something awful."

"Your brother Lloyd?"

"Yup. Figured they had it in for me too but as luck would have it I wasn't down at the harbour this evening. See, my young fellow Willard cut his hand and I had to take him to Grindstone, to the hospital, to get stitched up. Otherwise they'd likely have got me as well."

"What do you mean...got you as well? Who's out to get you?" Farley wanted to know.

Kenny's eyes narrowed. "I know the bastards."

"Then you'd better call the police," said Farley.

"How badly is Lloyd hurt?" I asked.

"Pretty bad. Beat with an iron bar around the head."

"Head injuries! That's serious," Farley said urgently.

"We should call the nurse," I suggested.

There was a public health nurse in Grosse Île, one of those legendary, plucky British nurses who had come over to serve in a Red Cross outpost just after the war. This one had married a local man. Her clinic was only twenty minutes away. The hospital would be a journey of an hour or more.

"I didn't want to phone her from my place 'cause all the youngsters are home. Might make them feel something real bad is going on."

"But something bad *is* going on," Farley retorted.

"Anyway, nurse'd likely call the police. That could mean more trouble."

"Damn it, there could be worse trouble if you don't," Farley almost shouted.

"But we don't have a phone," I lamented.

"Rhoda and Wesley do. I'm going over and calling the nurse. Then I'll call the cops."

Farley reached for his rain jacket, but Kenny put out a hand to stop him.

"Farley boy, you stay out of this. You don't know the Quebec police like I do."

"So?"

"They don't give a damn what happens to us English. They don't like us and we don't like them."

"Well, I'm going to call the nurse anyway. We owe Lloyd that much."

Farley made the call and was told the nurse would come at once. Then he did phone the Quebec Provincial Police station. They were not so obliging. They told Farley the only available officers were investigating a traffic accident at the other end of the islands. *"Demain matin,"* was the best they had to offer. Angrily Farley hung up, then he and Kenny took our car and drove to Lloyd's house to await the arrival of the nurse.

I finished my supper by lamplight as the wind rattled the windowpanes and the rain drummed on the roof. Out on the road there seemed to be more traffic than usual. Headlights glimmered as cars and trucks swished past. I noticed a vehicle had stopped just across the road. There were no houses over there, just the path to the beach. Surely no one would be going to the beach on a night like this. The headlights were turned off and in the dark I couldn't tell what sort of vehicle it was. Was someone watching our house? I decided to lock the front and back doors. I was greatly relieved when, after what seemed like an interminable time, the headlights came back on and the vehicle drove slowly away.

Perhaps it was simply kids, I thought. It was Friday night, after all, and it could be some guys out with a six-pack of beer or maybe some young couple making out. Still it didn't make sense for anyone to stop right there.

As a precaution I blew out the flame in the lamp. Sitting alone in the dark left me with absolutely nothing to do. I would have appreciated the company of a radio but we didn't have even a battery-operated one. During our weeks in that house we would occasionally go and sit in the car in order to catch up on the news of the world on the car radio from the CBC English-language station in Moncton. But Farley was away with the car so I simply sat there watching the passing of blurred headlights and wondering what on earth was going on and how we got mixed up in it.

Eventually Farley and Kenny returned. They had stayed with Lloyd until Mrs. Goodwin, the nurse, arrived and administered emergency aid. She also arranged to have Lloyd driven to the hospital. She was particularly concerned he might lose the sight in one badly injured eye.

"Kenny, you could probably use a drink," Farley offered, retrieving a bottle of rum from the pantry.

I lit the lamp again and the three of us sat together in the parlour. I told them about the vehicle parked across the road. Farley shrugged as if I was imagining things. Kenny made no comment but listened carefully to what I was saying. Farley ate some cold lobster but Kenny didn't want anything to eat. Mostly he wanted to talk.

He told us he had grown up in a big family with four sisters and five brothers. His sisters had all moved away to other parts of Canada. One brother had died in childhood. The other four had remained on the islands. Two had never married. His carpenter brother, Ernest, had married and produced twelve children. Another brother, Carl, had died at the age of thirty-four, leaving behind a widow and four children who lived in the house east of us. I had noticed some teenagers coming and going there but I hadn't realized it was a one-parent family.

"How sad for them," I said. "What happened to Carl?"

"Murdered," Kenny replied darkly.

"Oh," was all I could manage to say.

Kenny was silent for a while, then slowly he described how Carl had quarrelled with a fisherman from Grosse Île over who had the right to certain fishing grounds. Their dispute festered for several years until one day it broke out into a brawl at a dance.

Carl had been drinking and was knocked to the ground, where, the police claimed, he hit his head on a rock. Kenny said Carl had had his skull kicked in. He lived four days in a coma before he died.

His killer was charged with assault, not murder or manslaughter, and served seven months in jail at Gaspé on the mainland. After that he moved to Ontario for a few years but eventually returned to Grosse Île. Kenny refused to tell us his name.

"You're convinced it was deliberate, that he intended to kill your brother?" Farley asked.

"Everyone here knew the truth of it. He got away with murder, plain and simple. There's no justice. Not for us. Did you never hear about the trial of Wilbert Coffin?"

We nodded. Wilbert Coffin, an innocent man as it later turned out, was sent to the gallows in 1956 in Montreal for allegedly having murdered three American hunters in 1953 in the Gaspé interior. His trial in Percé was a terrible miscarriage of justice that, far too late, became the subject of several books and films. The fact that he was a poor man and a member of a linguistic minority in eastern Quebec only added to the sense of persecution many people like Kenny had who did not trust the police or the courts.

Had there been another miscarriage of justice in the trial of the man who had allegedly killed Kenny's brother Carl? Or was Kenny simply paranoid, believing that English-speaking people in eastern Quebec could never be treated fairly by a judicial system that was administered by officials whose language and heritage were French?

The electricity came back on abruptly and our small parlour was harshly illuminated by the single electric light bulb dangling from the ceiling. This brought an end to the spooky mood and Kenny's sorrowful tale. Farley began to yawn. I could no longer ignore the mess in the kitchen. Kenny gulped down another drink and headed for home.

As I washed the dishes I pondered the story Kenny had just told us. Everyone likes a mystery. Was Carl's death, ten years earlier, the result of an accident or by intent? Was the assault on his brother Lloyd part of the same vendetta? The storm raged on and I went to bed with many unanswered questions.

We didn't see Kenny the next day. Farley was immersed in the conclusion of his film script. I was packing our belongings and cleaning the house. When we did see Kenny the following day it was down at the harbour, where he was loading lobster traps onto an ancient, unlicensed truck that he shared with Lloyd. Kenny was moving Lloyd's 275 traps to storage. Lloyd, who had been sent home from hospital with a concussion, multiple bruises, and some fractured ribs, was unable to do any work.

"I'm nearly done here," Kenny called. "Come on over to Lloyd's place with me."

Lloyd's home was out on the Old Harry headland, a short walk from the harbour. It was a long, low structure with few windows, and it looked more like a garage than a house. I had noticed the building before but had assumed it was some sort of storage shed. Lloyd, a hefty bachelor in his fifties, lived alone in this strange version of a home.

He was leaning against his front door as we approached. He looked dreadful. His head and his left eye were covered by bandages and the entire left side of his face was a mass of yellow, blue, and greenish bruises. He moved cautiously, in the way of someone in pain.

"Hard luck, Lloyd me son," offered Farley in his best version of a Newfoundland dialect. It wasn't the way people talked here but somehow there seemed to be more sympathy in a statement that ended in "my son."

"Yeah," Lloyd muttered in a low voice.

Clearly he didn't want to talk about what had happened—at least, not to two strangers.

"You like gardens?" he asked Farley.

"Sure," Farley replied, surprised but agreeable.

"C'mon then," he beckoned, pushing open a door in a high, plywood fence adjoining his house. It was a rambling barricade of the sort that surrounds auto-wreckers' yards. These wooden walls surrounded an area the size of a tennis court, enclosing a skinny forest of young trees, each carefully planted in a bed of rich, brown earth—a fertile contrast to the thin, sandy soil of the headland.

Lloyd pointed out apple trees, plum trees, cherry trees, and peach trees, all in their infancy; the beginning of a fruit farm, he explained proudly. He had built the fence to keep the everlasting wind from destroying these vulnerable saplings, convinced he could succeed with the right kind of soil, most of which he had patiently gathered by the bucketful from miles around.

Kenny, who was obviously skeptical, made some good-natured jokes about it. "A cranberry farm would be more like it." He winked at us, doubtful, as we were too, that these fragile trees, if they survived the long winters and the hurricane-force winds, would ever bring forth fruit.

"Pick me a basket of plums," Kenny said as Farley and I meandered about admiring Lloyd's optimism in trying to grow fruit in this windswept little orchard. Despite his physical discomfort he was clearly enjoying showing it off to us, rare visitors to his inner sanctum.

On our way home from Lloyd's place, Kenny finally told us the names of the two young men who had beaten Lloyd, one of whom was already in trouble for having skipped out on his creditors in Sudbury, Ontario, where he had been living for the previous two years. He had returned to the safe haven of these islands, where it was more trouble than it was worth for collection agencies to track him down. Both men were sons of Ethel Kincaid at whose shop I had been buying our groceries. They were also nephews of the man who had fatally assaulted Lloyd's and Kenny's brother ten years earlier.

I had hoped to establish some sort of rapport with Ethel, even though she wasn't particularly friendly. However, I now realized we could never be more than acquaintances. From her point of view Farley and I were entrenched in the opposite camp—that of Kenny Cook and his extended family.

"I still don't get it," I remarked naively. "Why would they attack Lloyd? What were they after?"

"Those bastards," Kenny spat out the words, "claimed Lloyd cut the moorings on a boat that night so's she'd drift out to sea. They say they caught him doin' it and he pulled a knife on them. That's when they hit him, they said, in self-defence. That's what they told the police."

"Lloyd surely wouldn't do such a thing," Farley protested.

"'Course not. What the Kincaid brothers done was to cut somebody's boat loose—some fellow they were mad at—and then blame it on Lloyd. Only Lloyd never done it."

"Old Harry appears to have a lot of old grudges," I said to Farley when we got back to our house.

"Maybe it's one of those territorial things. Maybe somebody was stealing the other guy's lobsters. Maybe some fellow set his traps on ground claimed by another fisherman. It's highly competitive. Lobsters are worth a lot of money. The stakes are high. I picked up some undercurrents during the filming. I think there's a lot of poaching, for one thing. Somebody is trapping lobsters in the lagoon, which is illegal because that's spawning ground. Other people know about it but they don't tell the authorities..."

"For fear of being beaten up?"

"Possibly, or else they might get caught doing something illegal too. And then there's animosity between the French and the English fishermen; a fierce rivalry over how many licences are issued to each group. It's a complicated way to make a living. In the film we've been emphasizing the hard physical work, the long hours, the danger. The other side of the story, the seamy side, would be very difficult to get. These guys aren't going to talk about that to a camera. Anyway, it's none of our business."

It wasn't. But it would be a long time before I would forget the sight of Lloyd's bruised face and injured eye—as well as his brave and improbable dream of creating an orchard on Old Harry's desolate sands.

Chapter Three

RHODA TURNER HAD BEEN more than generous to us, showing up every few days with some home-baked treat from her kitchen. She and Wesley had one son, who lived in Charlottetown with his wife and two children. She missed them a lot and perhaps we were treated like family members as compensation. I told Rhoda how much we had enjoyed our time here and that we were going to miss her and the islands very much once we had left.

"You'll have to come back, then," she invited.

"I hope so," I said.

That was when she mentioned that she knew of a house for sale—in Grand Entry, a mainly French-speaking community a few miles down the road. The house belonged to her cousin Lena Reid, a widow who had moved to Charlottetown eight years earlier and only rarely returned.

Lena's brother, Murray, another cousin, had been keeping an eye on the place for years. Every Sunday afternoon he and his wife drove up from his home in Grindstone to make sure everything was all right. He kept the key. Rhoda phoned him and Murray offered to be there that afternoon. Why not take a look, we thought?

We drove up there before he arrived, which gave us time to examine the outside of the house and explore the property. The two-storey frame house was rather stylish. It stood well back from the road in the middle of eleven acres of gently undulating land covered with wild grass that rippled in the breeze. The grassy expanse was dotted with white daisies, purple irises, and yellow buttercups. We ambled up a hill past a small copse of stunted spruce trees until we reached the edge of a sienna-coloured cliff that sloped abruptly down to a wide and pristine sandy beach about three city blocks in length. There wasn't a sign of a human presence anywhere upon it, even though this was a balmy summer day.

We lay on the grass at the cliff's edge and gazed down at the surf rolling in far below us, listening to the mesmerizing rush of waves crashing on the

The view from our hill, Grande Entrée

shore. Bank swallows darted in and out of their burrows only a few feet under us. Black-backed gulls soared past, screeching and hovering in the updraft, so close we could almost have reached out and touched them. They made us poor earthlings wish we could fly too.

"I have the feeling I'm somewhere else, someplace not in Canada," I told Farley when we walked back down the hill.

"Where do you think you are?"

"Mmm. A place I must have seen in a travel magazine. Maybe Australia. Maybe West Africa. Maybe Fiji," I dreamed.

"Similar beaches. But the wrong kind of birds. I'll tell you what the Maggies remind me of: Bermuda. About the same size. All this sand...but without Bermuda's hordes of people. The Bermuda of the Gulf, that's how I'd define it."

"Only not the same climate."

"Just as well. With Bermuda's climate this place would be overrun."

Rhoda had told us that the four homes on the extreme western end of Grand Entry had all belonged to "English" people. There had even been a one-room English school on the little peninsula, though it had long since been closed. Only one of the four houses remained occupied year-round. Two were used in summer by former inhabitants who had moved off the island. The house we had come to see had stood empty for eight years, with a few infrequent visits from Lena or her family.

In his sixties, Murray Agnew had the pale, freckled complexion of a redhead but his hair had become white and thin. Murray and his wife, Gladys, arrived in a brand-new Dodge. Gladys didn't bother to get out of the car. She had seen the inside of her sister-in-law's house before. She gave us a nod, but no smile. We nodded back and then waited while Murray hunted in his pockets for the house key.

He didn't say much. He was well aware of who we were and why we and the CBC crew were on the islands, but he evinced no interest in the film. Perhaps, having been a general merchant most of his life, he considered the lives of men who fished for lobster to be of little interest. Finally he located the key and we went in.

Like all Maritime houses of that era, this one had a large, welcoming kitchen. The kitchen was the heart of every home, the chief source of heat, and the place where food was prepared and eaten. The mother of the family practically lived there.

Beyond this hub was a dining room—with pretensions. It contained a large, polished, wooden table and eight matching chairs. It was a room set aside for celebrations such as weddings, birthdays, and Christmas. An archway flanked by a pair of cylindrical wooden pillars led into a pint-sized parlour.

The parlour was in mint condition. The bulky chesterfield and chair, upholstered in a harsh shade of lime green, appeared never to have been sat upon. In the corner was a small round table topped with a lace doily displaying a few framed photographs and several china knick-knacks: Lena's small treasures awaiting the day she would return.

A solid balustrade of varnished hardwood bordered the stairs leading up to the second floor. There we found three middle-sized bedrooms and one small one. There was also a full bathroom containing one of those comfortable old porcelain tubs with a sloping back and claw-shaped feet.

There were hardwood floors throughout the house and many windows offering lush and grassy views and glimpses of the sea. To the north were

The Mowat's house in Grande Entrée

the harbour and the community of Grande Entrée. Or, as the English-speaking islanders called it, Grand Entry.

I tried to picture myself in this charming clapboard house, putting my personal stamp on it. The dingy walls would be painted in new, exciting colours. I could envision huge bouquets of freshly picked wildflowers, the good smell of homemade bread, the laughter of visiting friends who would delight in this surprising place.

Farley was on the back porch talking to Murray. "Any idea what sort of price she might want for this?"

"Nope. Gotta talk to her yourself," he insisted, showing no interest in whether we wanted to buy or not. "Never told me what her plans are. Didn't come home last year at all. Must be a coupla years since she was here."

We thanked Murray for showing us around, then we lingered outside after he and Gladys had driven away.

"So what do you think?" Farley asked.

"It's a nice house, all right. It's just..."

"What?"

"Well, to say the least, it's an offbeat location."

"So? Burgeo was a lot more isolated than this. And it changed your life for the better—so you said."

True. The five years we had lived in the outport village of Burgeo on Newfoundland's southwest coast had been an enlightenment of sorts for me. Human relationships there had been inconceivably different from those

35

I had grown up with in Toronto. Like it or not, everyone was part of everyone else's life. In a community like Burgeo, which had no road to any other place, you couldn't isolate yourself in your shiny new car, or your office cubicle, or your high-rise apartment. No matter where you were or what you did, you were part of a community. No one was anonymous.

Burgeo also had an intact culture composed for the most part of descendants of the original settlers who had arrived there a century and a half earlier. That posed a barrier for us. Much as we loved the place, we eventually realized we could never truly belong to it. In the end, after five marvellous years, we had sold our little house there and moved back to Ontario to try living in the town of Port Hope.

I had not reckoned on how much I would miss life in Newfoundland. After a year I wanted to go back and try again, but Farley wouldn't do it. He was still agonizing over the conflict we had endured in Burgeo over the death of the trapped fin whale, Moby Joe. The wanton destruction of that seventy-foot female whale had brought a torrent of condemnation down on Burgeo, and Farley had been the one who had unleashed it. We were torn between our admiration for outport people and our shock at some of their attitudes toward animals.

We wandered back up the hill to take a second look at Grande Entrée's sublime view. When we came back down we inspected the small, collapsing barn where a horse or two might once have been stabled. Next to that was a larger, sturdier barn with enough room in it for a workshop.

"This place has possibilities," Farley acknowledged.

"Mmm-hmm," I agreed, dreamily.

"The house seems in good shape and the property is spectacular. And this is a community that makes a living from the sea and the land; survivors of all kinds of adversity—even shipwrecks! There must be a hundred miles of beach and surf on these islands, along with all those lagoons just full of sea life. It's all here, and it's far from the madding crowd."

Farley was beginning to sound like a real estate agent.

"It's like Newfoundland in a lot of ways," he added.

"Doesn't feel the same though," I countered.

"Do you know what I saw on the beach yesterday? A piping plover. First one in my entire life."

Right then I knew he was hooked.

The next morning we left on the flight to Charlottetown, but instead of catching the connecting flight to Montreal we booked into a hotel and phoned Lena Reid in her son's suburban home to ask if we could visit her to discuss the possibility of buying her Grand Entry house.

Lena, who was about seventy, had the same pallid complexion and white hair as her brother, Murray...and the same unsmiling demeanor. She was living with Clifford, her younger, unmarried son. Her other son, Reg, was visiting from his home in Moncton. Clifford, who had red hair and looked to be about thirty, was friendlier than the rest of his family. He made us some tea and brought the tray into the modern living room, where a picture window overlooked a tidy lawn.

"After my husband died," Lena told us, "the children wanted me to come and live here. You see, they had all moved off the islands by then. I might have stayed there by myself even if it was difficult, in the winter especially..."

"Ma, you know you never coulda stayed there alone," Reg interrupted wearily.

She ignored him.

"...but the summers—the breeze was so cool and fresh. It's not the same here at all. The heat in Charlottetown in summer is simply terrible. You can even see it, the air shimmering in the heat. That never happens in the Magdalena."

"Ma, none of us is ever going back there to stay," Reg insisted.

"Well, there's summer holidays."

"Yeah, but Betty and the kids like to go to her folks' place out at Shediac. It's lots closer if you're looking for a nice beach. And Cliff can't be taking much time off, now that he's getting his car dealership going."

Clifford shook his head with a bemused smile. "Jeez, I can't believe this. Not so long ago we were all screaming to get off those islands. I mean... who wants to *live* out there when they could live here?"

His mother gave him a look of chastisement. She, at least, wanted to be back on the islands in the Gulf.

And...so did we.

We could see we had an advantage, insofar as Lena's two sons were on our side.

"Our house was the first of its kind in the islands," Lena explained with pride. "It came ready to assemble. We sent away to Victoriaville for it in 1925. It arrived on the steamship *Lovat*. John and I had been married for one year. He and two men put the house together from the plans. They had it up in just over two months. After that quite a few families copied us and sent away for the same kind of house."

I sympathized with Lena's reluctance to discuss selling. Her house was full of memories. She had moved into it as a bride and raised four children there. No doubt she had baked bread, picked berries, milked the cow, fed the hens, and hung out the wash in the ocean breeze; and at the end she had tended her ailing husband until the time came to bury him. Then she had reluctantly moved away. Now, here were a couple of strangers wanting to buy what she had never wanted to leave.

No decision had been made by the time we left Charlottetown the next day. Reg, who appeared to be in charge of things, said he would be in touch with us.

I had been uncomfortable during our visit with Lena. I felt as if she had been looking me over, resenting the possibility that I might take her place as the mistress of her home.

Over the next few months our life back in Ontario was very busy and I put the house—and Lena—out of my thoughts. But that view, the colossal sweep of sand and surf and the red cliffs, found its way into my dreams from time to time.

By the following spring Lena had decided to sell her home to us. I was sure she had done so unwillingly, coerced by her family. I could imagine their conversations: "The house needs repairs. Sell it now. The money will come in handy. What's the use of keeping a house you'll never use and all the while it's falling to rack and ruin?"

Yes, there would have been rational arguments, but there would also have been Lena's sense of loss.

Should we buy the place? We weren't ready to abandon Port Hope, but on the other hand we needed a retreat where we could spend part of the year away from the tensions and demands which kept increasing as Farley's literary fame grew.

"Let's do it," I said bravely. "It's such a unique place." But I still wasn't sure how we were going to fit it into our lives.

We were to take possession on the first of August 1970. Farley wanted to be there much earlier in the summer but Lena said she needed time to clear out her belongings, so we arranged to rent Rhoda and Wesley's extra house in Old Harry for a few weeks before taking possession. In July we drove our heavily laden station wagon from Ontario to Souris at the eastern end of Prince Edward Island, where we had booked passage aboard the *North Gaspé*, the only scheduled ship linking the Magdalen Islands to the rest of the Maritimes. A sturdy little vessel, she sailed once a week between Grindstone and the small port of Souris, carrying assorted freight, wholesale quantities of groceries and hardware, as well as passengers.

There was only enough space on deck for four motor vehicles—ours and three small trucks. Farley and I, and our two black water dogs, Albert and Victoria, stood on the wharf and watched with mounting horror as our car was hoisted high into the air in a rope sling and swung over the *North Gaspé*'s deck. Suddenly the overloaded vehicle slipped sideways in the sling and threatened to capsize. Somehow the crane operator managed to gradually lower it so that all four wheels touched safely down on the steel deck.

There was no place on board for dogs so we put them back in the car with the windows half-open to catch the sea breeze. Then we settled down in the small saloon for a blessedly calm six-hour crossing that would carry us to our new home.

Rhoda greeted us like long-lost relatives, a reassuring welcome because I was still apprehensive about this move. I remembered the tensions that had plagued us in Old Harry the previous summer. There seemed to be more friendliness in the air this time. After all, we had bought a house and planned to stick around, unlike last summer when we only had visitor status—nosy, prying visitors at that.

This July we got slightly acquainted with Rhoda's husband, Wesley, a man of few words whom we had seen little of the year before. Lobster fishing was over for the year so Wesley and other local men could now be seen painting and fixing their houses, fiddling with lawnmowers and chain saws, and painting trap boats that had been hauled up on the land.

Kenny Cook brought us up to date about his newest venture—a strawberry farm! He told us a scientist from the Quebec Agriculture Department had done a feasibility study of the Magdalens and had concluded that the soil and climate could produce strawberries in commercial quantities. Kenny owned five acres of land, which was actually a lot on these relatively crowded islands. All but the youngest of his seven children would be involved in the backbreaking job of clearing three acres covered with scrubby spruce trees. Then the berries could be planted and next summer, he forecast, there would be bushels of plump strawberries.

By the end of July Lena and her daughter, Lois, had dealt with the accumulations of forty years of household flotsam and little remained in the house except some basic furniture. They were offering to sell us three beds with mattresses that had seen better days, two chests of drawers that dated from the 1920s, the lime-green chesterfield and chair, a substantial wooden desk, a fairly new refrigerator, and an aged wringer-washer.

I hated the crass, clumsy chesterfield set and declined to buy it, despite the problem of trying to find a replacement. However, we were interested in some of the other items and I inquired about prices.

I was stunned when Lena asked the same prices quoted in Eaton's catalogue for brand-new beds, mattresses, refrigerators, and desks. She had us over a barrel and she knew it. She knew, all too well, what a slow process it was to furnish a house on these islands where delivery had to be made by the *North Gaspé* whenever space might be available.

When Farley and I had settled in Burgeo we had been faced with the same problem of furnishing a house in a community that couldn't be reached by road. We had inquired among our neighbours if they had any household furnishing they wanted to sell. I was offered an old, but sturdy, varnish-encrusted table by one family, who protested that they didn't want me to pay for it at all and I had a job to persuade them to take five dollars. Another neighbour had given us a cast-iron Franklin stove, another gave us a legless tabletop, which Farley turned into a coffee table. Someone else gave us a couple of wooden chairs that only needed paint. No one in Burgeo tried to profit from our need.

Lena and Lois were cut from a different piece of cloth. "Take it or leave it" was their unapologetic attitude. I had little choice but to buy one bed (with the newest-looking mattress), the refrigerator, the desk, one of the jerry-built chests of drawers, and the wringer-washer—even though I loathed wringer-washers. Fortunately, the oil-fired range in the kitchen was considered a fixture that came with the house.

Lois, a tall, blonde woman in her thirties who had somehow missed the family gene for red hair, was slightly more convivial than her mother. She told me she had left home at the age of nineteen to find work on the mainland, first in Halifax and later in Ontario. She had been married for ten years to an Ontario farmer and would never be coming back here to live.

She proudly pointed out the forty-gallon hot-water heater that had been installed only two years before her mother moved out and the fairly new refrigerator, which was one of the last single-door models before the two-door kind became the norm. It had a foot pedal with which you could open the door if your hands were full, a brilliant invention that has since been abandoned by the designers of refrigerators in the race to reinvent everything.

Lois had special memories of the big, wooden desk, which was the same shape and size that teachers used in every classroom where I had gone to school.

"It was Daddy's," she explained, "from the days when he was the Fisheries officer. That's why these holes are here," she said as she pointed to two small round holes in the frame of the archway that separated the living room from the dining room.

I stared at them, not understanding.

"After we moved away someone—some idiot—sat up on the hill there...and fired a few rounds. Out of badness," she frowned.

What I was looking at were bullet holes.

"There're two more upstairs," she added. "Uncle Murray got the broken windows fixed. We never found out who did it."

Fisheries officers are not popular in fishing communities. It's their job to police the fishery, to watch for people fishing out-of-season, fishing without a licence or taking a larger catch than the quota allows. It is a government job that pays fairly well but it does not make that person beloved by his neighbours in a place where fish mean money. Violations can mean fines, seizures of boats and gear, and even imprisonment. It appeared that Lena's late husband had trod on someone's toes, and his posthumous punishment was to have bullets fired into his empty house.

"We always figured it was someone from the reserve," Lois remarked.

"Reserve?" I repeated. What was she talking about? There were no indigenous people on these islands.

"Up the road. You must have noticed," added her mother from the adjacent room, her thumb pointing in a northerly direction.

I had noticed a cluster of small, rundown homes about a half a mile away at the junction of our gravel road and the paved main road. There was always a swarm of small children running around these houses, much laundry on the line, and several abandoned, rusting cars nearby. The people who lived there spoke French. This was what the two women meant by the word "reserve."

I didn't respond. I didn't want to confront them for insulting both the French and the native people in the same breath. Small wonder there were bullet holes in the wall, I thought.

Their bigotry made it easier for me to move in later that week. I felt less guilty about displacing Lena. I have always experienced pangs of guilt buying someone's house, even if they were eager to sell. A home is a home, in my sentimental mind, and not merely a sum of money. Lena's parsimony and prejudices had expiated my guilt.

Now it was our home and we were going to put our imprint on it. We would get acquainted with all our neighbours—English- and French-speaking. However, my first project was to learn how to make jam. I was going to harvest the bonanza of wild strawberries that grew amid the grass on our hill—fantasizing that I might resemble a character from Ingmar Bergman's *Wild Strawberries*. Small wonder that some agronomist had advised Kenny Cook to start a strawberry farm. The wild ones grew in such abundance, and in this soil and climate so would the domestic variety.

I resolved to learn the name of every wildflower that grew here. Who knows—someday we might even decide to live in this beautiful spot year-round. Maybe I would become pregnant again and help reverse the shrinking English community. We looked forward to becoming Quebecers. Québécois.

I could picture us climbing down the side of the cliff and lolling on the beach, watching the waves roll in. Then, hot and covered in sand, we would plunge into the foaming surf. Ah, what dreams I brought with me to that enchanted spot.

Chapter Four

THE ONLY OCCUPIED neighbouring house belonged to the McQuaid family: Elva, a widow in her eighties; her son, Morris, who was a boat builder; and her daughter, Rose. Morris, in his fifties, was a widower. Rose, who had never married, had lived a large part of her adult life in a psychiatric hospital in Montreal. She was now able to live at home because of the new drugs that were improving the lives of so many of the mentally ill.

The McQuaid house was tall and weather-beaten, positioned like a monument on a cape a short walk from our house. Withstanding a century of Atlantic storms, the original clapboard had been frequently repaired with whatever materials had been available—sometimes plywood, sometimes pressboard. The roof was a patchwork quilt of unmatched shingles. Near the house stood an equally weather-worn barn, to which an extension had recently been added. This was where Morris McQuaid built wooden boats, single-handed.

Morris was excessively shy of strangers but Farley got acquainted with him by watching him at work in the cavernous barn. At first Morris hardly said a word. Eventually the ice began to melt and he did talk, though awkwardly as if he was not used to it. He explained that he was now building a much larger boat than the Cape Anne lobster boats he had been making for local fishermen for years. The new one was going to be over fifty feet long, a hull of Morris's own design with a large hold and an after-cabin. It would have two masts for sails but its main propulsion would come from a big diesel engine.

Because of the size of the vessel, Morris had had to build an extension onto his barn to shield his work-in-progress from winter gales—work he estimated would take three full years. When Farley ventured to ask what the boat would cost, Morris replied, "Ten thousand was what I agreed to take." Farley asked what the new owner intended to use the boat for. Morris answered flatly, "I never asked."

A few days later I walked over to the boatshed with Farley. Although I hesitated to intrude into what was clearly a men's enclave, I wanted to get acquainted with Morris and his family. He nodded a greeting, but kept on planing a length of board.

He was even less forthcoming to a couple of teenaged boys who arrived shortly after and stood silently watching.

"You fellas steer clear of them boards," he admonished them as they lingered beside a pile of lumber. "I don't want them planks toppled over."

They glanced at him but said nothing.

"You boys thinking about building a boat some day?" Farley enquired, trying to be friendly.

They looked at him for a mute instant. Then one muttered something to the other boy in rapid-fire French. They stayed for a few more minutes and then left without saying a word to any of us.

Morris's mother appeared on the porch of their house, yelling something in the direction of the shed.

"Awright, Ma," Morris called back from the doorway.

"Supper," he muttered as he dropped a handful of nails back into a tin and hung up his hammer. As we headed for our house he issued an invitation. "Come and visit sometime. Ma would be glad of the company."

On the day we chose to visit, we tactfully arrived at three o'clock in the afternoon, assuming this would be an appropriate time, midway between the noon meal and the evening meal.

The inside of the McQuaid house proved a sharp contrast to the weary outer shell. A large, well-tended kitchen smelled of home baking. The Formica-and-chrome table was covered with a lace cloth topped with a bouquet of plastic flowers. The wallpaper had a motif of teapots. Someone cared about this room.

That person was Elva, who had snow-white hair, walked with a slight limp, and had a tendency to scowl. This kitchen had been the centre of her life for a long time and it was still her responsibility to keep the household running.

Her daughter, Rose, was a heavy woman with straight, dark, greying hair held back from her face by a child's barrette, a style she had doubtless acquired at the Douglas Hospital in Montreal, her home for twenty years. Rose did the heavy work around the house. We knew she did the laundry because we had often noticed her hanging it on the clothesline. However, we learned that her real pride was in baking pies.

"Morris loves pie," Rose explained quietly, so she baked one for her brother every single day. "Rhubarb, raspberry, blueberry, cranberry, apple," she recited shyly, recalling the seasonal progression of fruit becoming available.

We chatted briefly about our newly purchased house. Obviously the McQuaids would have known the Reid family. However, nobody offered any information about them. I was hoping they would as I am interested in knowing about the lives of the people who have occupied a house before I came along. Elva's only comment was to say they were glad someone "English" had bought it.

I found it difficult to get used to this definition of who I was, who we were: English. I think of myself as a Canadian and nothing else, even though three-quarters of my ancestors traced their roots to England. Farley's roots are in Scotland, Wales, and Ireland, with not a single gene from England. But in this corner of Canada, "Canadian" wasn't an adequate definition.

Elva did most of the talking. Rose only spoke when spoken to. We soon discovered there was little that met with Elva's approval. Her sharp tongue harangued the government, the Co-op store, the local children who sneaked into her field and picked strawberries, and the new clergyman who hadn't bothered to call on her yet. Despite her great age, Elva still ruled the roost.

This lonely little family seemed reasonably well off. They owned several tracts of land, which Elva's late husband had bought over the years as pasture for the cows they had once kept. They also owned the small, boarded-up schoolhouse up the road. Fifty years earlier Mr. McQuaid had donated an acre of his land so a school could be built for the local English-speaking children. Morris and Rose and their siblings, along with all the Reid and Agnew children, had been educated there long before the era of school buses. When there were no more "English" children, the school closed and the one acre and the wooden building reverted to the McQuaids.

Morris had lived briefly in the schoolhouse half a dozen years earlier, during his short-lived marriage. At the age of fifty-three, he had married a woman from Grosse Île who had spent twenty-five years in the Canadian army before retiring back to her original home. Morris made a home for his bride in the one-room school, but only a year and a half later his wife died from a heart attack. Morris therefore boarded up the school and moved back home with his mother and Rose.

Elva had had seven children but only three had married and then not until they were in their forties and fifties. There were no grandchildren.

The small enclave of English-speaking people at Grande Entrée was now facing extinction. We were the first new "English" to move into this corner of the Magdalens in fifty years. Sometimes I tried to picture the place when the one-room schoolhouse had been filled with children, when Elva and Lena had been young mothers.

As well as groceries, we had to buy a lot of other supplies that first summer. We needed to find out which stores sold what and we also wanted to get to know the people who ran them.

Grand Entrée had three general stores, the biggest being the Co-op, located near the government wharf. The manager, Paul-Émile, was a short, effusive man who spoke some English and a version of French I couldn't understand. In Grand Entrée the concept of self-service in a store was still years in the future so in order to buy anything I had to face Paul-Émile, or his one assistant, across a counter, and ask for every single thing I needed.

"*Des carottes et des pommes de terre, s'il vous plait*," I requested.

"Carrots an' *patates*," Paul-Émile verified as he headed for a room in the back where a few basic vegetables were stored.

"*Des mouchoirs en papier...la...*" I pointed to it. "*Et papier en ciré.*"

"Ah, Kleenex an' *papier waxé*," he said as he turned to reach them from the shelf behind him. No matter how I persisted in shopping in French, Paul-Émile always responded in English or in a blend of the two languages.

The Co-op store was where men hung around to exchange news and gossip. In the absence of a pub, or even a coffee shop, this building was more than just a place of commerce. Community notices were tacked to the wall by the door. Children were sent here to buy a few items when their mothers ran out of things. Some people appeared to come in for no reason, apparently just to see who else was there.

I was a target of their furtive glances, a stranger in this familiar shop where they expected to know everyone. When I attempted to make eye contact, they quickly looked down at their shoes or out the window. Their darting glances were not menacing but neither were they friendly. I hoped this attitude would quickly pass, that in a matter of weeks I would be part of the scenery. Farley, who was less self-conscious about being an outsider, could always quip and joke with Paul-Émile and the other fellow but I couldn't do that. As the weeks passed and nothing changed, I began to feel uncomfortable shopping there alone.

"Don't be silly," Farley would say to me.

"I can feel them looking at me."

"They like to look at a pretty lady."

"Thanks but...I can tell the difference between an admiring glance and..."

"What?"

"A stare."

"Hey, you're being paranoid. We're the new kids on the block. It's only natural they're going to look us over."

"I guess," I sighed.

I decided to try shopping in the general store in the English community of Grosse Île, which was a twenty-five-minute drive on that always-under-construction highway. I reckoned it would be easier for me to shop where my halting French was not the butt of anyone's jokes.

Creighton Richards, General Merchant stated the sign on a wooden addition built on one side of a two-storey house. The store wasn't as big as the Grande Entrée Co-op but it stocked much the same assortment of canned goods, flour, sugar, tea, instant coffee, pop, root vegetables, powdered milk, and a big assortment of candy. There was a chest freezer where I unearthed some frosty packages of chicken legs and some unidentifiable chunks of meat buried under a layer of popsicles. A thin, teenaged girl tallied up my bill but said not a word beyond stating the sum of money I was to pay.

I thought I would at least get a smile or a nod of recognition. Surely she would be pleased to greet a new customer even though I assumed that it wasn't her store, that she only worked there. Two other women came in to buy something but said nothing to us, not even after Farley bid them good morning. A little boy who came in to buy chewing gum stared at us and then looked away—just as the French children had done in Grande Entrée. I left the shop with no sense of having allied myself with anyone.

Disappointed, I concluded it would be better to make a weekly journey to the centre of the islands, to the larger communities: Grindstone, House Harbour, or La Vernière, where, despite the long, dusty drive, I could perhaps find anonymity. The big Co-op stores were largely self-service and usually had a meat counter with a butcher. They also sold hardware and building supplies. Having stood empty for so long, our house needed a lot of fixing.

The tall promontory of grey rock that gave Grindstone its name made a dramatic backdrop to the unattractive buildings that had been built below it. Not far from a phalanx of giant Irving Oil tanks, a long, sprawling building housed a fish plant. Strung along the main road was an assortment of plain structures for various shops and businesses. A few small, older homes were located here and there—remnants from an era before Grindstone/Cap-aux-Meules had grown into the commercial centre of the islands.

Only two structures in the town had any architectural interest—the large Roman Catholic Church and a small Anglican Church—but they were located on a side road and were not part of the streetscape of this tawdry little town. The Anglican Church was now rarely used for regular church services; more often for funerals. It had been the spiritual home of the English-speaking merchant class who had once dominated the economy of the entire archipelago. They were all gone now—having decamped for greener pastures in mainland Canada or simply died off. There were a few Anglicans left, like Murray and Gladys Agnew, but of the remaining parishioners hardly any would see sixty again.

The Co-op stores, which had replaced the shops owned by English-speaking merchants, were well-run, well-stocked, and staffed by friendly, French-speaking people, some of whom spoke English. The merchandise was displayed on shelves and counters, so I could hunt for what I needed and pile it into a shopping cart. It was a relief not to have to find the French words for such things as a dustpan, a hammer, a spatula, or thread. The Co-op in La Vernière became our favourite and here we bought most of our household equipment. Over time we came to be recognized as familiar customers and as summer turned to autumn I began to feel, if not exactly at home, at least a little more comfortable shopping there.

In most northern latitudes September is a sublime month. It was especially so in the Magdalens. Dramatic clouds hurried across the sky as the autumn gales gathered strength. The verdant summer grass that rippled across the contours of the land gradually turned the colour of wheat. Rose hips dotted the bushes with crimson. Goldenrod and smoky blue asters were the final flourish. It was a season of mixed feelings because the onset of autumn signalled the time for us to depart from this dreaming landscape and return to our other life.

That fall we returned via Quebec City on a locally owned freighter with the unromantic name *C.T.M.A.* The initials stood for the company that operated it: *CoOperatif Transport Maritime et Aerian* (it had once owned a small airplane). This nondescript cargo ship looked seaworthy but scruffy. She sailed back and forth between the Magdalens and Quebec City and Montreal, with various ports of call along the way depending on what freight had to be collected or delivered. The ship had room on deck to carry three or four vehicles. There were half a dozen passenger cabins and a small dining saloon where the crew and passengers ate together. The ship's schedule was flexible. The voyage would likely take two or three days, the purser told us.

I was looking forward to sailing the Gulf of St. Lawrence, that mighty inland sea that is such a dramatic entrance into the heart of Canada. It had been the first glimpse of Canada for hundreds of thousands of immigrants, but with the demise of transatlantic passenger ships in the 1960s very few new Canadians were seeing it any more.

Our ship had been scheduled to leave on a Tuesday but for some undisclosed reason we had to wait two extra days before she could depart. Travelling by freighter requires patience and lots of time, but by then I was in a hurry to get going. It rained every day, which curtailed the walks we liked to take around the headlands. And I had run out of anything to read.

Not one place in the islands sold English-language magazines. I knew there wouldn't be a bookstore but...not even magazines? I found that I truly missed them: news magazines, women's magazines, house-and-garden magazines. There were scarcely any in French for sale either, beyond the ever-present copies of *Allo Police*, a trashy Quebec equivalent of *The National Enquirer*. And there were no libraries in the Magdalens in either language.

We were finally summoned to the wharf on a Thursday evening, to sail at midnight. Again our car had to be hoisted on board with a crane. On this dark, windy night a steward ushered us to a small cabin with one porthole, an upper and lower berth, a sink with cold running water, one chair, and a small closet. The bathroom was along the corridor. We were the only passengers. No one objected to us bringing our two dogs into the cabin with us.

Farley and I stayed on deck for a while watching the hurly-burly of barrels of smoked herring being loaded on board, men in oilskins scurrying, shoving, and shouting. One of the ship's officers was standing beside us smoking a cigarette.

"Nex' year…gon' be better," he remarked, waving his arm toward the open ocean.

"Better?" Farley asked.

"Car ferry. Arrive in de spring."

"A car ferry? Really?" I repeated, surprised that we hadn't heard anything about it.

"She gon' make one voyage each day. From Souris then back again. Forty cars. Per'aps me, I take my car and make a *vacances* on PEI. Possible to drive to Montreal." His face lit up with pleasure at the thought of lots of future travels by car.

It bothered me that we hadn't heard about the impending car-ferry service, but there was no newspaper and I wasn't fluent enough in French to follow newscasts on the radio. The English-language CBC station in Moncton, which came in loud and clear on the Magdalens, didn't seem to know the islands existed.

"A car ferry would make our life a lot easier," I said to Farley, as we were getting ready to bunk down for the night.

"Yeah. Easier—for us and for everyone else. Forty cars a day. Could be the end of this little paradise once the hordes discover it."

"You think they will?" I asked. "Hey, have you noticed we are the only passengers on this ship? How many people do you think would ever want to come here anyway?"

"We'll find out," he said, and snapped off the light.

Chapter Five

WE ARRIVED BACK AT OUR HOME in Port Hope on the last day of September. Less than a week later we heard startling news on the radio. The British trade commissioner in Montreal, James Cross, had been kidnapped from his home by a group of people calling themselves the Front de Libération du Québec—the FLQ. I could hardly believe what I was hearing. A political kidnapping in Canada? This kind of thing happened somewhere else—in Latin America perhaps, or the Middle East—but surely not here.

There had been indications of underlying discontent in Montreal during the 1960s. Several bombs had exploded in mailboxes as a protest against the British symbols in the Canadian coat of arms, which at that time was emblazoned on all mailboxes across Canada. The 1960s had also been the decade of the Quiet Revolution in Quebec. Now, suddenly, it was anything but quiet.

The tense days wore on, bringing no release for the unfortunate Mr. Cross. Instead, harsh demands from the FLQ were being broadcast from a Montreal French-language station. The FLQ issued fierce diatribes against "English" institutions in Quebec—everything from Eaton's and Morgan's and General Motors to the Iron Ore Company of Canada. They also blamed the Roman Catholic Church for the impoverishment of the French because the Church, they claimed, had collaborated with the enemy, the hated English. Their list of arch-enemies included Quebec Premier Robert Bourassa and Prime Minister Pierre Trudeau, as well as all the leading Montreal captains of industry. The FLQ demanded that the people of Quebec take control of their destiny so that their "slave" society could become free.

They promised that Mr. Cross would remain unharmed on condition that their manifestos continued to be broadcast. Their final demand was that they (whoever *they* were) should be given a safe passage out of

Canada to a sympathetic post-revolutionary country such as Algeria or Cuba.

They were heard, not only by the people of Quebec, but also by people all over the world. Suddenly Canada, a country with an international reputation for beautiful scenery and peaceful, boring people, was making the front pages everywhere. Terrorists in Canada!

"Why the hell would they kidnap a British diplomat?" Farley wondered. "The guy is a trade commissioner, not some colonial viceroy."

Britain had no jurisdiction over Quebec, or any other part of Canada. The final strings had been cut back in 1931, when the Statute of Westminster established Canada's own Supreme Court. We Canadians were effectively on our own after that. But who was going to explain to armed terrorists there was a difference between the country called England and the millions of people in Canada who *spoke* English.

As it turned out, James Cross wasn't even English. He was Irish, but had made his career in the British diplomatic service. The irony was that Irish was the ancestry of many thousands of Québécois. I thought about the shipwreck of the *Miracle* and the orphans who had blended into the population of Les Îles de la Madeleine. I wondered how this news of the terrorists was being received on the islands. And what about us? We had just bought a house there, for heaven's sake. Were we now *les Anglais maudits*? The enemy?

Five days later there was a second kidnapping. This time of Pierre LaPorte, the Quebec Minister of Labour and Immigration. This kidnapping made even less sense than the first one. Apart from being a provincial Liberal politician who had to adhere to his party's policies, there was no apparent reason why LaPorte would be the target of kidnappers.

A week after he was abducted LaPorte's body was found in the trunk of a car. It was feared that James Cross might also have been killed.

The Government of Canada now invoked the War Measures Act. This little-known but drastic piece of legislation was intended for use in a wartime crisis. Its implementation shocked the country. The civil rights of every Canadian were suspended for as long as the act remained in effect. Any of us, anywhere in the country, could have been arrested and detained with no recourse to justice.

This draconian act seemed so out of character for Pierre Trudeau, a man of liberal ideas rather than repressive rules. Farley and I disagreed over the use of the War Measures Act. I believed that Trudeau had done what he had to do, considering the extraordinary circumstances. Farley believed it was an over-reaction, a violation of our rights, however valid the cause.

In the middle of October Farley began a cross-Canada author's tour to promote his newest book, *Sibir*. By now such gruelling tours had become a fixture in the world of book publishing. Farley had, at that point, survived five of them. They were a mixture of exhilaration and exhaustion. Any author who hoped to find his or her latest book on the best-seller list had to endure several weeks of radio, television, and newspaper interviews in a number of major Canadian cities.

Farley had a natural bent for media appearances. He could be funny when it suited him, serious when it was required, or angry when the occasion arose. I never worried about his ability to engage an audience, but I did worry about the stamina that was needed to survive these long, wearisome junkets across Canada.

That year there was an additional concern: his book tour was to begin in Montreal.

I usually joined Farley for trips to Montreal. It was a city I loved to visit and we had friends there. Back then, Montreal had several good English bookstores, an assortment of English-language radio and television shows, and two major daily newspapers in English.

Farley's tour had been organized by McClelland and Stewart's publicity department many weeks earlier; otherwise, we would not have chosen to arrive in Montreal on the evening before the day of Pierre LaPorte's funeral. It was not officially a state funeral but it was an occasion that would have done credit to a dead pope.

Montreal was normally a busy, bustling place—day or night. That October day it was ghostly. Most people who would normally have been downtown had cancelled their business lunches and postponed their shopping trips. Armed Canadian soldiers stood at all major intersections. I glanced in disbelief at these grim-faced young men as Farley and I were being whisked by taxi from one radio station to another. This was not a military exercise. This was real. From whom were the military protecting us? What was going to happen next?

In the radio and television studios there was little talk of anything except the startling and violent events that had recently taken place. Interviews with Farley were taped, to be broadcast at some later date. That day all of Canada was focused on the burial of an innocent man who had been the victim of some dark force that could, for all we knew, strike again, anywhere and at any time.

Sibir is about Siberia, a vast region that very few Canadians, or others in the western world, knew much about apart from the horror stories of Stalinist labour camps. We had travelled there together for two months in 1966. In 1969 Farley had gone back for a second tour of this enormous land whose geography and climate so closely resembled the Canadian far north.

He had discovered a lot about contemporary Siberia and the intention of his book was to enlighten readers about this much-maligned region of the USSR. Siberia was the Soviet Union's new frontier, the land where young, ambitious people from the European west of the country went to build careers in science, mining, construction, and the arts. Furthermore, Siberia was ahead of Canada in progressive social programs to protect the culture and languages of the many indigenous peoples who lived there. Farley thought this information might change the attitude of people who had long believed there was nothing in Siberia but prison camps, frozen mammoths, and the bones of Russian nobility assassinated in 1917.

There was something uncanny in listening to Farley talking about Siberia on radio and television that day when our own country was being subjected to repressive legislation. Canadian political activists had killed a man and they were still out there somewhere, shattering the myth of our peaceful nation.

On air, Farley let the Quebec audience know that we had recently bought a house in Maritime Quebec and intended to make a home—part-time or possibly full-time—in that province. This news didn't seem to capture the interest of anyone. To most Montrealers, les Îles de la Madeleine were almost as remote as Siberia. They lay a thousand miles to the east and were troublesome to reach, so it didn't make a lot of sense for Montrealers to go there for holidays when there were so many attractions that were much closer: the Laurentians, the Saguenay, the Eastern Townships, the Gaspé Peninsula. The landscape of Quebec is so varied and spectacular, ranging from the fertile farmlands that border the St. Lawrence River to the mountains and tundra of Ungava. Geography has bestowed grandeur on Quebec. History, at least as it was unfolding that day, did not seem to be so benevolent.

Farley was drained of energy by the end of each day. As usual on these tours, we had our supper sent up to the hotel room. There we watched a re-run of Pierre LaPorte's funeral on television and then went to bed, tired and dispirited.

Apart from fellow authors and people who worked in book publishing, there was a perception that a book promotion tour was a series of parties and autographing sessions. I suspect the notion came from the way popular authors have been portrayed in American movies—the celebrated author is the centre of attention amid adoring fans in glamorous surroundings. The reality was nothing of the sort.

Prior to the 1960s, Canadians who bought hardcover books at all generally chose the works of American or British writers. One reason English-speaking Canadians had difficulty defining ourselves as a nationality was that we rarely read books about ourselves by our own authors. However, by the 1970s we seemed, at long last, to be finding our way out of the literary desert and discovering one another.

Sibir: My Discovery of Siberia became a top seller in Canada. That same season also saw the publication of another very popular book: *The Last Spike* by Pierre Berton—the story of the building of the Canadian Pacific Railway in the nineteenth century, which was fundamental in linking the new western provinces to the east. Mordecai Richler launched a new novel that year titled *St. Urbain's Horseman*, a family story set in the old Montreal Jewish neighbourhood in which he had grown up. In Toronto a distinguished historian named William Kilbourn assembled an anthology of essays called, ironically, as things turned out, *Canada: A Guide to the Peaceable Kingdom*.

We had endured periodic American raids when we were still a collection of British colonies, rare uprisings like the Riel Rebellion in the 1880s and a few bitter industrial strikes over the years, but Canada had indeed been a reasonably peaceful place in which to live. The violence that had exploded in Quebec caught us off guard.

A book by a Quebec author, published in 1968, had described some unsettling realities. *Nègres Blancs d'Amérique* by Pierre Vallières was a bitter story of the author's own joyless, impoverished upbringing in working-class Montreal. This book touched a chord in Quebec. It quickly became the bible of young, angry, marginalized Québécois.

After the kidnapping of 1970 the book was published in English as *The White Niggers of America*. When I read it I began to understand why an earthquake was shaking our smug Canadian foundations.

In the United States that same year a new book by James Michener was published, *Kent State*. It was his investigation into the May 4, 1970, attack by the American military on a crowd of Ohio university students who were staging a peaceful protest against the war in Vietnam. Guns were fired. Four students died and thirteen others were injured. Canadians, along with people all over the world, were horrified. The shooting of innocent young people who were exercising freedom of speech was an alarming indication that justice was not being well served in the country next door to us. Yet here we were in Canada with terrorists at large and the War Measures Act imposed on all of us. Were we, as a nation, heading down the same slippery slope?

James Cross was finally released early in December, somewhat thinner but unharmed. In exchange, his five kidnappers, plus the wife and child of one of them, were flown by the Canadian military to Cuba, their choice of political asylum. After they had gone there was a national sigh of relief.

The War Measures Act was duly revoked after a few weeks. The murderers of Pierre LaPorte were captured, tried, and given sentences of life imprisonment. Our collective panic subsided. We were more than ready to return to that relatively unruffled kingdom we had taken for granted.

Chapter Six

WHEN FARLEY FINISHED his book tour we tried to settle into our winter routine, which for him meant starting in on his next book: a tragic account of a whale stranded in a cove in Newfoundland. However, his public persona brought innumerable intrusions into our life. There were requests from reporters and journalists who wanted him to comment on a whole range of subjects from politics to pets. From time to time he was approached by aspiring writers who wanted to know how they could get their work published. Environmental activists became frequent visitors, hoping to get Farley's endorsement for their plans to defeat the many poisonous assaults being made on our planet. Along with all of this, residents of Port Hope wanted one, or both, of us to get involved in community issues. Then there were people we didn't know at all who showed up at our front door simply because they wanted to meet Farley Mowat, as well as strangers who called on the phone just to have a chat.

We talked about getting an unlisted telephone number, although in the end we always decided against it. There seemed to be something both snooty and hostile about an unlisted number. We concluded we would simply have to put up with some unwanted phone calls. Most of the time I answered the phone and tried to screen the sincere callers from the nuisance ones.

In addition to reporters and curiosity seekers, as well as our friends and neighbours, we had other demands on our time. Farley's seventy-five-year-old mother, Helen Mowat, lived alone in her Port Hope house four blocks away from ours. Farley's father, Angus, had left his marriage to Helen a few years earlier, when he was seventy-two and Helen sixty-nine, to go and live with his long-time mistress, a former librarian named Barbara Hutchinson.

Like a lot of marriage break-ups, this one had appeared amicable at the outset. Angus and Helen had in fact being going their separate ways for many years but had always managed to preserve the façade of a marriage.

Farley and Angus Mowat, 1970

During this time they had been raising two children whom they had adopted fairly late in life. John and Mary were in their late teens when Angus left for good.

In some ways it must have been a relief for Helen to have him gone. He had been living a double life since his retirement as Director of Public Libraries for Ontario—staying home for a few days and then going off for a week or so. His excuse was that he was visiting Indian reserves in order to help establish local libraries. The reality was that when absent from Port Hope he had been spending his time with Barbara. I believe Helen had well-founded suspicions but preferred not to see them confirmed.

I was very fond of Angus. It would have been difficult to find anyone who wasn't. I often said to Farley that his father should have been an actor because he fairly swaggered across life's stage, energetically living the roles of soldier, farmer, librarian, yachtsman, novelist, civil servant, and finally boat builder. In later years he embraced his part-Scottish ancestry with a passion, dressing variously in a kilt, Scotch bonnet, plaid "troos," and an Inverness cape.

It was Angus's passion for all things Scottish that led Farley to purchase a complete kilt outfit for himself a year later, when we were touring Scotland. I loved his new clothes. To me, men wearing the kilt look sexy. However, I didn't share Angus's obsession, or Farley's more moderate affinity, with Scotland. For one thing, I have no Scots ancestors at all. More importantly, I was concerned with defining myself as a Canadian—a much more challenging pursuit in a country that had only recently shifted from the British Empire into a quasi-colonial wing of the American Empire. It was just that—our growing affinity with the culture of the United States— that had spurred Angus on his nostalgic quest for the rugged land that had been the home of about half of his ancestors.

At the age of sixty-six Angus had gone alone on a walking tour of Scotland, completing his journey in the northern county of Caithness, from which his paternal great-grandfather had emigrated. Born in 1892, one year older than my own father, Angus was so unlike all the other men I had known from my father's generation that he shone like a comet.

Farley was sure there had been many women in Angus's life and it was easy to see why they had been attracted to him. Whether they were the cause of the gradual demise of his marriage to Helen or the result of it is hard to say.

Helen was a gentle, philosophical, religious woman who read several books every week, with a preference for British authors of the early twentieth century, including every book by C.S. Lewis. She was well-liked by a circle of loyal friends and neighbours, but had little practical knowledge of how to live on her own. Born in 1896, she belonged to a generation of women who had little choice but to leave the finances of the home to their husbands: mortgages, taxes, insurance, house repairs, vehicles. Helen had never paid a telephone bill until Angus moved out. She never did learn to drive a car.

We did what we could to help her. We gave her moral support and located tradesmen and snow shovellers as they were required. The charming clapboard cottage in which she lived was 130 years old, and something in it always needed to be fixed.

By 1970 it was obvious she needed more financial support than Angus had agreed to provide. Helen lived very modestly. Nevertheless, Angus and Barbara questioned the cost of her minor household requirements. Who authorized a new porch light fixture? What was wrong with the old one? Too much money was paid to the fellow who repaired the broken fence, they claimed. When the dining room ceiling fell down we had to endure long, nit-picking discussions with Barbara about getting it fixed the cheapest possible way.

Sometimes during the winter, when we had a couple of undemanding days, we would drive east to Prince Edward County to visit Angus and Barbara, who were living near Northport in a modern log house overlooking the Bay of Quinte. Farley had always had a close, complex relationship with his flamboyant father and none of us—not even Helen—wanted to see that erode. Visiting him on the shore of the frozen Bay of Quinte was a treat. It removed us temporarily from the tangle of obligations in Port Hope.

Angus and Barbara made an odd-looking couple. Barbara was in her early forties and Angus in his mid-seventies. She was taller than Angus by quite a bit and had red hair. Angus was a slightly built man with white hair and, later, a white beard. Although they never married, Barbara referred to herself as Mrs. Mowat for the sake of respectability. "Living in sin," as it was generally called at the time, was not socially acceptable in rural Ontario.

Barbara was only half a dozen years older than I—much closer to my age than to Farley's mother's. I had assumed she and I would become good friends. We shared many interests: books, recipes, CBC radio, dogs, gossip. And, of course, Angus. For a long time the couple urged us to move closer to them, insisting that Farley would have more time to write and fewer distractions if we lived in rural Prince Edward County—which is a very pleasant part of Ontario. We were tempted. Barbara sent us real estate advertisements from the local papers, featuring gracious old stone farmhouses that were picturesque and affordable. I have since wondered if she was truly eager to have us living close by or simply wanted us not to live in the same town as Helen.

Farley, however, wasn't sure he belonged in Ontario at all. He was toying with the idea that we make the Magdalen Islands our permanent home—with brief trips back to Ontario for business purposes and to visit friends and family.

From the beginning of our life together, Farley and I had to make a decision that circumstances dictated for most people. We could live almost anywhere in the world we chose. Farley earned his living working from home and could make enough money at it to support his first wife Frances and the two boys and ourselves; not lavishly but adequately. But where exactly, given so much choice, would we choose to call home?

We agreed that we would never leave Canada permanently. We knew we would never feel the attachment—the same emotion—for any other nation. The food may have tasted better in France, the architecture of Italy was more inspiring, and the ancient history of Scotland was more engrossing, but Canada was where we belonged.

Our dilemma was that Canada was huge. In which corner of it should we make a home?

I thought about our Magdalen Island house many times during that winter. I had been gathering furnishings, trying to picture each room and how improved it would look with a braided rug on the floor, an Indian cotton spread on the bed, Marimekko draperies framing the window, and an art poster tacked to the wall. I've never been much of a seamstress but I did own a sewing machine and when I could find the time I managed to sew some pillow covers and drapes.

In May that year Farley would turn fifty and we decided to throw a large party to celebrate the occasion. It was to be a weekend affair with a recommendation that Toronto guests book accommodation at a local motel rather than make the long drive home after an evening of revelry.

Max Braithwaite was a longtime friend and fellow author then living in Orangeville with his wonderful wife, Aileen, and the youngest three of their five children. When Farley and I had first moved to Port Hope, Max had given us some good advice. If you live in a small town, he said, but also have friends in the city, you should never invite the two groups to the same party. They don't mix, he explained. It's not that they dislike one another; they simply have nothing in common. The city people will huddle together with other city people who share their concerns. The town people will do the same.

This was true. The only time we blended Toronto friends with local friends was when we were giving a dinner party small enough for everyone to get acquainted.

Our house, at 25 John Street in downtown Port Hope, was a Victorian brick building. It was rundown when we bought it but its spacious rooms appealed to us so we became part of the wave of gentrifiers of old downtowns everywhere: Cabbagetown, Gastown, Old Montreal. These were neighbourhoods architecturally neglected for nearly a century. We didn't have enough money to give our house the facelift it deserved but we did manage to get rid of most of the brown linoleum on the floor, strip off the worst of the 1940s wallpaper, fix the leaks in the roof, and apply fresh paint to doors and windowsills.

We loved the house, though our immediate neighbourhood left a lot to be desired. We were across the street from a busy Canadian Tire store. Beside us was a parking lot for the patrons of a nearby beer parlour. Directly behind our small back yard was a rarely used spur line of a railway and, beyond that, the town's municipal parking lot. It was a far cry from the grassy hill, the auburn soil, and the ever-changing ocean that surrounded our Magdalen Island house.

But it was a perfect house for a party. It had elegant double front doors with a broad, welcoming centre hall. The rooms were laid out in such a way that guests could easily circulate. A wide stairway led up to another spacious hall on the second floor, which turned out to be the ideal place to set up the bar.

The guests at Farley's fiftieth birthday were mainly from the Toronto world of radio, television, book publishing, magazines, and newspapers, which constituted a village of its own. In 1971 there were not a lot of Canadians making a living writing books or hosting television shows. The handful who had become celebrities had been dubbed, by one Toronto reporter, "The Comfortable Few," a word play on the title of Pierre Berton's recent book, *The Comfortable Pew*, about organized religion in Canada.

Our guests were Max and Aileen Braithwaite, Pierre and Janet Berton, Bill and June Frayne (known professionally as Trent Frayne and June Callwood), and Stephen Franklin, a popular journalist at *Week-End* magazine, and his wife, Elsa. Farley had a passion for the voice of singer

Catherine McKinnon, so we invited her and the man she had recently married, actor Don Harron. Helen Hutchinson, who hosted her own television show at CFTO, attended with her husband. They brought a friend they had known since university days in Vancouver, a west-coast newspaper columnist named Alan Fotheringham. Morton Shulman—who had made a name for himself as the fighting Ontario coroner and who was making an even bigger splash as an author, with his book *Anyone Can Make a Million*—came with his charming wife, Gloria. Sylvia Fraser, a journalist whose star would soon be rising with the publication of her first novel, *Pandora*, came with her husband, Russell. That marriage would soon crumble. And so would the marriage of another pair of guests: TV host Adrienne Clarkson and her husband, University of Toronto professor Stephen Clarkson.

The one cherished friend who declined to attend was Jack McClelland, Farley's Canadian publisher. Elizabeth, his supportive wife, came to the party but Jack, she apologized, was too despairing to spend a gala evening in the midst of so many of his authors. His firm, McClelland and Stewart, which his father had founded in 1906, had recently been listed for sale. It had been hovering on the edge of bankruptcy for the past few years. Trying to stay afloat while publishing Canadian books was a dicey business, then as now. In view of the overwhelming avalanche of American books, it was miraculous that Canadian literature existed at all.

Jack, a Canadian nationalist like the rest of us, refused to sell his quintessentially Canadian business to an American conglomerate. Such had been the recent fate of the Ryerson Press, a long-established Canadian publishing company that had been sold to the American firm of McGraw-Hill. Eventually the province of Ontario would come to McClelland and Stewart's rescue with a one-million-dollar loan, which, with some subsequent grants from the federal government, would keep the barely solvent company alive for another fifteen years. However, on Farley's fiftieth birthday it appeared that the flagship of Canadian publishing was about to sink. Jack, who had contributed enormously to Farley's career and to the careers of many authors, was profoundly depressed.

We served Ukrainian food at the party, an ethnic novelty for these worldly people, who had more often dined on the cuisine of France or Italy.

There were no caterers in Port Hope then but we had discovered the culinary talents of the Wladyka family. Bill and Mike Wladyka ran the Queen's Hotel and Beverage Room just up the street from our house. Their wives, both named Mary, prepared the most delicious cabbage rolls and perogies, a legacy of their Ukrainian heritage. We persuaded them to provide our supper.

Most of our guests stayed overnight at the Greenwood Tower—the only motel in town—and returned to an outdoor gathering in our garden the next morning for a brunch of scrambled eggs cooked by Farley.

When the last guests had departed and we had cleaned up the mess, I was tired but happy. Our friends had travelled an hour or more from Toronto to celebrate Farley's half-century. It was one of those moments when it dawned on me that, in the orbit of Canadian writing, Farley was a genuine celebrity.

Fame is an intangible phenomenon. You are only famous among those people who acknowledge that you are. I, for instance, who do not follow professional hockey, would not have recognized the most celebrated hockey player even if he had appeared at my front door. Among people who did not read Canadian books nor listen to the Canadian radio nor watch Canadian television, Farley was not famous at all. Whenever there was a new clerk at the drugstore or the dry cleaners, I usually had to spell our last name for them. This I took to be a lesson in humility. It would save us, as my late grandmother would have admonished, from getting "a swelled head."

As my life with Farley got busier and busier, I felt badly that I wasn't spending enough time with my mother, Winnie Wheeler, then a seventy-year-old widow living in an apartment in the Colonnade on Bloor Street in Toronto. My mother didn't often complain about my long absences from her life. She had many friends. She did volunteer work, travelled a bit, and cherished her summer cottage in Muskoka. When Farley went off to Montreal one spring day to finish the script for a National Film Board film, I went to Toronto to spend a few days with Winnie.

We went shopping at Eaton's College Street store, where I helped her choose a new carpet. Just being inside that store was a pleasure in itself. A classic art nouveau building, it was so much more elegant than the creaky old Queen Street store. Eaton's College Street was built in 1931 and should have become the firm's flagship store. It failed to do so for two reasons: the Depression of the 1930s put a stop to full completion of the building and then College Street was soon supplanted by Bloor Street, further north, as Toronto's newest upscale commercial district.

One evening Mom and I played Scrabble, a game we both loved. Another evening we went to see *Klute* starring Jane Fonda and the great Canadian actor Donald Sutherland. This was the first time I had watched a movie that featured a nude love scene, and I can still remember how uncomfortable we both felt.

Some days later I boarded the overnight train from Toronto to Montreal and in the morning Farley met me at the Dorval station. By evening we were at Pier 47 at the foot of Pius IX Boulevard, ready to board that grungy old ship with the unimaginative name *C.T.M.A.* I could hardly wait until they cast off the mooring lines and we got underway.

Chapter Seven

W HEN OUR SHIP DOCKED at Grindstone, Father Frédéric Landry was on the wharf waiting to welcome us back. It was early evening, under a threatening sky, so he invited us to stay overnight at his *presbytère*, only a few miles away. Our house, an hour's drive, would be cold and damp and without food.

Frédéric lived alone in a well-appointed house with four bedrooms. His housekeeper, he told us, would arrive in the morning to make breakfast for us. This was a welcome invitation. After a three-day voyage that had taken us to several ports on the north shore of the St. Lawrence, as well as six hours in the rain at a wharf near the town of Gaspé, the prospect of a clean bed in a warm house was an offer we accepted without hesitation.

We slept in the bedroom usually reserved for the visiting bishop, complete with a prie-dieu and a huge portrait of Christ. A large wooden cross presided over us on the wall above the bed. Our two dogs slept on the floor.

At breakfast Frédéric told us that the museum that he had been trying to establish was soon to become a reality. He had obtained a grant, and construction would soon begin on the building in which he would display his burgeoning collection of artifacts and photographs. We were as pleased as he was that his vision was finally taking shape.

Frédéric also told us that the *North Gaspé*—that sturdy little ship that for so long had maintained the link with Prince Edward Island and Nova Scotia—had been sold.

"We 'ave a new car ferry. Bigger. Faster," he nodded approvingly.

"I didn't know it was in operation," Farley said, "and I asked my travel agent to check. She couldn't find any mention of it."

"Ah, *pas encore*. She was suppose' to commence now, in the spring... but..." he shrugged, "not ready."

"How are we going to get food—milk and potatoes and everything—over from PEI?" I asked.

Claire, Grande Entrée, 1971

"The airplane bring that," Frédéric reassured us.

Later that morning we made the long drive from Havre-Aubert to Grande Entrée and, once again, were captivated by the beauty of the cinnamon-coloured cliffs, the white sand beaches, the broad lagoons, and, that day, heavenly blue skies. Our house was waiting. Soon it would come alive with the sound of voices, the aroma of cooking, new curtains fluttering in the breeze, laundry on the line, dogs barking, and friends coming to visit.

How we savoured the magic moments when first we stepped inside. But then we had to deal with reality.

The plumbing, which Farley believed he had fully drained the previous fall, refused to function. Some hidden section of it had frozen and burst. The water pump in the cellar wouldn't work, nor would the hot-water heater.

Farley is a handyman. For years I had watched him fixing all sorts of household machinery—often in other people's homes, which made him a welcome guest. He got to work straight away, removing panels and fiddling with the pipes. The real setback came when he went out to the barn to retrieve some wrenches and discovered someone had broken in and stolen the tools he had left there.

"Bloody hell," he muttered. It was no great financial loss. They were second-hand tools and not worth much. It was the inconvenience that was so annoying. It hadn't occurred to either one of us that anyone would bother to break in to an almost-empty barn with a padlock on the door. A dozen tools, hanging on a wall over a work bench, were the only things that had been taken. The thieves hadn't attempted to steal the lawn mower or the garden chairs. "Kids, I guess," Farley concluded. "I should have known better than to leave tools in there. I'll go and see Isaac. He'll lend me a pipe wrench."

Isaac LaPierre operated the only garage in Grande Entrée. A young man in his twenties, he had recently returned to the islands after spending five years working in a downtown Montreal garage, an expensive place catering to owners of sports cars. Now he fixed trucks, school buses, and the engines that powered the lobster boats. He may have earned less money than he did in Montreal, where he had been a cog in a big machine, but here in Grande Entrée he was indispensable.

When Farley told him of our plumbing problems he immediately offered to come over and help solve them. The two of them soon managed to get the cold water running to the kitchen and bathroom. Nothing could be done about hot water until we got a new heating coil. Isaac said he knew of a place in Moncton to which he could send for one.

It was discouraging to have things go wrong on our first day back, but I was determined not to let it spoil our pleasure at being there. The dogs, relishing their freedom, raced around the property, sniffing, exploring, and searching for last summer's bones. Far offshore I caught a glimpse of a flock of gannets plummeting into the ocean in search of fish. Closer to shore a clutch of coal-black cormorants flew by. On the ground around me a galaxy of wild strawberry plants were in bloom. Ah, this was why we were here. Plumbing be damned! I relished the view for a few moments, then returned to the house to look for a can of soup for lunch.

At least the stove was working.

And so was the telephone. We hadn't even unpacked our car when the first call came in. It was from an official at the Department of Parks in Ottawa. Farley had written to them several weeks earlier, complaining about the wanton slaughter of ducks and geese—mainly out of season— that took place on the many ponds of East Point. He was advocating the establishment of a marine wildlife park there to protect both the birds and the entire ecosystem.

To Farley's surprise the Feds were actually interested in his proposal. The call was to tell him that Robert Shaw, deputy minister in charge of national parks, would be arriving in the Magdalens in a few days, accompanied by two men from his department. They were coming to look at the marine park possibilities and wanted Farley to be their guide.

For years Farley had been badgering government officials about a multitude of problems that needed attention immediately, including starving Inuit, endangered wildlife, and the U.S. threat to Canada. Most of the time the response had been a polite letter thanking him for his concern. This time it appeared he had triggered a real reaction.

I was hardly ready to welcome visitors. The house was a shambles of unpacked cartons and exposed plumbing. We still had barely enough furniture for two people to sit down together. All I really wanted was to be left alone for a while to put my house in order.

"Relax," Farley told me. "These guys are on expense accounts. They won't expect you to look after them."

"Sure, but *where* are they going to stay, and eat, if not with us?"

I needn't have worried. Things were starting to change. A spanking new motel had opened in Grindstone just in time to accommodate the three men from Ottawa. And we were pleasantly surprised to find a little café had recently opened in Grosse Île. Its limited menu offered only soup, burgers, and fries, but this satisfied our visitors, who hospitably took Farley and me out to lunch there.

Afterwards the five of us hiked to the top of the isolated monolith called East Cape. East Cape, about as high as an eight-storey building, had been sculpted by the sea but the water was no longer near it. Over the centuries the ocean had built, in front of East Cape, a vast peninsula of sand that now formed the great sweep of dunes, ponds, and beaches of East Point, the place we hoped the government would protect and preserve.

We all marvelled at the sensational view, feeling like monarchs of all we surveyed. Sculpted clouds were rolling past. The ocean, dotted with distant fishing boats, was a dramatic shade of metallic grey. Even these men, whose work took them to so many spectacular places, were impressed. Bob Shaw was convinced that the Point should be protected. However, he warned it was no easy matter to establish national parks or wildlife refuges in Quebec. Quebec preferred to administer its own protected spaces and resisted setting aside any large tracts of land that would come under federal control.

Perhaps, he said, the fact that Farley, a local resident, had initiated this project might help. Farley replied that he hardly qualified as a local person, having spent only a total of five months on the islands over two summers. Nevertheless, Shaw seemed optimistic, though he warned it might be a long and tedious process. At any rate, he would begin right away to try and have East Point turned into one of Canada's first National Marine Parks.

A week or so later we went over to say hello to Morris McQuaid in his boat shed. We were interested to see what progress he had made with his masterpiece. The ship now had ribs and a keel and we could more easily imagine how she would eventually look.

Laconic Morris rarely gave more than a nod in greeting and perhaps some comment about the weather. This day, however, he had something else to say. "Duck huntin's always been the way we lived around here," he proclaimed out of the blue. It seemed a strange remark to make in June, when we were months away from hunting season.

"Fishin' too. That's what these fellas do. Always done. Long as I can remember. Long as my father could remember."

"True enough," Farley agreed.

As we walked back home we wondered why Morris had mentioned these subjects since he neither fished nor hunted himself.

The following day Farley answered the telephone and got a tirade from an anonymous voice—in English—warning him to "Keep offa my land!"

We dismissed this as a crank call, or a wrong number. Apart from climbing East Cape we hadn't been trespassing on anyone's land. We had, in fact, been staying close to home. I was busy painting walls and putting up drapes. Farley was writing his whale story in the mornings and in the afternoons he was slogging away in the field next to our house to establish a vegetable garden.

It wasn't until a few days later when he had an unexpected visitor that we finally realized what was going on. The visit was an angry young woman from Grosse Île who immediately began yelling at Farley.

"My husband's ancestors came here years and years ago! They worked hard to build their homes and their boats and make a living. The land is theirs! They won't let you take it away from them!"

I was flabbergasted. What was she shouting about?

"Hey, hey, calm down. Who's taking anything away from anybody?" Farley asked.

"The government. They were here. So were you. You showed them around. Everybody knows what you're up to," she insisted.

Now we understood. While eating our lunch in the café in Grosse Île we had been chatting about such things as the enforcement of the International Migratory Bird Act, what sort of waterfowl protection would be needed in a marine park, and what could be done to stop people trapping lobsters out of season. Our conversation must have been of great interest to the waitress and anyone else within earshot. Farley and I were already suspicious outsiders and the three men with us looked precisely what they were—government bureaucrats. We could scarcely have generated more alarm had we been Russian spies. And to add fuel to the fire we had innocently climbed the Cape without asking anyone's permission. The people of Grosse Île had concluded we were planning to drive them off their lands.

Rumours, we were discovering, whipped around these islands faster than grains of sand in a gale.

When Joan Richards calmed down enough to identify herself, she proved not quite so formidable as she had seemed. We offered her tea and gradually, grudgingly, her mood improved. She was plucky. It had taken courage to drive right up to our house and beard the lion in his den, as it were. Joan was not a Magdalen Islander herself but was married to one. She was from Prince Edward Island, where she had met her husband during his student years at the University of Prince Edward Island. Stuart Richards, born and raised in Grosse Île, was now about to become the principal of the local school.

Farley carefully explained that the federal government did not plan to uproot anyone. It was merely investigating the possibility of a national marine park, something that would be good for these islands and for the people who lived here. It would conserve the natural resources of East

Point and would likely become a destination for tourists. "Tourists bring money into a community. Why would anyone be opposed to that?"

"That's not what the people think. They think the government is going to confiscate their homes and their land and turn the whole of Grosse Île into a park. Like they did over in the Gaspé. You know what happened there. People were forced out of their homes and their houses were burned to the ground. It was brutal!"

This was true enough. Real injustices had occurred in the recent past during the creation of new national parks in eastern Quebec and in New Brunswick. People had been paid compensation for their homes and lands but no amount of money could put a rural community back together once it had been dispersed. Bureaucrats who make decisions about expropriation live in cities and rarely understand the deep bonds in a village where the same families have lived for generations.

Farley's involvement seemed to some islanders like the missing piece in the puzzle. It explained why he had bought a house here on the islands. He was part of a sinister plot to turf everyone off the northeast end of the islands—specifically the English community—and to ban all hunting and even the fishing that was the economic base of the place.

Joan appeared to grasp that this was not the case, so we asked her to explain things to her family and neighbours. We also said we would like to meet her husband and maybe we could get together for a meal.

"Not till fishing's over. Right now Stuart is helping his father fish lobster. That's what he loves. Once he takes the principal's job he won't have time to fish any more," she explained, a bit sadly.

After she left we wondered if Joan's enlightened version of the facts would be believed. She was an outsider too, although being married to a local man would give her more credibility than we had.

The whole thing made me squirm. I was accustomed to being an outsider, but not one accused of being an accomplice in some dark plot.

We encountered an additional difficulty that summer: a shortage of food. Because the *North Gaspé* had been sold and the new car ferry had yet to be delivered, basic supplies, most of which came from Prince Edward Island, were reduced to what could be flown in. Milk, eggs, and dairy products became very scarce. So did fresh vegetables. Oranges, bananas, and apples were rarities. The plodding *C.T.M.A.* could bring in flour, sugar, canned goods, soft drinks, beer, wine, and liquor from Montreal, but the supply of air-lifted perishable food did not meet the demand.

Farley had planted an impressive array of vegetables in his garden but it would be the end of July before it would yield anything to sustain us.

Shopping became an even worse ordeal. I still felt I was being stared at—and suspected of some treachery—yet I had to visit more stores than usual in my search for items of food I had always considered basic necessities. I am an inventive cook and I had learned to make do with powdered milk instead of fresh and canned milk instead of cream, but I found it a real obstacle to try and cook without such ingredients as eggs or onions. We could, of course, buy all the lobsters we cared to eat but finding butter to melt as a dipping sauce was no easy matter.

I tried not to complain. We weren't going to starve. I thought of my relatives in England during the Second World War, and remembered my mother constantly sending them food parcels. Living on a beleaguered island, they had to endure food shortages because of insufficient shipping. Now, on an island in peacetime Canada, we were reminded how vital ocean transport is.

There was a significant difference between the efficiency of marine transport in Quebec and in Newfoundland. The outport of Burgeo on Newfoundland's southwest coast, where we had lived in the 1960s, had been every bit as isolated as the Magdalen Islands and both places relied on ships to bring much of what people ate as well as a host of other goods. The difference was that Newfoundland was served by an organization called Marine Atlantic, which was operated by the federal government of Canada. If one of their ships went out of service, they always seemed able to find a replacement and more or less keep the schedule. Except during the worst storms of the winter, we could rely on one ship eastbound and one ship westbound every week.

That summer, in the Magdalens, where shipping was in private hands, no scheduled ships from the Maritimes reached us until the autumn.

Chapter Eight

WE DIDN'T EXPECT TO SEE very many visitors that summer. As it turned out, the hippies had discovered the Magdalens. Hitchhiking had taken on a new respectability and drivers of cars and trucks were generously offering rides to the roving young people who stood on the shoulders of highways, begging for a lift. Highway travel, if you weren't in too big a hurry, had never been easier for the young and footloose.

The Canadian East Coast—land of sea breezes and down-home folks—had become a popular destination, especially remote places like the Magdalens. There were two affordable flights a day from Charlottetown. As well there was a newf airline called Air Gaspé that linked Quebec City with several communities in eastern Quebec, including this one.

The Quebec department of tourism had also discovered the islands and was advertising this sandy haven as a great place for a vacation. The promoters no doubt believed an influx of tourists would make us more prosperous. They had not paused to consider that there were as yet no campgrounds, there was only one motel and one antiquated hotel, there were no restaurants worthy of the name, and the new car ferry had yet to arrive.

As the weeks of summer wore on there was seldom a day without strangers showing up at our door looking for a place to camp. Jean-Jacques and Annette, a pair of backpackers dressed in windproof jackets with multi-pocketed shorts and sturdy hiking books, knocked on our door one day to ask if they could fill their water bottles from our outdoor tap. They were a polite French-speaking couple in their twenties who also spoke precise English. Surprisingly, they were from France. European tourists were unusual in Canada in 1971. We chatted with them for a while and suggested a couple of good places nearby where they could pitch their tent sheltered from the wind.

However, it started to rain so we invited them in. We were curious as to what brought them here. Jean-Jacques, it turned out, was an officer in the

Claire in the kitchen, Grande Entrée, 1971

French army. As part of his military service he had the option of serving as an attaché in some other French-speaking country. Quebec—though not by definition a *country*—was on the list and he and his fiancée, Annette, had chosen to spend his overseas year in Quebec City.

I wondered exactly what he, a French army officer, would do in the provincial administration. Was it possible the French army was plotting a coup against the rest of Canada? It had only been five years since General Charles de Gaulle had shouted, *"Vive le Québec libre!"* from the balcony of Montreal city hall. However, we didn't discuss de Gaulle. Instead, we talked about the many species of birds to be seen in the Magdalen Islands.

From the beginning of their Quebec year this was the one place they had most wanted to see. I think they were, as we were, fascinated by maps and atlases, and on any map this lonely archipelago had a magnetic appeal. Jean-Jacques and Annette were the sort of travellers who took a keen interest in everything they encountered. Because the rain was pelting down by then, we invited them to stay for dinner and overnight even though they insisted they were quite capable of pitching their tent in the rain. I cooked a meal of spaghetti with Farley's homemade sauce, which he made in great quantities and then froze in small portions. It was my standby for unexpected visitors.

The next day the sun shone and the travellers made their camp on a hill overlooking our beach, but far enough from our house so they were discreetly out of sight.

A new Anglican minister had arrived a few months earlier—from South Africa. Anglican clergy have a portable profession, should they choose to serve in some far-flung corner of what used to be the British Empire. The previous incumbent here had departed for a posting to a church in Australia. The Reverend Richard Blythe had, for whatever reason, made a similarly long trek to tend a scattered flock of Anglicans in this nethermost corner of Quebec.

He dropped in to see us occasionally, a tall, thin bachelor in his thirties with the aura of a mystic who might have worn a hair shirt or endured forty days in the desert as part of his spiritual journey. I could hardly imagine how these windswept islands must have looked to him after his previous life in the lush landscape of South Africa.

Rhoda Turner told us she liked this new minister. She said he was a lovely speaker and his sermons didn't last too long. He was a man who did a lot of visiting. Visiting was a prized quality in a religious leader here.

One group of people who had no hesitation about simply showing up at our door were former Magdalen Islanders who had moved away to Canadian cities and were home for a summer holiday. Some of them had heard of Farley Mowat, the outspoken author, even if their country cousins had not. They were curious to meet him and, in the tradition of the rural Maritimes, simply dropped in for a visit when it suited them. It didn't always suit us.

At first Farley was patient and polite and signed autographs and tried to find something to talk about with this passing parade of complete strangers. However, as the summer weeks brought more and more of these people their visits became an intrusion. Farley—like it or not—was becoming a tourist attraction.

Farley's vegetable garden was also an object of local curiosity. Almost no one under the age of seventy was still growing anything to eat. Growing one's own food was considered old-fashioned and our neighbours must have wondered why we, who could obviously afford to buy all our food at the store, would make such an effort to plant and tend and harvest. People gazed at our garden as if it was a horse and cart, a curiosity from a bygone time. Farley proudly pointed out the green shoots that would soon become lettuce, green beans, peas, carrots, spinach, tomatoes, and a vegetable that few people here had heard of—zucchini.

I groaned whenever I saw an unfamiliar car turning into our driveway. Farley decided there was only one thing to do—close the gate at the end of our drive. Our land was fenced at the roadside but our gate, and everyone else's gate, was normally left open. To this day a closed gate is an unfriendly gesture in most of rural eastern Canada. It suggests that you think yourself better than your neighbours and that you'd prefer not to have anything to do with them. I didn't like being regarded as a snob but our open gate was an invitation both to the people who wanted to gape at Farley as well as to a few others who simply walked in and sauntered across our property en route to the beach.

Early in July we had a visit from Peter Davison, who was Farley's American editor. A charming, erudite man, who was then forty-three years old, he was big and handsome with a head of curly brown hair I would have died for. He had been visiting Farley, and then Farley and me, intermittently for about ten years. Wherever we happened to be—Palgrave, Toronto, Burgeo, Montreal, Port Hope, and now these remote Quebec islands—sooner or later Peter would turn up, sometimes alone and sometimes with his witty, dark-haired wife, Jane.

A book editor needs to keep in touch with a valued author. Authors work alone and most of them need a lot of reassurance from someone they respect and trust. Writing a book can be a very uncertain process.

Peter worked with Atlantic Monthly Press in Boston and edited the work of an impressive array of American authors, and he was soon to add the poetry of Margaret Atwood to his editorial roster. He was a personal friend of Robert Frost, John Updike, and, at one time, Sylvia Plath. He edited both prose and poetry but first and foremost he was a celebrated poet himself. Four books of his poems were in print by 1971 and he was often asked to read at poetry festivals all over the United States. His father,

Peter Davison with Claire, Grande Entré, 1971

Edward Davison, by then a retired university professor, was a renowned American poet as well. Very few poets—even in affluent America—can make a living by poetry alone. Peter's career as a book editor paid the bills, but poetry was his real life's work.

In Cambridge, Massachusetts, two blocks from Harvard University, Peter and Jane and their young son and daughter lived among other American intellectuals and artists. Theirs was a lifestyle I occasionally envied but Farley didn't. He enjoyed the company of gifted people as long as it wasn't in a city. Any big city made Farley both claustrophobic and melancholy.

Farley's work was not as widely read in the United States as it was in Canada. His books rarely made the best-seller lists in the States but he did have a loyal American following, particularly on the west coast.

When Peter stayed with us he spent much of his time discussing Farley's current work or the next book he intended to write. However, it wasn't all work. Peter had the capacity to enjoy himself wherever he landed. Like Farley, he was a keen bird watcher. But unlike Farley, Peter had a vast knowledge of music and a splendid tenor voice. In Cambridge he belonged to a group of madrigal singers and, as he wandered along the broad beaches of the Magdalens, he would sometimes burst into "Sweet Phyllis" or "The Merry Month of May."

I found Peter to be an easy house guest because he was so adept at amusing himself. Farley, on the other hand, knew him as a very demanding editor. Peter's intense scrutiny of Farley's work was both stimulating and stressful. Peter was sympathetic to Farley's great causes so there was never any philosophical rift between them. Their disagreements occurred over the question of what Peter believed the readers wanted to hear from Farley Mowat. A book editor has to gauge what the reading public wants...which is not always precisely what an author wants to write.

Whenever Peter came to visit us he would purchase a box of tea bags to take back home. Ordinary Canadian tea, of the supermarket variety, was, he claimed, far superior to any you could buy in the States. Americans, he lamented, simply had no concept of how to appreciate a good cup of tea. Canadians did.

Like us, Peter loved dogs and was full of admiration for Albert, the "water dog" we had acquired when we lived on the southwest coast of Newfoundland. Albert was a warrior, a unique entertainer, and very, very smart. Peter was always urging Farley to write a book about that dog. He persisted with that request for the next thirty years, until his death. That book has yet to be written.

Peter stayed for four days and had only been gone for a couple of days when our next guests arrived. During the previous winter Farley had been describing the wonders of these islands to most of our Ontario friends and had generously invited them to come and stay with us. Little did we imagine how many of them would accept.

Arnold and Vi Warren were treasured friends who had been Farley's neighbours when he lived on a side road near Palgrave, Ontario. They knew his first wife, Fran, and their two sons, Sandy and David. They had volunteered to bring David, then fifteen, with them that summer so that he could have a holiday with his father and me.

The Warrens—Arnold was about sixty then and Vi about a decade younger—had lived adventurous lives. Among other things, both of them had been pilots for about twenty-five years. Arnold, a slim, unassuming-looking man, had been a flying instructor in the Canadian Air Force and some time later in the Indonesian Air Force. Both Arnold and Vi had worked as bush pilots in northern Ontario.

Vi, a petite, alert woman, did not look the pioneer in aviation that she was. During the Second World War she had been a ferry pilot in England, a job that required her to fly any kind of aircraft (including damaged ones) from one airstrip in England to another. She was one of the few women in the British Commonwealth, if not in the entire world, who had flown everything from a Spitfire to a four-engine bomber.

When their flying days were over Arnold resumed his original career as a teacher of shorthand in a commercial high school in Toronto and Vi became a librarian in the Ontario civil service. But as they neared retirement they yearned for some more adventure in their lives. Like us, they sought out unheralded corners of Canada. The Magdalens proved irresistible.

Farley's sons, Sandy and David, did not get along with one another. Sandy had been born to Farley and Fran in 1954. David had been adopted three years later, when he was fourteen months old. It would be hard to imagine two boys less alike. Sandy was a self-reliant, skinny, pensive fellow who did well in school, read a lot, took great care of everything he owned, and showed scant interest in sports. David was a heavy-set boy who managed to lose or break almost everything he came in contact with. He liked hockey but cared not a whit for books, did poorly in school, but did have a sunny, outgoing disposition.

David found our pastoral life utterly boring. He was happiest when he could hang around with some pals and that summer there was absolutely no one his age anywhere nearby. Gardening, which took up a lot of Farley's time, did not interest him in the least. Mowing the grass was a chore he loathed. A rainy day indoors with a good book was a royal pain to him.

Eventually David and I found some common ground in the game of Scrabble and the two of us played a game every evening. I was hoping it would increase his vocabulary and improve his spelling. He had just failed grade nine.

A couple of weeks later, when it was time for Arnold and Vi to take David back to Palgrave with them, he broke down and sobbed, begging to stay on with us. He claimed that his brother hated him and that his mother always sided with Sandy against him. Whether it was true or not, we gave in and he stayed for two more weeks.

After the Warrens left, our friends Max and Aileen Braithwaite arrived to spend a month in the small house in Old Harry that we had originally rented from Rhoda Turner. Max and Farley had been bosom pals for about twenty years by then. Max and his family lived in Orangeville, which wasn't all that far from Farley's first home, near Palgrave. There were not many freelance writers living in the Albion hills in the 1950s so the few who did soon got to know one another.

Max and Aileen were about a decade older than Farley. Born in rural Saskatchewan, Max had started his working life in the 1930s as a teacher in a one-room schoolhouse, although all along he harboured the dream of becoming a writer. During those lean years he won a provincial short-story contest, which was just the boost he needed to keep him writing in the evenings and on weekends.

The Second World War interrupted his literary ambitions when Max, like a surprising number of land-locked prairie boys, joined the Canadian Navy. The navy dispatched him, and his schoolteacher wife and young daughter, not to the high seas but to Toronto, where he spent the war years as an instructor "on board" *H.M.C.S. York*—which was not a ship but a building on the grounds of the Canadian National Exhibition. After the war he stayed in Toronto, making his living as a freelancer writing magazine articles and radio scripts. When television arrived he wrote scripts for that too. It was a precarious livelihood, especially as Max and Aileen's family grew to include five children.

In 1971 Max was a big, portly man with an impish smile and some degree of literary success. He had just completed the final volume of a trilogy based on his and Aileen's lives as teachers on the prairies during the Great Depression. They were humorous stories that told both the light and the dark side of a sometimes harsh existence. *Why Shoot the Teacher* was published in 1965, *Never Sleep Three in a Bed* in 1969, and *The Night We Stole the Mountie's Car* was due to appear in the bookstores in the fall of

1971. *Why Shoot the Teacher* was later adapted for film and was a box-office success at a time when Canadian movies were rare.

Farley, more given to passion than to reason, had envisioned our new-found home in the Magdalens as the beginning of a colony of like-minded friends who were, for the most part, writers or artists of one sort or another. Along with the Warrens, the Braithwaites were among the people we most wanted to join us. We treasured their unstinting loyalty and their shared sense of humour. By this time all but the youngest of their five children were making their own way in the world. Orangeville had been a good place to raise a family but now they were looking for a more interesting spot in which to live. During the previous year, whenever we had got together with them Farley had extolled the virtues of the Magdalen Islands: the ocean, the beaches, the affordable real estate, the down-to-earth folks, and, in time, he hoped, a circle of friends with shared interests.

Initially Max and Aileen were as smitten with the islands as we were. The uncluttered horizon and feeling of limitless space reminded Aileen of the prairies. Max found the people in Old Harry intriguing, and may have sensed a potential novel revolving around the lives of this little-known English-speaking minority adrift in a sea of French speakers.

When Max heard that ten acres of land in Old Harry were for sale, he bought the property immediately. "Invest your money in land," he used to say. "They're not making it any more." Soon Aileen was daydreaming about the summer cottage they would build.

By midsummer my own rapturous affair with cliffs, surf, sand, and wild strawberries was being eclipsed by the more pressing matters of changing bedclothes, cleaning the house, hanging out the wash, and endless cooking. Cooking and baking are fulfilling occupations and I normally did not think of them as a chores. However, I would have given a lot that summer to have been near a delicatessen or some passable restaurants. It was a rare day when I wasn't baking bread and cooking meals for assorted guests.

With David Mowat's departure at the end of July, we actually had a few days to ourselves in our own home. The weather was perfect and I should have spent time on the beach, either swimming or sprawling on the sand with a good book. Instead, I spent three days in bed with the drapes drawn. I was utterly exhausted in a way I had never been before. Having non-stop visitors for over a month had taken its toll. The lingering hostility I felt from the English community and my alien status among the French had added to the sense of oppression. We continued to get occasional nasty phone calls, which, we concluded, were a local form of aggression, quicker and easier than writing a poison-pen letter and less harmful than physical violence. But I never got used to it. Those three dark days in midsummer were as close to what used to be called a nervous breakdown as I had ever known.

Farley was kind. He took over the cooking and simply let me rest. I read a couple of novels. I listened to CBC radio. I slept a lot. After the third day I was sufficiently restored to get up and tackle the mountain of laundry. We had recently bought a Hoover spin-dryer, a cleverly designed little washing machine that was faster and easier to use than the time-consuming old wringer-washer. However, it still took a fair amount of time to wash, rinse, and spin the huge accumulation of sheets, towels, and clothes. We didn't own a clothes dryer but I didn't consider that a hardship. During our years in Newfoundland, when we couldn't afford a dryer, I had developed a passion for hanging out the wash in a brisk, ocean breeze at any season.

As I gathered strength I went back to baking: bread, cookies, cakes, and pies, which, once they had cooled, I froze. More guests were going to arrive soon. Trying to bake when there were other people in the house was next to impossible. I could cook a dinner with people milling around me but baking was a job I had to tackle alone.

In early August our new friends Joe and Debbie MacInnis arrived with their camper-van, which they had shipped from Montreal on the *C.T.M.A.* This meant they had their own accommodation of sorts, which lessened the housekeeping. Joe, a lean, intense man in his thirties, was a medical doctor who had embarked on a study of the effects of the underwater world on human beings, whether they were divers in wet suits or people who were lowered into the depths in submersibles. This was coupled with an abiding interest in marine life, which was what had brought Joe and Farley together back in Ontario. Farley wanted to take up scuba diving, so he had enthusiastically invited Joe and his wife, Debbie, to visit us in the Magdalens in the summer.

In the oceanic world Joe had accomplished some amazing feats, including several descents under the ice of the Arctic Ocean. He had even escorted

Farley and Claire with Joe MacInnis, Grande Entrée, 1971

Prince Charles under the arctic ice during the prince's recent visit to Canada. Joe knew a lot of people who shared his marine interests, including our athletic prime minister, Pierre Trudeau. Joe had organized several private diving expeditions for the prime minister. Trudeau's girlfriend, Margaret, also a diver, had often been included in these brief holidays before she and Pierre were married. When Pierre Trudeau surprised the nation by marrying Margaret Sinclair in March of 1971 the MacInnises were among the handful of Canadians who were not surprised at all.

The Trudeaus were currently visiting Atlantic Canada aboard a Coast Guard ship. Pierre had expressed an interest in seeing the Magdalen Islands when Joe mentioned that he and Debbie would be there this summer. Joe asked if it would be all right with us if Pierre and Margaret dropped in at our place.

Drop in here to visit us? Well, I guess so. But I couldn't believe it. Surely the prime minister of Canada didn't simply "drop in" for a visit the way ordinary mortals did.

It would be a simple matter to arrange, Joe assured us. The Coast Guard ship would be leaving Port-aux-Basques, Newfoundland, on Friday, heading for Prince Edward Island. We were located at the halfway point in the voyage. The ship could anchor off Grande Entrée. A helicopter would bring the Trudeaus ashore and land them on our property.

Farley was concerned that the weather might not cooperate. Helicopters do not fly in conditions of poor visibility and the weather here, even in summer, was fickle. I remained skeptical, although I did begin making frantic preparations. Then the appointed day dawned—sunny and windless. Looking out to sea we could see the big red-and-white ship moving slowly toward Grande Entrée. The air was so still that morning that we could hear the helicopter's engine revving up a mile away.

Joe's instructions were that we were to stand in the field behind our house, waving a white sheet so the pilot could see where he was supposed to land. We waited there, in a state of tension, as the dot in the sky got closer and closer. In a matter of minutes a small helicopter was hovering above us and our white sheet. As we scrambled out of the way, it landed. The rotors wound down and stopped. The door opened and out stepped the prime minister of Canada, followed by his stunning-looking bride. One aide accompanied them, Tim Porteous. The pilot was the only other person aboard. There were no police or bodyguards.

I think Farley was as overwhelmed as I was, but naturally neither of us was going to show it. We walked calmly toward the visitors and introduced ourselves. There were warm exchanges between the Trudeaus and the MacInnises.

We had set up a circle of garden chairs down by the house where, Farley suggested, we might sit down and discuss plans. Like people greeting one another everywhere, we all remarked on what a lovely day it was. I kept reminding myself that famous people are merely people, after all, and there was no reason to feel apprehensive. I had met a fair number of literary and media celebrities by then and they didn't intimidate me. But Pierre Trudeau was in another realm.

He was a Canadian leader like no other. He had been known to quote Plato to surprised reporters. In the House of Commons he sported a fresh rose in the lapel of his jacket every day. He had been filmed doing a double gainer from a diving board into a motel swimming pool while the press looked on in awe. Whether you agreed with his politics or not, you simply couldn't ignore this man. And to cap it all he had astonished the nation only six months earlier by marrying this captivating twenty-two-year-old woman who was by then pregnant with their first child.

Margaret was even more beautiful in real life than in her photographs. She was dressed in the current fashion for peasant-style clothes: a flowered dirndl skirt, a white drawstring blouse with flowered embroidery, and leather sandals on her feet. Pierre wore sandals too, cotton slacks, and a cotton knit shirt. The first thing I noticed about Pierre (and Joe had told us to call them both by their first names) was how young he looked. He was fifty-one at the time, yet up close, in person, the age gap between husband and wife was hardly noticeable.

Joe began extolling the prospects for local scuba diving and explained that he and Farley had arranged for a boat to take us diving that afternoon if our guests were interested. I told them I had a picnic lunch prepared, which we could enjoy on our beach, where the swimming was superb.

We sat there chatting for ten or fifteen minutes then the pilot said, "Sir, if it's all right with you, I'll return to the ship now." Pierre smiled and nodded. I have wondered since if the two men had some secret understanding. Suppose Pierre, or Margaret, hadn't like the proposed plan for the day—or didn't like us—was the pilot hanging around at the ready to take them back aboard? The helicopter roared into action, lifted, and disappeared over the hill. The prime minister of Canada was marooned in Grande Entrée with us for the day.

I had prepared a fairly elaborate picnic: breaded chicken legs, a fresh shrimp salad, homemade bread, several bottles of wine, homemade cookies, and a thermos of tea, even though I had doubted until the last minute that the Trudeaus would actually show up.

Pierre and Margaret withdrew to an upstairs bedroom in our house to change into their bathing suits. Tim Porteous used the time to make a couple of phone calls confirming the PM's next appearance, which was to be in

Charlottetown that evening. I hastily packed our lunch into two canvas bags. Within minutes we had gathered towels, cameras, suntan lotion—all the paraphernalia that for a day at the seashore.

As we headed for the hill Pierre picked up one of the heavy haversacks. "Oh, I can take that," I protested, certain that he should not be called on to perform the menial task of lugging a bag of food to the beach.

"I'll take it," he insisted quietly and continued up the hill.

At the crest of the hill we all paused to take in the spectacular view of white sand and the pulsating surf stretching below us. There was not another person on the beach, I noted with relief. We had no idea if the news had leaked out about who had arrived at our place in a helicopter. Up until then only three people other than ourselves knew the prime minister might arrive. The owner of the lobster boat, who would be transporting the divers offshore, knew. So did Gerald LaPierre, a local man who was also a diver and would accompany them. Father Frédéric Landry knew who was coming because he had corresponded with the prime minister earlier that year regarding his fledgling museum and Trudeau, amazingly, had written back to say he might be visiting the islands and looked forward to meeting him.

These men had been sworn to secrecy but secrets have a way of escaping. Farley and I were not sure if local people, once they knew who was in their midst, would keep a respectful distance from the Trudeaus or whether the couple would be mobbed.

It was the perfect picnic. We lingered on the beach for two hours. There was plenty of time for forays along the shore, for swimming, for eating, and for conversation. For quite a while we talked about the Soviet Union. Pierre and Margaret had made a state visit there four months earlier. Farley and I had travelled there a few years before. Visitors from Canada to the USSR were infrequent at the time and those of us who had been there could always share anecdotes about a country that operated in ways quite unlike our own.

Their visit had been very different from the lengthy Siberian trek Farley and I had made in 1966. Nevertheless, Margaret and I found some common ground as we talked about the obstacles of shopping in Moscow. She told me the skirt she was wearing that morning was from a length of brightly flowered chintz she had bought in the GUM department store. She had made the skirt herself.

Farley and Margaret and Pierre Trudeau on our beach, 1971

From time to time I caught snatches of the men's conversation. I heard Pierre say, "...and if the Americans don't like it, that's too bad." American intervention in Canadian foreign policy had been growing for many years, imperialist meddling that infuriated Farley and me. It would take a lot more than a passing comment from any Canadian prime minister to reverse the trend, but at least Trudeau's attitude suggested something other than total compliance.

Our two dogs, Albert and Victoria, always came to the beach with us, liking nothing better than a picnic and a swim. Victoria—Vickie—was pregnant. So was Margaret Trudeau. Margaret's baby was not due until December but Vickie was only about a week away from delivering puppies. Albert—the father of the pups—was at the top of his form that day. You'd swear he knew he was giving a command performance. His greatest pleasure was to dive, often from considerable heights, into the ocean to retrieve whatever we threw for him.

Albert came from the tiny outport of LaPoile in Newfoundland. He was a descendant of a local Newfoundland breed known simply as "water dogs," the ancestors of which have come to be known as Labradors. The LaPoile water dogs were famous on the southwest coast of Newfoundland for their amazing ability to dive to depths of ten feet or more from the government wharf to retrieve bones that the cooks on coastal ships saved for them.

While Pierre and Margaret had been running along the beach like a pair of teenagers, Albert had positioned himself on a sandstone promontory high above the surf. Farley hurled a stick into the sea and Albert, like an Olympic athlete, dove fearlessly into the waves to retrieve it. He did this several times and the prime minister was impressed.

"Tell you what," Farley offered. "When Vickie's pups are born, we'll save one for you. If you're going to have a baby then you should have a dog too."

The Trudeaus smiled at the idea.

The only other person to join the seven of us at the beach that afternoon was Father Landry. He couldn't come for lunch because he had to conduct a wedding at eleven o'clock that morning and then drive for an hour to reach our place. He did manage to join us for the final fifteen minutes on the beach, looking oddly out of place dressed in his black suit and clerical collar.

It was surprising that on a hot Saturday in August no local swimmers or sunbathers had come to the beach. Only as we were leaving did we meet two little boys and their dog. Pierre said *Bonjour* to them and to their perky little dog, but they barely looked at him and had no idea who this man in a bathing suit was.

The men soon left for the Grande Entrée wharf to join the boat that was waiting to take them scuba diving. Margaret Trudeau was not going because of her pregnancy. I was not a diver. Debbie MacInnis was, but that day she chose to spend a quiet afternoon sitting on our lawn. She and Margaret had lots to talk about—notably about Michael Pitfield, another of Trudeau's aides, who had a new girlfriend. They liked her very much.

Margaret talked about their forthcoming trip to England, where Pierre was to attend a conference. She looked forward to shopping at some London store that specialized in designer maternity clothes. Then she asked lots of questions about the Magdalens: What did people here do for a living? What kind of transportation linked them to other parts of Canada and how long was the journey? The one aspect of the place that pleased her most was the absence of reporters or photographers. Apart from a small monthly newsletter dealing with local concerns, we had no newspaper, no radio station, no television, and thus no person on the islands whose mission it was to track down visiting celebrities. For people like Margaret who lived in the spotlight this was a genuine relief.

Later in the afternoon the men returned and Farley got busy lighting the barbeque, while I prepared the rest of our supper. Pierre dutifully packed up the diving gear while Margaret, Joe, Debbie, and Tim started a game of croquet.

I was setting the table in the dining room when I glanced out of the window and realized that the word was out. Our normally quiet side road was crawling with a slow-moving parade of cars and trucks whose occupants were trying to catch sight of their fabled prime minister. As a precaution Farley had closed our gate to discourage anyone driving in.

This, however, had not hindered a man named Graydon Dawson, who had unlatched the gate and was making his way slowly on foot up the driveway toward our house.

Graydon, a lobster fisherman, was a barrel-chested young man renowned for his belligerence. He came from the English community of Old Harry but he had married a pretty French-speaking woman from Grande Entrée. As was usually the case in such mixed French-English marriages, the Anglo moved to French territory. I did wonder if it was Graydon's peculiar status as the only "English" male in an extended family of French-speaking people that made him so ornery. Maybe not. Maybe he had simply been born that way. He was a man I had learned to avoid.

I was in a panic. I rushed outdoors to tell Farley that Graydon the Terrible (my name for him) was approaching. What should we do? I suggested phoning the police because he was, after all, trespassing. But what good would that do? The QPP detachment was forty miles away and might take hours to respond. At that point I wished the Trudeaus had brought some protection. I wondered if Tim Porteous, as part of his duties as a prime ministerial aide, carried a gun.

Farley quietly told Pierre that a rather bellicose neighbour, uninvited, was approaching our house. Did the prime minister care to step inside and avoid meeting him?

"No," Trudeau said decisively, "I'll talk to him…if that's what he wants."

Once Graydon reached the yard at the back of our house and realized he was actually face to face with the prime minister of Canada he did not seem as fearsome as he was reputed to be. I listened from the kitchen window as he blurted out, "…fishermen here getting a rotten deal…poor price for landed fish…our licences cost too much…What are you going to do about it?"

Trudeau listened patiently to Graydon's diatribe for several minutes, then he said, "I agree with you. The fisheries are in a mess. I am returning to Ottawa early tomorrow and I'll see what can be done about it."

That seemed to take the wind out of Graydon's sails. He left soon after, pleased, I imagine, that he alone of the islanders had had the nerve to confront the prime minister while everyone else had been content to smile or wave from a distance or simply stare.

After our supper of steak, salad, and dessert, Farley and I drove the Trudeaus and Tim Porteous to the airport. It was a superb summer evening—so calm that each great blue heron fishing in the lagoons was reflected like a pair of twins attached upside down. There was hardly any traffic on the gravel highway. Every time we approached another vehicle I thought smugly to myself, "If only you knew who was sitting inside our dusty Volvo.…"

As we approached the airport we could see a bright yellow RCAF search-and-rescue plane waiting on the tarmac. The airport security guard had been advised to watch for our car. He quickly unlocked a gate in the chain-link fence and signalled Farley to drive right out on the runway to the side of the aircraft. The prime minister stepped out of our car and immediately the flight crew stood at attention and saluted. Pierre had to return to the real world now. His day of virgin beaches and the aquatic kingdom beneath the waves would soon be a memory.

Margaret and Pierre talked to these smiling airmen, who were based in Summerside, PEI. These were young men whose training had been in how to spot missing ships, downed aircraft, and drowning people. They must have considered themselves lucky to have been chosen for this happier assignment of collecting the prime minister and his gorgeous wife and flying them to Charlottetown.

I turned to look at the airport terminal. There was a crowd of excited people at the window, craning to get a look at these unexpected, famous visitors.

"There are no facilities on board, Mrs. Trudeau," I heard the plane's captain say quietly to her—meaning there was no toilet in this utilitarian aircraft, which was intended for men on dangerous assignments.

She turned to me and said, "Maybe I'd better use those in the airport then."

I escorted her through the crowd in the terminal to the ladies' room on the far side. I prayed no one else would be in there and, fortunately, no one was. Then I stood with my back braced against the closed door, preparing to keep out any curious girl or woman who might dare to enter. No one tried.

Pierre—a politician, after all—had by then come into the crowded terminal too and was standing in the midst of a circle of onlookers while he talked to Farley. A few people dared to come forward and shake his hand or utter a shy *Bonjour*.

We said our farewells and our guests boarded the plane, which immediately taxied down the runway, took off, and disappeared into the sunset. In half an hour the Trudeaus would be facing yet another crowd of curious people over in Charlottetown. I did not envy them.

Chapter Nine

AS WE DROVE BACK to Grande Entrée I was on a high. The prime minister of Canada had literally dropped out of the sky and landed in our back yard.

When we reached Old Harry we decided on the spur of the moment to stop in and say hello to Max and Aileen Braithwaite. We were dying to share our excitement with some friends. This was where we learned a hard lesson about hobnobbing with the famous. The Braithwaites had been friends for years but they greeted us at their door that evening in a manner that was decidedly chilly. Aileen managed a smile but Max didn't. After an awkward moment they suggested we come in for a drink, but we could tell that something was wrong. The atmosphere in that little house was colder than the ice cubes in my drink. I had taken only two sips of my gin and tonic when Farley caught my eye and urged me to "Drink up! We should be on our way." There was no further mention of the Trudeaus.

We hadn't invited Max or Aileen to join us because Joe MacInnis had been told by the PMO that no one else should be included. It was to be a private day for Pierre and Margaret. We understood how the Trudeaus felt. We had occasionally been invited to visit the home of someone we barely knew, only to find that our hosts had also invited a large crowd of their friends to meet a celebrated author. We were not going to inflict anything of that sort on Pierre and Margaret.

However, we had effectively snubbed two cherished friends. We should have insisted they be included. It was our home, after all, and two more people would not have made that much of a difference. I felt absolutely dreadful about this for a long time. Aileen confided to me later that they felt "like the kids who had been left out of the birthday party."

Fortunately they were of a forgiving nature. We got together with them—for meals, for swims, for drinks—often during the rest of the summer. The Trudeaus' visit was never mentioned until a few months later, when

Max got a fan letter from former prime minister John Diefenbaker, praising Max's trilogy of novels set in 1930s Saskatchewan. As a young lawyer, John Diefenbaker had lived there during the Depression and he wrote to tell Max that he had captured perfectly the mood and the challenges of that era.

Not many authors get congratulatory letters from prime ministers, current or former. Farley never had. Diefenbaker's letter restored the balance in our friendship, and we remained close friends with Max and Aileen until their deaths a quarter of a century later.

Morris McQuaid came over to visit us the morning after the Trudeaus' visit, asking if he could borrow our barn for a day so he could paint his car. He drove the 1959 Prefect we had first noticed in 1969 and once a year painted it navy blue—with enamel and a brush, the way one might paint a boat or a house. He believed his car would withstand the weather better and last longer with a fresh coat of paint every year. Perhaps it did. He needed to do this under cover in case it rained, but his shed was filled to capacity with his ship-in-progress. We told him he was welcome to use our barn.

He added, as an afterthought, "We seen them getting out of that helicopter, there, yesterday. With my binoculars. Ma and Rose—they were real interested. Real interested."

We had been too busy and too preoccupied to think about our neighbours, who must have been watching our house like hawks. A chopper landing nearby was a big event. The prime minister stepping out of it was even bigger news. As far as anyone knew, no Canadian prime minister had ever set foot on these islands before.

I could only guess how the news of our visitors must have been received in the larger English community, where a lot of people already didn't trust us. They would be more convinced than ever that we had influence in high places and even more fearful that any day now the government would be turfing them out of their homes.

A week after the Trudeau visit, Vickie made it clear she would soon be giving birth. There was no veterinarian on the islands and my only guide to dealing with her pregnancy and delivery was a book titled *Raising Puppies for Pleasure and Profit*. It was reassuring to have a medical doctor close at hand. Joe and Debbie were still staying with us, and although Joe was not a vet, I assumed he would know what to do in an emergency.

My book stated that pregnant dogs usually stop eating between twenty-four and forty-eight hours before they begin to deliver. Vickie, not a dog ever to refuse a meal, did exactly that. After a forty-hour fast, she began her labour at ten o'clock at night. I stayed up with her beside the bed Farley had prepared in the laundry room.

The book warned that pregnant dogs often dig a secret burrow in which to give birth. Apparently Vickie did have a hidden dugout somewhere nearby because she became frantic to get outside. For a while I didn't know who knew best—the dog or me. I had to marvel at the way an animal that had never read a manual nor shared a conversation with another female on the subject of giving birth would have such a resolute notion of how, and where, to go about it. However, right or wrong, I insisted she stay in her pristine nursery and she did finally settle down. Eight black puppies were born between 11:00 p.m. and 5:30 the next morning: six males and two females. Vickie and I were both exhausted.

Mammalian birth, whether it's human beings, dogs, or hamsters, is a scary, miraculous business. In an instant we are transformed from an aquatic creature into one that breathes air. It's a wonder that any of us—from elephants to mice—survive this dicey process.

Vickie settled into motherhood like an old pro. All we had to worry about now was how we were going to find suitable homes for eight little black dogs two months later.

The MacInnises were the first to request one of the puppies. They left a couple of days later and we promised to bring their pup with us when we returned to Ontario. They phoned us a few weeks later to tell us that Pierre and Margaret had decided they would like one of our puppies as well, a lucky dog who would be moving to a new life at 24 Sussex Drive in Ottawa.

In September Farley's mother came to visit us, along with her longtime friend Dorothy Little. By then the puppies were almost a month old. They could waddle around and they entertained us for hours, playing with each other in the field behind our house. We had given them temporary names based on small differences in appearance: a white tip on a tail became White Tip, a touch of white on one foot or on the chest became Spot, the runt of the litter—a little female noticeably smaller than her six brothers—became Mini-dog. Everyone who came to see them fell in love with them. Morris

Claire with Vickie and her pups, Grande Entrée, 1971

McQuaid asked if he could have one and so did Kenny Cook. Before long we had prospective homes for most of them.

On Sunday Helen and Dorothy and I went to church at Grosse Île. I had considerable hesitation about showing up in a community where I was regarded as one-half of a couple who were planning to take over the world. At least I wouldn't have to face the people of Grosse Île alone. I would have two respectable ladies with me. Surely, I thought, no one would insult or assault me in their company, especially not in church.

And, of course, no one did.

When the service was over Joan Richards greeted me like a long-lost friend. It had only been a few months since she had accused Farley of treachery and treason. Now she was asking after him. Was he well? Was he writing? How long would we be staying? We should get together. I took it for what it was—an olive branch.

This was the beginning of an enduring friendship. Joan and Stuart had figured out that Farley had neither the inclination nor the influence to turn the village of Grosse Île into a national park. Stuart Richards was a quiet, thoughtful, red-haired young man and the first person from Grosse Île to have completed a university education. Now he was in charge of a six-room school that included grades one to ten. Any student who hoped to complete grades eleven and twelve in order to graduate would have to attend the English-language high school in the town of Gaspé, two hundred miles, by air or sea, to the west of us. There the student would board during the school year with a local family and study amid strangers in a huge new regional high school. Not surprisingly, very few Grosse Île students chose to endure the homesickness and the dislocation.

There *was* a regional high school on the Magdalens at Grindstone/Cap-aux-Meules but it provided instruction only in French. So far no English-speaking student knew enough French to attend.

I was puzzled as to why the English speakers here had not been taught French at school from an early age. They had been a minority since the early days of settlement. In the 1970s they only numbered about eight hundred people, not even ten per cent of the overall population. At first I thought it might have been arrogance, but I began to see it differently. Originally most of the communities on the islands—whether they were French or English—had been linked only by water. There had been no roads and little communication between them, so no pressing need for knowing the other language. Now, with the construction of the road, a lot of things had changed. As well there was the pending legislation in mainland Quebec that French, and only French, would be the language of business and government services in the future.

Stuart planned to reverse this isolating unilingualism. French was now on the school curriculum for all grades and he was organizing evening classes in French for adults. However, he was having trouble finding a qualified teacher. With ninety per cent of the islands' population speaking French, one wouldn't have expected that to be a problem but it was. The legacy of Quebec's segregated school system was still a factor. From the beginning of public education in Quebec, if your language was French you attended a Roman Catholic school. If you spoke English and were not

Roman Catholic, you attended a Protestant school. Quebec was phasing out church-oriented schools but it was still a new concept for a francophone teacher to teach French, or any subject, in an English school.

We had to leave the islands at the end of September, though I wasn't in any hurry to go. We had finally found some friends in the larger English community, where I had previously felt like a pariah. Had we been staying for the winter I would have enjoyed hearing about the ups and downs of Stuart's first year as school principal. I imagined his experience would be akin to those of Max Braithwaite's years teaching in rural schools in Saskatchewan.

Joan and I had a bond insofar as we were both outsiders. Like me, she had come from somewhere else and didn't quite fit in. Nor did she entirely approve of some of the customs and attitudes of the local women and she didn't hesitate to say so. I admired, and even envied, her spunk. She was sassier than I could ever be.

Another reason we were reluctant to depart was that we had to transport eight dogs—Albert and Victoria and six of their eight puppies. This was no easy matter. Farley constructed a two-room wooden crate that filled most of the back of our station wagon, leaving just enough room for the two parent dogs. Our personal luggage had to be tied to the roof. The night we prepared to board the ship I felt as if I was part of a travelling circus.

I doubt if anyone before us had attempted to transport a vehicle full of puppies and dogs aboard the *C.T.M.A.* Fortunately the ship's officers did not have a lot of finicky rules about dogs. Albert and Vickie would sleep on the floor of our cabin, as they had before. The puppies, then seven weeks old, would huddle together inside our Volvo, which was lashed on the foredeck.

The ship sailed at midnight and by dawn we were somewhere in the Gulf of St. Lawrence, charging into the teeth of a fierce gale. The ship heaved and fell and shuddered, then rose and plunged. I tried to get out of my berth but every plummet and heave sent me flat on my back, trying to fight off waves of nausea. I was as sick as a dog. Farley, thank heaven, never gets seasick. He donned his rain gear and strode out on the pitching deck to tend to the needs of the bewildered puppies, who must have wondered where on earth they were.

The two-room crate was an ingenious idea. By herding the puppies into one half of it, Farley was able to clean up the mess in the other half, then line it with fresh newspapers. The used ones simply blew away in the gale. With both halves of the crate relatively spic and span, he then fed a mushy mix of oatmeal to the six hungry puppies. Later, when he was eating his own breakfast in the galley, he learned that his nanny manoeuvres with the puppies had been a great source of interest to the ship's officers watching him from the bridge.

By evening we had sailed past the north coast of the Gaspé Peninsula and into the St. Lawrence River, where we had some protection from the storm. In calmer waters, I was able to get up and help Farley tend to the puppies. The next day, rain and mist plagued us all day and the spectacular mountains and autumn colours of the St. Lawrence shoreline were invisible.

It was still raining when we docked at Quebec City the following morning. I was happier than Jacques Cartier had ever been to set foot on mainland Quebec. I took Albert and Victoria for a walk while Farley waited for our car full of puppies to be hoisted down from the ship. Soon we were driving out of the city and we didn't stop until we reached the first of the park-like rest areas that dot the Trans-Canada Highway through rural Quebec.

There we opened the back of our station wagon and then the puppy crate, and two large black dogs and six little black puppies poured out onto the grass. They must have been overjoyed to finally feel terra firma under their feet again. We let them romp around for quite a while, heedless of the rain and their collective thirty-two muddy feet.

A man and woman were getting into their car, which bore Massachusetts licence plates, when they noticed this parade of wet dogs and two damp people. They smiled at us indulgently but probably thought we were crazy. Maybe we were.

Chapter Ten

IT TOOK MOST OF A DAY to drive from Quebec City westward to Ontario because we stopped so many times to let the puppies out. By late afternoon we had found our way through the highways, tunnels, and bridges that make a nightmare maze out of the city of Montreal, and an hour later reached Ontario. I didn't feel any surge of emotion on our return. Highway 401 was no substitute for the Magdalen Islands.

While our gas tank was being filled, Farley phoned his father in Northport, who invited us to stop and stay the night, which we were thankful to do. As always, I had written a number of letters to Angus and Barbara over the summer. I love writing and receiving letters and so did Angus, who was a very entertaining correspondent. Angus and I had been writing to one another for nearly ten years. Having long since given up any thought of writing another novel, he channelled his literary talent into his letters.

I had of course told him about the visit of the prime minister. Angus and Barb respected Trudeau—a bit grudgingly, because they, as well as Farley and I, were longtime supporters of the New Democratic Party. We all liked to believe that, in his heart, Pierre Trudeau was further to the political left than the Liberal Party. I felt sure Angus and Barb would be curious to know more about our charismatic leader.

There was a golden sunset by the time we reached their house. It was one of those rare autumn evenings when the leaves have turned yellow and red but the air is still warm enough to sit outdoors. We sat on garden chairs by the peaceful Bay of Quinte and sipped our drinks and laughed at the antics of the romping puppies. I pointed out the one we had selected for Sussex Drive. I thought this would lead the conversation to Pierre and Margaret, the puppy's adopting family.

I especially wanted to mention that, in my opinion, the age gap between the Trudeaus, which was twenty-nine years, didn't seem to matter at all. I thought this might make Angus and Barbara more at ease with the thirty-three-year difference between themselves. However, it soon became obvious they did not want to hear about the Trudeaus' visit. I was genuinely baffled by this rebuff. I assumed that their indifference was due to their disapproval of Farley's "high-flying" lifestyle, which is the way they had often described it.

Angus came from a generation that regarded literature as a gentlemanly pursuit. He believed an author should live a reflective life somewhere in the countryside, dress in tweeds, make only rare public appearances and then only in dignified surroundings. That way of life may have been possible for John Galsworthy, who lived long before television and other modern media changed the way writers were presented to the public. Although Farley had understood the necessity of becoming a public person from the beginning of his career, Angus could not, or would not, accept it.

Angus Mowat's first novel had been published in 1938 and his second in 1944, at a time when there was scant interest in serious Canadian fiction. His books were well-written but they had unfortunately sunk without a trace, largely because it was not fashionable, nor were there any outlets, for an author to use his or her personality to sell books. I was sure that Angus was proud of his son's ability as a writer yet he and Barbara were resentful of any acclaim that came from "showing off" in public.

As the evening wore on I realized they were administering a reprimand. I regarded our encounter with the prime minister as unique . . . even historical. They saw it as more evidence that Farley was—as our grandmothers would have put it—too big for his britches.

The talk turned to Angus's will, to what was going to happen to his worldly goods after he died. Angus Mowat was not wealthy, but neither was he poor. He had a small disability pension from the First World War due to a badly wounded right arm. In 1936 he had inherited a few thousand dollars from the estate of an unmarried aunt. By 1971 he could afford to live a middle-class existence with Barbara—and send a meagre household allowance to his wife, Helen.

Angus's will was becoming an obsession with Barbara. We understood her need for financial security because she no longer had an income of her own. Five years earlier she had resigned her position as librarian in charge of the Smith's Falls library in order to live with Angus. Nevertheless, Farley and I both wished they would sort out money matters when we were not there.

I tried to change the subject to dogs and puppies since we were all fond of dogs. They shared their home with a cherished old Springer spaniel named Molly. When the subject of dogs petered out Farley began to tell them about the book he was writing, which he planned to call *A Whale for the Killing*. Despite Farley's efforts to save the whale back in 1967, it had died from gunshot wounds inflicted by some local yahoos. This had been a turning point in our lives, one which we had already shared with them through letters and conversations. They listened politely for a few minutes but before long we were back to the subject of money.

Finally, wearily, Farley and I herded the puppies into the crate for the night. We all went to bed that night with the details of Angus's will still unresolved.

The next day we arrived home in Port Hope and began settling in for the fall and winter. Joe and Debbie MacInnis came to collect their puppy, which they named Moby. Since they were en route to Ottawa they offered to deliver the Trudeaus' puppy, who was destined to be called Farley. Farley Trudeau.

Before long we were down to one pup still needing a home. A unique destiny awaited him. Alexei Kosygin, then the premier of the Soviet Union, was in Canada on a state visit, a reciprocal visit for the one Prime Minister Trudeau had made to the USSR the previous spring. The Cold War was starting to thaw and Canada and the Soviet Union—two northerly nations with many concerns in common—were trying to establish a better relationship.

Farley had long believed it was time Canadians rejected the hysterical, anti-communist mentality of the United States. We Canadians should make our own decisions about our relationship with the Russians, and with all countries. His two long journeys through Siberia and his book *Sibir* had been his contribution to a better understanding of a country that shares much of the top of the world with us.

"I wonder if Kosygin would like a dog," Farley mused one morning as he read *The Globe and Mail*.

"You mean...one of ours?"

"Why not?"

"We've no idea if he likes dogs. Or maybe he already has one. Besides, how would you be able to give it to him? He's surrounded by a battalion of police wherever he goes, not to mention all the protestors," I countered.

"I'm going to make a few phone calls," my husband said, and left the kitchen for his office.

In the process of organizing his two Siberian journeys Farley had made the acquaintance of a few people in the Soviet embassy in Ottawa. It took him a couple of days to contact them and get a reply to his question. Yes, Premier Kosygin would like to have one of our puppies. He would be in Toronto in three days. Could we take the dog to his hotel and present it to him?

The people whose job it is to make decisions about public relations in the Soviet Diplomatic Service could doubtless see the advantage of a noted Canadian author presenting a cute little puppy to the leader of their country. I only hoped that Mr. Kosygin, or Mrs. Kosygin, or some member of their family, really *did* want a Canadian dog and were prepared to look after him.

Kosygin and his considerable entourage were staying at the Inn on the Park hotel Toronto. The security surrounding them was probably the most extensive in Canadian history. Plenty of people in Canada had legitimate grievances against the Soviet empire. Assassinating visiting heads of state was not the Canadian style, but our police were not taking any chances.

Farley had named the puppy Red Star as soon as he knew the gift would be accepted. When we drove off toward Toronto with Red Star that afternoon I had my doubts we would ever get through the police blockades to deliver our furry gift to his new owner. As we approached the hotel there were hundreds of protestors along both sides of the highway waving signs at passing vehicles. Among them were Ukrainian nationalists who wanted independence. Another group was protesting the imprisonment of dissidents held captive in camps in Siberia. Others were campaigning to "Free Soviet Jewry."

I had never seen so many uniformed police in one place before. There was a barricade manned by policemen at the foot of the driveway leading into the hotel grounds. We stopped and they rushed toward our car. Farley calmly explained why we were there. One officer stepped a few feet back and spoke into his radio. The others looked us over as if we might be either a pair of terrorists or else a pair of kooks trying to unload an unwanted dog. The first officer soon returned, evidently convinced that we were who we said we were. Nevertheless, they searched our car very carefully—even looking under the hood to make sure there was no bomb hidden in our engine.

We had been to this hotel many times. It was a favourite drinking and dining place for Jack McClelland, whose book-publishing firm was not too far away. However, on this day it was not the bustling place we were accustomed to. The few people we saw in the lobby were mostly men with sombre expressions, either police or diplomats.

The Soviet ambassador spotted us as soon as we entered the lobby. An informally dressed couple carrying a puppy was almost as conspicuous in that scene as a clown act would have been. We shook hands with the ambassador and with the plainclothes RCMP officer accompanying him. Then the two of them ushered us through a doorway and down a flight of stairs to the lower level of the hotel. We walked past kitchens and laundry rooms and air conditioning ducts in order to reach the service elevator in which we were to ride to the top floor, where Kosygin was staying.

When the elevator door opened another Soviet diplomat and another Mountie greeted us. There were police at every door and every stairwell in sight. The ambassador and the other diplomat disappeared down the corridor, leaving us standing in the quiet hallway with a friendly cop who actually wore the proverbial trench coat with a gun and holster bulging under it. He chatted with us in a Scottish accent.

I had been holding little Red Star in my arms all this time and he was starting to fidget. The one thing I had neglected to do amid the commotion of entering the hotel was to take him for a short walk so he could have a leak. Now he chose to do it on the orange-coloured carpet. The policeman looked amused. His job was guarding a foreign leader, not fretting about the housekeeping details of the hotel.

Ten minutes later the diplomat returned to usher us into a spacious suite where he introduced us to the leader of the 225 million people living within the Union of Soviet Socialist Republics.

There is something unreal when you meet, in person, someone whose media image has been front and centre for a long time. I had felt the same when I met Pierre Trudeau: a momentary intimidation, followed by the realization that this was a mere mortal who lived and loved and suffered just like the rest of us.

Kosygin was not a large man—as we always imagine that famous men are. He spoke no English, so our conversation was through his interpreter—a svelte, black-haired fellow in a pin-striped suit. I handed the puppy to the premier, who smiled and cradled him like a man who was genuinely fond of dogs. His first question was whether this breed of dog could withstand cold weather.

"Definitely," Farley assured him. "This breed came originally from Labrador, where winter can be as cold as Siberia."

Kosygin said something to the interpreter, who then told us that they had visited Newfoundland just one week earlier to tour a pulp-and-paper mill. Farley added that we had lived in Newfoundland for several years and has also travelled extensively in Siberia. That gave us some common ground for a few minutes with a man whose life was so very different from our own.

The room had a huge window overlooking a highway where the protestors kept up their vigil. We could easily see them and so, of course, could Premier Kosygin. I wondered what he thought about them. In his country this kind of demonstration would not be tolerated. However, he had visited Western countries before and perhaps he was accustomed to our demonstrations of dissent.

We said our farewells to both the man who led the world's largest country and also to the puppy who was heading for a new home a long way from Toronto.

While we waited for the elevator I glanced back down the hallway. A Russian diplomat in a dark grey suit was leaving the VIP suite carrying the puppy on his shoulder—heading, I hoped, for some place more suitable for a dog. I had to smile, wondering if that tight-lipped fellow had ever envisioned himself transporting a puppy as one of his responsibilities when he embarked on his career in the Soviet Foreign Service.

Later we would learn that Kosygin gave the pup to his daughter, who lived in the countryside near Moscow. She named him Druzhba, which translates as "friendship."

Chapter Eleven

ON CHRISTMAS DAY 1971, Margaret Trudeau gave birth to a son. It seemed to be one more magic ingredient in their fabled marriage that she and Pierre should have a son on the day the birth of Christ is celebrated. Canadians, even if they didn't agree with Pierre Trudeau's politics, were captivated by the ethereal photos of his wife and child.

Margaret still wasn't giving interviews to the media, which, considering her youth and her recent arrival in public life, was wise. Photographs alone were enough to turn her into an icon. It would be hard to imagine any Canadian who wasn't pleased at the birth of Justin Pierre James Trudeau and that, for the first time since the days of Sir John A. Macdonald, there would be a nursery in the prime minister's official residence. I sent them a card, undoubtedly one of thousands they received. I never expected to hear from or see them again.

But we did. To my everlasting surprise they invited us to spend a weekend with them the following spring. Margaret wrote to us, describing the route from Ottawa to Harrington Lake in Quebec, where the prime minister's summer residence is located. She said they loved the place and spent almost every weekend there.

I didn't know what we should take with us. Did they dress for dinner? Joe and Debbie MacInnis, who had been there several times, gave us some tips. Life at Harrington Lake was much as it would be at any summer cottage, they told us. We were to wear casual clothes and be sure to include a bathing suit. Pierre disapproved of smoking so if we were going to smoke it would have to be in our bedroom with the door closed and the window open. Pierre drank very little alcohol—at the most, only one glass of wine with his dinner. If we cared for a pre-dinner drink, or an alcohol-based drink at any other time, we should take a bottle of our favourite tipple with us. Apart from these few restrictions, we would be free to enjoy the house, and the great outdoors surrounding it, any way we liked.

We drove through Ottawa on a hot Saturday afternoon in late May, accompanied by two of our four dogs: Albert and his son Edward. Then our route took us across the Ottawa River past Hull and beyond Meech Lake. We continued for a few more miles until the road became narrower and unpaved. It ended in a woods with a locked gate and a sign that stated simply "Private."

We got out of the car and waited for a few minutes, unsure how to proceed. We didn't want to blow our car horn. It seemed presumptuous, considering whose home this was. Finally Farley climbed over the metal gate and headed along the trail. I stayed in the car with two panting dogs and played Mozart on the tape deck to calm my jittery nerves.

Within a few minutes Farley encountered a plainclothes Mountie whose job was to protect the prime minister and his family and admit only people who had been invited. Unlocking the gate, he casually waved us on and we drove to the end of the trail that led to the Harrington Lake house. It was large and rambling, imposing but not ostentatious. I had seen many like it in the Muskoka Lakes region north of Toronto.

I expected a butler would greet us and show us into the house, where there would be a chef, some housemaids, and a nanny for the baby. We parked our car and the first person we saw was Margaret, dressed in jeans and a T-shirt, standing on the lawn waving at us. She greeted us like old friends. Five-month-old Justin was asleep in his cot on the screened verandah. Pierre was in the lake swimming with their dog, Farley. There wasn't another soul in view anywhere. Several Mounties, who were based in a separate building, stayed out of sight.

We let our dogs out of the car and naturally they plunged into the lake and joined the splash party.

Harrington Lake, in the Gatineau region, is long, narrow, and surrounded by high, wooded hills. There is only one home on its shore. The white, sprawling cottage was built in the 1920s by a family who had made a fortune in the lumber business. In the 1950s it was bought by the Canadian government as the official summer residence for prime ministers. John Diefenbaker was prime minister at the time and it apparently had been his wife, Olive, who had urged the government to buy the place. Apart from the fact that John's favourite form of relaxation was fishing, Olive knew how important it was for him, and for future prime ministers, to get away, now and then, from Ottawa and the pressures of running the country.

Margaret ushered us into the house and down a hallway to our bedroom, a modest room furnished with twin beds and sturdy Vilas furniture manufactured in Quebec. On one wall hung a large painting of a Quebec village in winter. As I unpacked our clothes, I thought about all the people—celebrated as well as unknown—who had slept in this room.

The only indication that the house had been occupied by Canadian prime ministers was the display of artifacts. A huge elk head, mounted on the verandah wall, had a brass plaque stating it had been an official gift to Prime Minister Lester Pearson—who had sensibly chosen not to take it with him when he left office. Margaret said she didn't like it; she preferred live animals. On the living room floor, under the wicker chesterfield, was a brightly beaded replica of an alligator, a gift from the president of the Cameroons. In one corner of the living room was a miniature version of an Easter Island statue that, I guessed, had been a gift to some Canadian prime minister from his counterpart in Chile. On another wall hung a native Canadian cradleboard, decorated with an intricate design of porcupine quills, intended for carrying a baby on its mother's back. Among the books on the bookshelves were four lavish art books from France.

Margaret seemed very much at home here. She said she hated "Sussex"—the official residence at 24 Sussex Drive in Ottawa—and wished they could live at Harrington Lake all the time. Pierre emerged from the lake and greeted us, soaking wet, wearing only his bathing suit. He had a trim, athletic body and once again I marvelled at how boyish he looked in real life. He suggested we might take a boat ride down the lake. There was a good place to swim about ten minutes away. We donned our bathing suits and grabbed towels and sunglasses. Baby Justin was tucked into his carry cot. Soon we were travelling at moderate speed down the lake in a roomy outboard motorboat driven by the prime minister of Canada.

Margaret and I were both wearing bikinis. She looked like Miss Universe in hers; I felt self-conscious in mine. She was twenty-three; I was thirty-eight. Bikinis were the ultimate in swimwear fashion at the time but I have never been entirely comfortable with too much of my flesh exposed. As well, bikini bathing suits—for those who have never worn one—are not particularly comfortable. The under-wire in the bra jabs you in the ribs when you swim and the skimpy little panties tend to slide down your thighs if you dive into the water. I longed for my sleek one-piece suit that day, but was sufficiently vain to want to be regarded as fashionable by our hosts.

Luckily I have been a good swimmer since childhood. I am not athletic by anyone's yardstick but swimming is one of the few sports I love, and so does Farley. Pierre dropped the anchor in a small, shallow bay far from the eyes of the police who were supposed to have him under surveillance at all times.

I tried not to be obvious about it but my eyes kept following him. He was so perfectly at ease, it seemed to me, in his role as husband and father. I concluded that marrying Margaret was the best thing that could have happened to him, maybe even more fulfilling than becoming prime minister. Margaret, and baby Justin, somehow made him seem more human.

After our swim we sat on the shore for a while. Farley, as ever, became interested in a couple of small birds that were darting among the trees.

"I believe those are warblers—in migration," he said to no one in particular.

"Magnolia warblers," added Pierre.

"Mmm-hmm," Farley nodded.

So Pierre was also a bird watcher. This gave the two men something neutral to talk about, I was glad to note because I had been concerned that Farley might get argumentative over some political issue as he so often did. I was sure Pierre got quite enough arguments in the House of Commons and didn't need more from his house guests. As long as we stuck to bird watching everything would be all right.

Harrington Lake is idyllic as a retreat for a weary head of state. All the forested land encircling it is owned by the National Capital Commission, so no prime minister will be irritated by the roar of speeding outboard motors nor kept awake at night by neighbours hosting a noisy party. The only irritation in this private paradise were the trillions of blackflies.

Back at the house, Pierre departed to his study for a couple of hours with a stack of House of Commons reports. Farley and Margaret and I settled ourselves in the large verandah. Justin contentedly drank mother's milk while Farley and I sipped some dry vermouth we had brought with us.

A telephone rang in a distant room and Margaret rose to answer it. It was a wrong number, she told us, sounding annoyed. The number at Harrington Lake was, of course, unlisted and known only to a few family members, some of the PM's staff, and the police. Yet someone else, speaking in French, kept dialling it. This struck me as funny: somebody was speaking either to the prime minister or his wife and didn't know it. Margaret found it a nuisance because the calls sometimes came early in the morning or late at night.

Farley and I had returned from a trip to Europe only one week earlier. Our travels had included Scotland—notably Caithness at the northern tip, the place from which Farley's great-great-grandfather had emigrated to Canada in 1812. Margaret Trudeau also had distant roots in Caithness. Her father had emigrated from Scotland to Canada as a small child but had kept in touch with his relatives in the old country. We told Margaret we had met one of them.

"You met Auntie Grace!" she exclaimed.

Aunt Grace, her great-aunt, was a cheery woman in her sixties who ran a newsstand in the town of Wick. She had become a bit of a local celebrity since her great-niece had married the prime minister of Canada. Pierre Trudeau was the first Canadian leader to cause a flurry of excitement in the self-absorbed British press, which had long been convinced that all Canadians are boring.

For our evening meal Pierre cooked a steak on a run-of-the-mill barbeque of the sort that could be bought in any Canadian Tire store. All four of us liked our steak rare. Margaret had assembled a delicious salad with hearts of palm as the main ingredient.

Margaret was, I thought, as amazing in her own way as Pierre was in his. At twenty-three I could not have begun to handle the life she was leading with such aplomb.

After dinner Farley and Pierre took the dogs for a walk along the lakeshore. I helped Margaret clear away the dishes, which she loaded into the dishwasher in the large, efficient kitchen.

We all went to bed early.

Around four o'clock in the morning Farley was awakened by the sound of a dog barking. It wasn't one of our dogs, who were sleeping soundly on the floor of the bedroom. He concluded it must have been Farley Trudeau. Eventually the barking stopped and Farley fell back to sleep. I, who sleep the sleep of the dead, had not heard a thing.

Sunday morning, we had been advised by the MacInnises, was a quiet time in the Trudeau household. Pierre liked to sleep late and then spend a couple of hours reading those endless reports.

We tiptoed outdoors on a still, sunny morning. There was a nice old-fashioned, canvas-covered canoe on the shore. Harrington Lake was the perfect place for a paddle that day so off we went—Farley in the stern and I in the bow.

Eventually hunger brought us back. We had not had any breakfast and there's nothing like an hour or two on the water to whet one's appetite. It had been a splendid paddle.

"What we need," I mused as we hauled the canoe ashore, "is a lake of our own. Something like this."

"Mmph," Farley snorted. He was in no mood to think about searching for yet another rustic paradise.

Margaret had cooked a sumptuous quiche for brunch. Pierre emerged from the study by then and was pleased to hear that we had paddled around the lake. Canoeing had long been a treasured part of his life. He told us he intended to write about some of his expeditions when this job came to an end. We didn't dare ask when that might be. Margaret had definite ideas about how long they would be living "this crazy life," as she called it. One more term? Possibly two at the most. After that they planned to build a home on land that Pierre owned in the Laurentians.

"Sometimes we drive up there and just look at it," Margaret reflected, "and try to decide what sort of house we should build."

I smiled. It sounded so ordinary, the sort of thing a lot of us do as we envision the house of our dreams which, in most cases, will never be built.

"What was all that commotion last night?" Farley dared to ask. "All that barking around four o'clock. Did anyone else hear it?"

Pierre nodded. "Yes, I did and I came down to see what was going on. There was nothing amiss that I could see. I don't know what Farley was barking at. All I did discover..." and a hint of a smile crossed his face, "...was a police officer asleep on the kitchen floor."

What a shock! A Mountie, who is supposed to get his man—or, in this case, guard his man—had literally fallen asleep on the job. And this particular Mountie must have slept as soundly as I did, not to have heard the barking dog.

"So did you wake him up?" Farley asked.

"I did, inadvertently. I tripped over him."

"And now he will be banished to Ellesmere Island," Farley quipped.

Pierre had no intention of reporting this lapse of duty. He sympathized with the difficulty of staying awake all night when virtually nothing was happening save a dog barking at the moon.

We discussed what we might do during the afternoon. We could go canoeing or we could go cycling. Margaret didn't feel it was safe to take the baby in a canoe—although she could phone "Sussex" and have one of the nannies dispatched here to look after him. However, they liked to include little Justin in their activities as much as possible, so cycling, with Justin in a baby backpack on his father's back, won the day.

I was apprehensive. I was at home with canoes and swimming but I had not been on a bicycle for at least twenty years. I had never been much of a cyclist even in my teens. As our bumpy journey progressed along what had once been a logging road, I soon lagged far behind the others, with my knees trembling. My only companion was our dog Albert, who was slowing down in his old age.

A couple of miles along, I spotted them waiting in a clearing. Nearby stood the foundation of what had once been a log house, perhaps an immigrant family's home a century or more earlier. I wandered around, speculating what sort of life they had lived here long before cars, electricity, and telephones. Their circumstances may have been humble but they had the advantage of living amid these magnificent Gatineau hills. They could never have imagined that their meagre homestead would one day be a corner of a prime ministerial retreat.

Not far from the crumbling walls of the stone foundation we came upon the remains of a small outbuilding. It sheltered a spring with icy-cold water cascading over rocks. We knelt down in succession for a welcome drink. It felt like being on a pilgrimage to a place arduous to reach where one might drink the healing waters of a mystical stream.

I wish I had a photograph of us drinking this sparkling water but I had left my camera back at the house. I took very few photos that weekend, feeling it would be intrusive to take snapshots of this much-photographed family in their private domain. We were guests, not snooping reporters. In retrospect I don't think the Trudeaus would have objected, but at the time I wasn't going to risk offending them.

After Justin had been put to bed on Sunday evening we four gathered for a Japanese meal cooked by Margaret. I wasn't familiar with Japanese cuisine, nor was Farley, but we are adventurous eaters and were ready to try anything put in front of us. However, what Margaret had not put in front of us was a knife, fork, or spoon. There were only chopsticks.

Pierre, who turned up for dinner dressed in an authentic Japanese kimono, seemed surprised that neither Farley nor I knew how to eat with chopsticks. He evidently assumed we were as worldly as he was and that we would have acquired this skill. We had indeed travelled to a lot of places. We had dined on horse ribs in Siberia, whale blubber on the shore of Hudson Bay, boiled squid in Italy, and turtle soup in Mexico—but none of these had required chopsticks.

The meal was served in a large tureen in which little pieces of chicken were floating in a soy-flavoured broth. Four small bowls contained our individual portions of boiled rice. How was I supposed to get any of this into my mouth? I was too proud to ask for a spoon, but I could not dip my fingers rudely into the sea of soy sauce to grasp a chunk of chicken. And I had no idea how anyone could eat rice with chopsticks either.

Pierre must have seen the look on my face.

"Here, it's simple. I'll show you," he offered, placing the two chopsticks just *so* between my thumb and two fingers. Indeed, it did turn out to be fairly simple and after a few tries I got the hang of it. Slowly I picked up pieces of chicken and mixed them with the rice in my china bowl and ate them. I consumed far less food than if I had had a fork. It occurred to me that one way to lose weight would be to limit yourself to using only chopsticks.

Farley was not as compliant as I was. He simply asked Margaret for a fork and a spoon and ate his dinner with his accustomed tools.

"Just think," I said to him when we were in the privacy of the guest room, getting ready for bed. "Some day I could appear on one of those television quiz shows...you know...the kind where the guest has an interesting secret and the panel has to guess what it is."

"And what's your big secret?"

"The prime minister of Canada taught me how to eat with chopsticks. I'll bet not too many other people can make that claim."

"It could be you're the only one in the world," he laughed.

Many years later, shortly after the death of Pierre Trudeau, renowned photographer Peter Bregg put together an exhibit of the best of the countless photos he had taken of Pierre Trudeau over the years. In an accompanying article, he reminisced about the first time he had been part of a delegation travelling with the prime minister. They were heading to the Arctic. Peter was only nineteen years old and had just started his career with Canadian Press. A Chinese meal was served on board the plane and the steward handed him chopsticks. Peter didn't know how to eat with them. And guess what? Pierre Trudeau leaned across the aisle and showed him how.

Chapter Twelve

SHORTLY AFTER OUR VISIT to Harrington Lake, Farley and the dogs headed off to the Magdalen Islands, leaving me to spend a few weeks alone in Port Hope. I saw it as a chance to regain my balance in the midst of a life where there was always too much happening.

Farley took his son Sandy, then eighteen, with him so they could have some time together away from stress and schedules. That year the journey to the islands had become much easier with the long-delayed arrival of the car ferry. The ferry was not a new vessel, having previously linked two Quebec towns—one on the north shore of the St. Lawrence River with one on the south. She bore the vaguely threatening name *Manic*. No doubt it had some significant meaning in an aboriginal language, but in English it was hardly a reassuring name for a ship.

I had had an uneasy relationship with Sandy Mowat. Our first shared summer holiday, three years earlier, had been in a rented house on Cape Breton Island when Sandy was fifteen and his brother, David, was thirteen. At the time Sandy resented my presence in his father's life. I don't think he disliked me personally, but he blamed me for the fact that his parents' marriage had ended. I understood his attitude. I had read that children of separated or divorced parents—and this included Farley and his parents—have a blueprint somewhere in their psyche of their mother and father always belonging together.

David Mowat, on the other hand, was a happy-go-lucky boy who apparently couldn't have cared less if I was his father's second or seventh wife.

However, since that somewhat tense Maritime holiday, Sandy had stayed with us in Port Hope several times and his frosty attitude toward me had thawed considerably. The only misery I had to cope with that summer morning, as I waved goodbye to them, was the departure of our dog Alice.

We had kept two of the puppies from the last litter, Edward and Alice, but it was several months before we discovered both were deaf—born deaf, due, the vet told us, to a genetic defect. We anguished over what to do. Both were smart, affectionate, and obedient young dogs and most of the time one would never have known they were deaf. By observing what their parents, and we humans, did they managed to fit into our lives almost as well as dogs that could hear. Nevertheless, the prospect of coping with two deaf dogs, as well as the hearing ones, while leading the peripatetic life we led, promised to be too much.

It was my idea to contact the Ontario School for the Deaf in Belleville and ask if someone there would like to adopt one of these good-natured, deaf dogs. Right away one of the teachers said she would take Alice, who she thought would be a perfect mascot for the hearing-impaired students.

Farley had arranged to deliver her the same day that he and Sandy were heading east to the Maritimes. However, when it actually came time to part with little Alice I couldn't stop weeping. I am sure I felt as sorrowful as any parent of a deaf child who was heading off to a special school to learn how to live with their disability. In a way, it was worse because Alice wouldn't be coming back to us at the end of the term.

It turned out to be a story with a happy ending for Alice. She was greatly loved by the students and the staff and lived at the school for many years. From time to time the students sent us letters with photos and drawings of her. However, the morning we parted I couldn't know what was in store for her, a young dog who was all the more endearing because she never stopped watching us. When Farley, Sandy, and the dogs departed a spooky silence settled over the house.

It became our pattern that Farley would depart for the East Coast two or three weeks ahead of me. I needed the time to deal with chores like putting away winter clothes and arranging for household repairs and someone to cut the grass. It also gave me time to visit our mothers— Farley's and mine.

Helen Mowat spent a fair amount of time ruminating on the wickedness of the world and often told me that if she could have lived her life over again she would like to have been a nun. However, she acknowledged that if that had been her destiny she would not have had Farley, whose existence she felt somehow validated the way things had turned out for her. She was a regular churchgoer and sometimes I accompanied her to the Anglican

Church down the street from her house. At the time I wasn't sure how I felt about organized religion but, for reasons I didn't try to analyze, I got something back from being in that old church, even though I could never be as deeply religious as Helen was.

"God has a plan for you," she used to say to me. I often wondered what it was.

Angus Mowat had been gone from Helen's life for seven years by then and I think I was the only person to whom she could speak about him. Farley was too busy, too impatient, or too conflicted for long, introspective conversations with his mother. He preferred to help her with practical things—like house repairs. Farley's adopted brother, John, was twenty-six by then, married, and living with his wife, Dianne, and their infant son in Picton, Ontario. His adopted sister, Mary, then twenty-five, was in Toronto with her husband and two small children. Neither John nor Mary had the time nor the inclination for therapeutic sessions with their mother about the break-up of their parents' marriage. In fact, Mary had formed a close friendship with Barbara Hutchinson and it was never clear to us whose side she was on in the ongoing family war games that Barbara had instigated.

So it fell to me to become Helen's confidante. Although she had many friends, I doubt there was anyone else to whom she felt able to disclose her pain at losing her husband to another woman after forty-seven years of marriage. There was no psychiatrist or therapist anywhere near Port Hope then, but even if there had been I doubt that Helen, then seventy-six, would have considered consulting one.

Over a cup of tea in her charming house, or else sitting out on the back verandah on warm June days, she talked about her life with Angus. I couldn't tell if she was suffering more from his departure or from the humiliation of being deserted. Her early married life sounded so happy that I could never figure out why, over the years, it had unravelled.

While I listened to Helen I tried to picture them—Angus, Helen, and a very young Farley—living in Trenton, Ontario, long before it became home to an air force base, long before Highway 401, and long before television and every other electronic gadget we now take for granted. People sat on front verandahs on summer evenings. Sunday afternoons were reserved for visiting relatives and friends. The Mowats were poor, she told me, but it didn't seem to matter. People were kind and tried to help one another. It was the way Helen would have wished things to stay.

Had they remained in Trenton would things have turned out differently? Moving away from one's roots takes its toll on marriages. Perhaps if Angus hadn't been so successful there wouldn't have been so many temptations. Over a period of twenty years and many moves to other places, he had risen from being the Trenton town librarian to Director of Public Libraries for all of Ontario. He had an office in Queen's Park in Toronto. He was good-looking and charming. Barbara Hutchinson was not his first dalliance.

Helen claimed that Angus changed as he got older, and no doubt he did. She was also convinced he was no longer in his right mind.

"That Miss Hutchings (Helen never did get her name right) is only after his money. What can she see in an old man like him?"

Helen wanted to talk to Angus once in a while—in person or over the telephone. Her life had become more peaceful without him but he was still her link with the past, with those long-ago, happier years. But Angus refused. He told us he had decided never to set foot in Port Hope again, not even to visit us.

We were sure this had to be due to Barbara's overweening influence in his life. She wasn't going to risk any possibility of Angus returning to Helen, or of Helen getting a better deal in financial support. Angus must have carried his own load of guilt. Perhaps it weighed less heavily if he let Barbara make all the decisions about his life and his money. When it became necessary to communicate with Helen he did so through one of us and eventually through a lawyer.

Even though they were my parents-in-law and not my parents I felt as torn as any child of divorce because I truly cared for them both. I had been captivated by Angus's wit and style right from the beginning, but over time I had become just as fond of enduring, pious Helen.

My own mother was not a bit like Helen. Winnie was an optimist and an extrovert and only rarely given to reflection about her place in the scheme of things. Unlike Helen, my mother did not have sentimental memories of her early married years. She and my father, as cash-strapped as the Mowats had been, had begun their marriage in a narrow row house on Keystone

Avenue in east-end Toronto, a house that they shared with my father's mother, my father's grandmother, and a step-brother who came home on weekends and slept on a couch in the dining room.

Winnie was only too glad to leave all that behind while they struggled to "climb the ladder," as she was fond of saying. After sharing their cramped home with relatives for eight years they bought their first home, a bungalow in East York, where my brother, Fred, and I grew up. My father, who worked for the same hospital-equipment company for forty years, gradually moved up from stockroom clerk to salesman and finally became the vice-president. By the time my parents were in their fifties, and we were teenagers, they were able to buy a large house in Rosedale, where we lived for a dozen years. After my father's death in 1962 my mother sold the Rosedale house and moved to an apartment on Bloor Street near Avenue Road. Like Helen Mowat she had never learned to drive a car but unlike Helen she adored living right in the middle of the noise and activity of a big city. In her high-rise apartment she was, she firmly believed, sitting on top of the world.

My mother relished hearing about my life. Barbara Hutchinson may have deliberately steered the conversation away from news of where we went and who we met. Helen Mowat did listen but she merely smiled an enigmatic smile, which implied that earth's proud empires would pass away and what did any of this matter. Winnie, on the other hand, would settle down with a cup of tea and a cigarette, eager for anecdotes and details about the life I was sharing with Farley.

Among Winnie's many passions was the theatre. One evening I took her to the Tarragon Theatre to see a play called *Leaving Home* by David French, a drama about a Newfoundland family who had moved to Toronto in 1950. In the big city, they earned more money than they had back home, but they had to live without the support of the culture they had left behind.

I was profoundly moved by that play. I knew what it was like to live in a Newfoundland outport. I knew what those people had abandoned. But my mother didn't. She sympathized with the struggles of that working-class family but she couldn't understand their sense of loss. To her they had only left poverty.

City life was normal for my mother. When she married my father in

1920 she had exchanged one British city, London, for another British city, Toronto. In England she had started working full-time at the age of four-teen in a draper's shop, where she worked long hours for little pay and shared a room in an unheated dormitory above the shop with two other girls. She felt no nostalgia for those years or even for England. From the June day she stepped off the boat in Montreal she became an unflagging booster for all things modern and Canadian.

Conversely, Farley's mother, an eighth-generation Canadian who had only visited Britain twice in her life, nevertheless considered herself a British subject first and Canadian a distant second. The only real dis-agreements I ever had with Helen concerned her lack of enthusiasm for Canadian institutions. Her son was fast becoming a celebrated author in this country, I had to remind her. Canada was on the brink of an exciting era in literature. She was unimpressed. She continued to read several books a week from the Port Hope Library, but her favourite authors were, with-out exception, British.

Chapter Thirteen

AT THE END OF JUNE IN 1972 I took the train to Montreal, where I boarded the Ocean Limited train heading for the Maritimes. I have always loved trains and especially enjoy sleeping on them as they rumble through the night while I snuggle down in one of those compact sleeping spaces called a roomette. Early the next afternoon the train reached Amherst, Nova Scotia, where a bus awaited those bound for Prince Edward Island. It took us to Cape Tormentine, New Brunswick, where we boarded the ferry to PEI.

The crossing of the Northumberland Strait lasted for one dreamy hour during which I ambled around the deck and watched the coast of New Brunswick fade into the distance while the rust-coloured shores of Canada's smallest province drew closer. That pleasant experience is gone now—unless you have your own boat. Since its completion in 1999 the longest "fixed link" in Canada, joining New Brunswick and Prince Edward Island, makes it possible to drive across the strait in about ten minutes. The tranquil interlude aboard the ferry, with all its intimations of history and a calmer, quieter world, has been abandoned in pursuit of speed.

The bus deposited us at Charlottetown, where I boarded an Eastern Provincial Airways flight to the Magdalen Islands. But my two-day journey was not over yet. The Magdalens were obscured by thick fog—an all-too-frequent obstacle in early summer. In 1972 neither the airport nor the airplane had the technology to permit landings under conditions of poor visibility so the plane returned to Charlottetown, and I spent the night in a motel. Next morning we took off again and this time the pilot was able to see the airport.

Had I arrived on schedule I would have had one evening in which to visit with Sandy Mowat. As it happened, that visit lasted only a few minutes—at the airport—since he was booked to return on the same flight on which I had arrived.

Sandy had not had his father entirely to himself during his weeks on the islands. A young couple we had earlier befriended in Ontario had been staying with them. The previous December we had met Chip and Lindee Climo in Port Hope, where they had opened a candle shop. Hand-crafted, artfully designed candles were very popular then. Candlelight was symbolic of the counter-culture's rejection of the technological world.

Chip and Lindee had spent the winter living in a room at the back of their small, rented store. They slept on a mattress on the floor, cooked their meals on a hot plate, and produced candles of all shapes and sizes. That spring we had asked them if they would care to house-sit and dog-sit while we were away on a trip to Italy, France, and Scotland. They had been pleased to escape from their dismal room and spend a few weeks in our comfy house, with such luxuries as a bathtub, a washing machine, and upholstered furniture.

Chip had grown up in Saint John, New Brunswick, the son of a prominent photographer, but he had been drifting around the Caribbean for close to ten years. Linde grew up in an affluent family in California. I never knew how they met but they were classic hippies, part of a mobile population of young people who were rejecting the materialistic life and seeking something they believed would be more meaningful. Many of them were choosing to live in the very places that so many Maritimers were leaving behind.

In June Chip and Lindee closed their small Port Hope shop and headed east, hoping to buy a few acres of land in the Maritimes. They had all their worldly goods, and their dog, in the back of their ancient red truck. They had managed to save one thousand dollars. It wasn't in cash. It wasn't in any bank. It was in the form of a gold bar that they kept in a small leather bag sewn into the waistband of the long wool skirt that Lindee always wore. A lack of trust in financial institutions was another tenet of hippie philosophy.

Their long-range plan was to become subsistence farmers and artists. Lindee had graduated from an art college in California. They were both hard workers. Chip was confident that once they had bought some land he would have some sort of shelter built for them before the winter closed in. Lindee had a passion for farm animals, especially sheep, and was eager to acquire a flock of them as soon as possible.

Farley had suggested the Climos might find something in the Magdalens. He had encouraged many of our friends to come and join us in what he hoped might become a new kind of collective Shangri-La.

However, the Climos decided the Magdalens were both too isolated and too densely occupied for their needs and, as well, neither of them spoke a word of French.

While it didn't appear obvious to an outsider, the Magdalens, with a population of about fifteen thousand people, bordered on being crowded. Most visitors—and we were no exception at the outset—tended only to see those great empty stretches of sand and surf. But you cannot build your house on sand—something I learned in Sunday school. The actual landmass of the islands was barely sufficient for the number of people living there.

The Climos departed to investigate real estate in New Brunswick. After they were gone Farley concentrated on his vegetable garden while I began reorganizing the house. It had been occupied by several people since I had left the previous autumn. They had kept the place clean, but the problem with lending your home to anyone, I was discovering, is that inevitably things get moved around. I had to hunt for my favourite paring knife, my clean dishcloths, my measuring spoons, and my butter dish, and put them where I could find them before I felt I was truly in charge.

In July Max and Aileen Braithwaite returned to Rhoda's rented house in Old Harry and settled in for a month. This time they had the youngest of their five children, Colin, aged nineteen, with them. Colin had brought his guitar and he soon found a group of friends of his age. A guitar was a passport to acceptance almost anywhere in those days.

One sunny day we four set off in our small motorboat to examine the shoreline of the ten acres the Braithwaites had purchased the year before. Their land consisted of a long, narrow strip, mostly covered with a tangle of spruce trees, extending from a cliff facing the Gulf at one end and as far as the shore of the Grande Entrée lagoon at the other. They were trying to decide if it would be best to build a house facing the ocean or on the more sheltered waters of the bay, although I sensed Max and Aileen now had reservations about this project. They were then in their early sixties— young at heart for sure, but whether they truly wanted to commit themselves to spending a lot of time and a fair bit of money in this remote place was a matter for second thoughts.

After investigating the lagoon shore of their land we headed for a small island about half a mile away. Most of the island was covered by a forest of spindly spruce trees but there was a short stretch of beach at one end beyond a grassy clearing.

Cormorants were circling around the centre of the island and Farley guessed the birds were nesting there. He wanted a closer look. We followed him as he pushed his way through a tangle of trees. We stumbled over roots and scratched our hands shoving branches aside and eventually came upon a surrealistic scene.

We had reached the nesting grounds of about a hundred pairs of cormorants and a smaller number—maybe twenty—pairs of great blue herons. They and their ancestors had been using this place for generations and had so drenched the trees holding their nests with droppings it was as if the trees had been stripped of all their leaves and then whitewashed. This resulted in lichens taking advantage of all that nitrogen and so the dead trunks were covered in slimy patches in a shade of green I associated with decay and death. The stench of the place matched the gruesome colours.

The birds were not happy to see us down below intruding into their community of high-rise, scraggy nests. A clutch of adult birds whirled and screeched above us, while half-grown fledglings craned out of their nests. There was something hypnotic about the piercing, continuous noise. Then Farley noticed something worse. Scattered across the clearing were the corpses of a dozen or more adult birds. Among them was a scattering of empty shotgun shells. Somebody had been using the nesting birds as targets.

We stumbled and pushed our way back out to the little beach, which, fortunately, was upwind. There, in the warm sunshine, we enjoyed a picnic of crackers and cheese and iced tea. Max said it felt like coming to Heaven after a brief visit to Hell.

When Farley and I got home later that afternoon our phone was ringing. I rushed in to answer it.

"You stay offa my island or you'll be sorry!" yelled a woman's voice. Then she hung up.

"Oh Lord. It was one of those calls," I sighed.

Farley could cope with menacing calls more stoically than I could. "Just forget it," he shrugged.

I should have, but I couldn't. Who had yelled at me and why? Who could object to the four of us innocently enjoying a summer afternoon on an island in the middle of the lagoon, unoccupied (except by the birds)?

A few days later someone pitched a small tent on the beach in front of the McQuaids' property. Farley was irritated that strangers would settle themselves where he could see them without a by-your-leave from anyone. However, they weren't on our land so there was nothing he could do about it. The McQuaids, on the other hand, seemed pleased that someone from far away had chosen to spend a few days at their place. In fact, Rose McQuaid baked extra pies and generously shared them with the three young campers: one man and two women.

Farley, on one of his morning walks around the cape, stopped to talk to them. He concluded they were nice kids who appreciated the beauty of this place so he invited them to drop in and visit us that evening.

The young man who owned the tent and the camping gear turned out to be a veterinary student at the Université de Montréal. He had long wanted to visit these islands. While driving through New Brunswick he had picked up two hitchhiking girls. When he told them where he was going they said they would like to visit the islands too. They were pretty girls with long, straight hair, faded blue jeans, baggy shirts from India, and lots of beads. They told us they were from British Columbia.

They said they were heading for an eastern Canadian seaport to look for a freighter heading for Europe. They intended to work their way across—cooking, washing dishes, laundry, swabbing decks—doing anything at all.

"Well I admire your spunk," Farley remarked, "but you're about thirty years too late. It's almost impossible to work your way across the ocean nowadays. First, you'd have to acquire some seagoing qualifications, then join a seamen's union, and then wait your turn for a position. And they're not looking to hire one-way crew. In the shipping business they want people who will sign on for a guaranteed length of time."

The girls looked crestfallen.

"The cheapest fares to Europe are on charter flights—mostly out of big cities like Montreal or Toronto," I added.

It struck me as odd that these girls didn't know all this. The young people we knew who went to Europe usually got there on some sort of airline seat sale. This pair seemed to be living in a time warp. Maybe they had been watching too many old movies.

As the evening wore on it became clear they didn't know much about British Columbia either. We had been there many times and it seemed the hospitable thing to do to talk about their home province. We asked them what they thought about Dave Barrett and the possibility that the NDP might win the next provincial election.

They looked blank. That was when they finally admitted that they were not Canadian. They were actually from California, although they had once been to Vancouver for a few days.

This was the first time we had encountered the phenomenon of Americans passing themselves off as Canadians. The ghastly Vietnam War was giving Americans a bad reputation all over the world. Many young Americans who travelled overseas did not want to be identified with what their country was doing and in those days Canadians were looked on as good guys almost everywhere. The word had got around among the young down in the States that it was almost impossible for Europeans, and others, to tell the difference between a Canadian and an American. And it usually is, until you have to show a passport or get into a conversation. I felt sorry for these two young women and, at the same time, glad that I could still be proud of the way my country behaved internationally.

The girls were trying to live off the land, and to do them justice, they did have a fair knowledge of botany. They came to the door the next day with a small bag of leaves: wild strawberry, yarrow, and chamomile. They told me if I boiled the leaves it would produce a delicious, fragrant tea and, because these plants grew all over our property, I would never have to buy tea from the store again. Furthermore, they wanted me to know, commercial tea plantations exploited Third World workers.

After the trio had packed up their tent and moved on, I did brew a concoction of the leaves. It made a dreadful drink. It was so bitter it puckered my mouth. I concluded that if the world's tea pickers went on strike for a better wage I would simply have to adapt to drinking gin.

Chapter Fourteen

MAX AND AILEEN ARRIVED at our door a few days later, looking uncharacteristically solemn.

"We are the bearers of bad news," said Max. "It's about Garnet Cook, Kenny and Marlene's son. There's been an accident. He's dead."

"Oh God, what happened?" I cried.

"Seems he was asphyxiated—on board his father's lobster boat. He and Kenny had been hauling traps way offshore near the Bird Rocks. On the way back Kenny was at the helm so Garnet lay down on the bunk in the forepeak and fell asleep. But there was a leak in the exhaust system and carbon monoxide filled the cabin. When Kenny got to shore, maybe an hour later, and tried to wake Garnet...well...he was dead. He was only fifteen."

It was hard to imagine anything more tragic than the death of this boy. When Kenny showed up at our door the following day he was forlorn and bedraggled.

"We're so sorry," I managed to say.

Farley clapped him on the shoulder, too choked to say anything.

Kenny had come to borrow some money. He needed one hundred dollars to pay for a suit to wear to his son's funeral. The suit was in a COD parcel in the post office. Ironically, it had been Garnet who had ordered it to wear to his cousin's wedding the following week. Now, in a terrible twist of fate, his father—who didn't own a suit—would be wearing it to Garnet's funeral.

Kenny also admitted he desperately wanted to buy a bottle of rum from Farley. He didn't think his truck could make it as far as the liquor store. Farley gave him the rum and a hundred dollars for the brand-new suit.

The tiny church in Old Harry could seat sixty or seventy souls and on the day of Garnet's funeral it was full an hour before the service began. Another seventy or more people were solemnly standing around outside. I had never before seen so many people gathered in this small village. We joined the group of mourners in the churchyard, people of all ages from both the English and the French communities.

Everyone wore their best clothes for this unhappy occasion, including the four of us. Max and Farley had donned white shirts and ties and pressed their summer trousers. Aileen and I both wore cotton dresses—clothing which felt unfamiliar because we lived our summer days in slacks, shorts, and T-shirts.

It was a brilliant, sunny day that somehow made the occasion even more grim. Funerals, it seems to me, ought to take place when clouds obscure the sun and a cold wind blows fallen leaves across the ground—an image that surely comes from a lifetime of watching movies. No filmmaker would ever have chosen such a perfect summer day as this for the funeral of a fifteen-year-old boy.

A large black hearse from the islands' only funeral home arrived and slowly backed up to the door of the church, where six men unloaded the coffin. Soon after, a black limousine arrived carrying the summer replacement clergyman, an Episcopalian minister from New York who, along with his wife and six children, was having a working holiday here during the month when the Reverend Richard Blythe had gone back to visit South Africa. Next came Kenny Cook and his family, who walked the short distance from their house to the church. Kenny was dressed in the ill-fated navy blue suit. They entered the church and the service began.

Noticing that Aileen and I were among those who stood outside, Rhoda Turner beckoned to us to come into the church and stand at the back amid the crowd of women. It was only the men who were expected to wait outside.

On the altar, flanking a simple brass cross, were two huge bouquets of wildflowers—daisies, purple vetch, and red clover—the abundant blooms of midsummer. The American minister conducted the funeral with great dignity. He was obviously a worldly man who tended a sophisticated, affluent parish in the suburbs of New York, a far cry from the people he was facing that day. But death and grief are the same for rich and poor.

I had been told by Richard Blythe that it was only at funerals that Magdalen Islanders sang lustily. At Sunday services very few people sang at all, but at funerals they belted out the hymns. It was a release for the sorrow they were otherwise unable to express. Indeed, the closing hymn that day (which was always the final hymn at local Anglican funerals) was a mournful dirge called "Till We Meet Again." Everyone knew it by heart and sang it loudly and passionately as the coffin was being carried out of the church.

What I had not expected to hear was the heart-rending wailing and crying as Garnet's coffin was lowered into the waiting grave. At funerals as I had known them elsewhere, mourners did not pour out their grief in loud lamentation. Garnet's mother and five sisters did. They were inconsolable and the depth of their sorrow was enough to break your heart.

Ten days later we were once again inside a church, this time celebrating a happier occasion: the marriage of June Dawson (who was Garnet's cousin) to Hubert Bourgeois. June was an English-speaking Anglican and Hubert a French-speaking Roman Catholic and such "mixed" marriages always took place in the Roman Church. This time, however, something new was allowed that had previously been forbidden—the presence of a non-Roman Catholic priest.

Vatican II, in the 1960s, had decreed this could happen. The Reverend Frank Mahlau, the Anglican priest from New York, had participated in "mixed" marriages in the United States and was glad to officiate at this one. However, he did not receive a welcome from Father Gregoire Bélanger, who was only twenty-eight years old and recently appointed priest-in-charge of the Grande Entrée church. He refused to permit a Protestant clergyman to be included in the wedding Mass in his church.

June and Hubert had both been born and raised on these islands and had, for the previous six years, been schoolteachers in Montreal. They knew what was going on in the larger world. They were not going to be intimidated by an ultra-conservative local priest. June phoned the Catholic bishop of the Gaspé and complained. A reluctant Father Bélanger had to obey and permit an Anglican priest to stand beside him at the altar and participate in the wedding.

This was the first time I had been inside Grande Entrée's Roman Catholic Church and as we waited for the wedding to begin I had plenty of time to look around. It was much bigger than the Anglican Church down the road. This white clapboard church had a steeple, gothic windows, and an imposing double doorway. Inside, it had to be one of the least inspirational houses of worship I had ever seen. The walls were sheathed in plywood that had been varnished in a shiny shade of brown that cast a murky gloom over the whole interior. Not even the glimmering votive candles could compensate for the depressing hue. At one side of the altar a statue of the Virgin Mary with a jaundiced complexion gazed down at us with pity. On the other side stood a large bouquet of plastic flowers that had faded to dusty shades of fuchsia and olive green.

I take an interest in religious décor whether it is medieval or modern. It is intended to transport us out of our everyday surroundings and enhance a sense of spirituality. Those dark, plywood walls did not lift my spirits. And what was in the thinking of whoever it was who chose plastic flowers in midsummer when there were so many wildflowers and garden flowers growing outdoors?

Once the wedding began I did my best to overlook the surroundings and focus on the bride and groom and the two priests, who conducted the ceremony alternately in French and English. It was a historic moment in the religious life of Grande Entrée, although I doubt that everyone there realized it. Youthful Father Bélanger, assuming that he remained a priest for the rest of his life, would have to live with enormous changes, both in his church and in Quebec, in the years ahead.

Early in August the Braithwaites headed back to Ontario, still undecided about what they should do with their ten acres of land in Old Harry. They drove their car aboard the ferry *Manic* fifteen minutes after our friends Arnold and Vi Warren drove off. The Warrens were heading for that same little house that the Braithwaites had just vacated. Our friends alone had kept Rhoda's extra house rented all summer.

A few days later we got a phone call from David Mowat, Farley's younger son, who had arrived unannounced and unexpected at the Magdalen Island airport. He had told us in the spring that he was uncertain what he planned to do with his summer vacation. Now, suddenly, he was here.

He had hitchhiked from Palgrave, Ontario, to Charlottetown. It had taken him almost six days. The highway verges, he reported, were dotted with kids begging for rides. He regaled us with tales of their subculture as they wandered, in fits and starts, across Canada, comparing notes about the places where rides were easy to get, or else were nearly impossible. Rivière-du-Loup, in eastern Quebec, he told us knowingly, was the worst place. He had been hanging around there for three days before a truck driver heading for New Brunswick picked him up and drove him all the way to Moncton. It was a point of honour among these young wayfarers that even if they could afford it they did not break ranks and buy a bus ticket to get them over these stretches of unfriendly highway. Reaching one's destination without having spent a penny on transportation was the goal. It was only on the final leg of his journey, where hitchhiking was impossible, that David had bought a ticket for the flight from Charlottetown.

I was appalled to think he had been on the road for six days and nights, sleeping God knows where, and eating only sporadically. Yet in those times we did not consider that there was any real danger in what he had done. I was only concerned that he hadn't slept in a bed for five nights nor taken a shower. Farley drove down to the airport to collect him, after which I fed him a huge meal and dispatched him to bed. He didn't wake up until noon the next day.

For a few brief years in the 1970s a lot of young Canadians were eager to see the country and to get to know one another. Thumbing a ride was not a suspect activity. It was the hospitable thing to do to offer a lift to these trusting travellers. Even women driving alone sometimes picked up hitchhikers. It provided company, a diversion in those days before there were tape decks or talking books.

Those were halcyon times for adventurous people like the two American girls we had met earlier that summer, young people with little money but a yearning to see the world. Like all golden ages it would soon end. Before long we would be hearing horror stories about people being assaulted on our highways or ghastly accounts of hitchhikers being murdered. Yet in 1972 I probably wouldn't have hesitated to hitchhike myself had we not owned our own car.

Arnold and Vi Warren had been seduced by these islands the previous summer. They had both retired that spring and were ready to try living on the Magdalen Islands. They were searching for a house or some land on which a house could be built. Like us, they wanted a place with a view of the ocean and enough space so they wouldn't be living cheek-by-jowl with their neighbours.

Buying property was not easy. We had been singularly lucky to be able to buy our place and so had the Braithwaites. For a long time, the Warrens had not been having any luck. Most islanders did not want to part with any surplus land they might own—they might need it for their children's families someday. As well there were no real estate agents on the islands.

Our neighbouring house to the north belonged to Ivan Agnew, a descendant of one of the original English-speaking families. Ivan no longer lived on the islands and only occupied the family house for a few weeks in summer with his wife and two teenaged sons. We had met the boys, who had become pals with David Mowat, but we had yet to meet their parents.

The Agnew house—also an early prefab—stood on a parcel of land slightly bigger than ours. It crossed our minds that the Agnews might consider selling part of the land, or even the house itself since they were so rarely in it. Along with Arnold and Vi we called on them one evening.

Ivan, his wife, Hélène, and another man were drinking beer in the kitchen. They invited us in and for a while we chatted about various local concerns. Ivan, who had evidently been drinking for some time, soon became sentimental about these islands and how strongly he felt attached them. "Best place in the goddam world," he stated emphatically. Although his career as a ticket agent for Eastern Provincial Airways had taken him away to Prince Edward Island, he intended eventually to return and live here in this very house. "Gonna die here, happier 'n' a pig in…" he declared.

Hélène, who was from a French family in Grande Entrée, sat there shooting dark glances at Ivan as he grew more and more maudlin. "Ee-van. Shut up," she muttered. Apparently she did not share his fondness for this place nor his desire to come back.

"I like living in Summerside," she said to me in an aside, letting me know she was a woman of the world. "A lot more going on there than out here."

There was no point asking if they wanted to sell the house, but Farley did ask Ivan if he had ever thought of selling some portion of his land.

Ivan shook his head. "Tell ya the truth, Farley, I don't rightly know where the old grant begins or where it ends. Daddy used to tell me our land ran over as far as those trees on the north and the other side was our land over as far as that hill runs up back of your place. But that can't be right because after Aunt Lena sold her place to you she claimed she still owned a strip of land between your property and mine."

"So where *is* the boundary?" Farley asked.

"Hard to say." Ivan shrugged and drained his beer bottle.

"Then how come Lena claims she owns it?"

"See, in the old days people here had an understanding with one another about what land was theirs. We never had a survey. Nothing like that," Ivan explained.

When we had bought our house and property a local lawyer had drawn up the deed and there had only been a verbal description of what we owned. In centuries past all land on the islands had been held in a kind of seigneurial tenure, mostly by absentee landlords. Even after the province of Quebec had abolished the feudal remnant a couple of generations earlier, property rights and boundaries had not been legally established.

"I hear talk the province might be bringing in a survey to straighten things out—what they call an 'adastre,' but who knows when that will be," Ivan added.

A week later a truck, with three men in it, pulled into our driveway. The driver asked permission to drive up our hill so they could complete a survey. Farley hesitated. We didn't like vehicles driving over the fragile meadow. However, he relented. A survey, as we had so recently found out, was badly needed.

Farley was furious the next day when he discovered the men had not been provincial surveyors at all, but prospectors staking claims for underground salt deposits with a view to establishing a salt mine. They had driven all over everyone's property, hammering in wooden stakes with fluorescent red ribbons attached to them. That afternoon Farley yanked out all the stakes on our land and threw them over the cliff.

"All we bloody need," he muttered. "Some corporate cowboys digging a mine on our land."

"Can they do that?" I asked.

"I'm afraid they can. There's something in law about mineral rights belonging to the Crown. I don't think property owners can deny them access."

"Lena could make a bundle if they dig their mine on her strip—right next to ours," I joked.

"What a pain in the butt, trying to sort out that boundary, salt mine or no salt mine," Farley grumbled.

"Let's just hope we get lucky and they won't find what they're looking for."

The possibility of a mine was the talk of the islands for the rest of the summer. A gold mine might have been better but any sort of mine meant at least some jobs in this isolated place where jobs were sorely needed. In any event, a salt mine would be underground—or under the ocean—and not the eyesore that open-pit mines are. Tourism was supposed to be the salvation of the local economy but there would always be limits because of the difficulty of access and the short summers. Jobs in a salt mine, however dreary they might be, could help fill the gap.

Chapter Fifteen

NEAR THE END OF AUGUST a large, elegant sailboat called *Veronica II* sailed into Grande Entrée. Her crew consisted of eight teenaged boys, most of them students at private schools in Ontario. They were on a voyage around the Gulf of St. Lawrence observing whales, dolphins, seals, and seabirds while at the same time learning how to sail. Rufus MacGregor, a marine biologist associated with an oceanographic organization in Halifax, was their captain, supervisor, and mentor.

It didn't take long for Dr. MacGregor to track us down. A visit with a noted naturalist and author was one more discovery for the expedition. He invited us to visit the graceful ship he had chartered for the month of August and asked Farley to give a talk to the boys.

For David Mowat, and his chums the Agnew brothers, this boatload of boys who were more or less their age was a source of great excitement. The fellows on the ship were a bright, well-mannered bunch and it was a pleasure to listen to them talk enthusiastically about their adventure.

Some of them dropped in at our house—partly for chats with Farley but also to ask to use our telephone to call home. Cell phones had yet to be invented and there were no pay phones in our village. We were glad to oblige these polite boys, who thoughtfully asked the operator for the charges and left the money on our kitchen table.

We even had a barbeque party for them and Dr. MacGregor, who was a man with some outlandish theories about whales and dolphins, and who claimed they "talked" to him from great depths and distances. Studying communications among marine mammals was a promising new branch of science, but Farley felt some of Rufus's conclusions belonged in the realm of fantasy.

David Mowat spent more and more time hanging around with the kids on the yacht, which was fine with us so long as he got back home before dark. One night, when he still wasn't home by 10:30, Farley drove down to the wharf to bring him back. David was below decks, as were all the boys, and the air was thick with marijuana smoke.

Next day there were several requests to use our phone. We made a point of not listening to what the boys said. The phone was in the hallway, and when we closed the kitchen door it gave the callers privacy. The following day David brought us the news that Dr. MacGregor had suddenly left the yacht and caught an early morning flight out of the Magdalens. None of the boys knew where he was going or how long he would be gone. Temporarily, at least, no one was in charge of the expedition.

That evening MacGregor phoned Farley from Charlottetown airport to say he was on his way back from Halifax and his flight to the Magdalens would be leaving in ten minutes. He wanted Farley to drive to the airport, pick him up, and drive him to the Grande Entrée wharf. He said he needed to talk to us. However, Farley had had enough of ferrying visitors around the islands that summer, so he refused. Rufus could hire a taxi for the forty-mile drive.

He showed up at our house very late that evening to let us know the *Veronica II* would be sailing at dawn next morning, two days ahead of schedule. This hasty departure reflected what he mysteriously called "The Farley Mowat presence."

"What the hell does that mean?" Farley wanted to know.

MacGregor was vague. "The Institute…they have their opinions…I have mine…" he shrugged.

"Opinions about what? About me? What's this got to do with your expedition?"

"You're a great communicator," Rufus replied. "And the boys have benefited from your company." Then he launched into another of his far-fetched discourses about the extrasensory perceptions of sea mammals.

"Good night, Rufus," said Farley with a yawn. "And bon voyage."

The *Veronica II* was gone when we woke up next morning. Gone…but not forgotten.

A few days later Arnold and Vi Warren headed back to Ontario, taking David Mowat with them since it was time for him to return to school. We had our lives to ourselves for a while. We celebrated our first peaceful evening with a barbequed steak accompanied by new potatoes and fresh green peas out of the garden. After dinner we sat outdoors and watched the changing hues of an apricot-coloured sunset.

It was while contemplating this pastoral scene that a dark suspicion dawned on Farley that he might have been involved in the abrupt departure of the yacht.

"Do you suppose..." he muttered, "all those phone calls—the day before Rufus took off for Halifax...several boys wanted to use the phone that day. Could it be they were getting nervous about what was going on aboard the boat so they phoned their parents and spilled the beans? Is that what happened? You can guess the rest. Angry parents phoned the Institute demanding an explanation. The Institute summoned Rufus by radiophone and he had to rush to Halifax to defend himself. How? By blaming the infamous Farley Mowat, of course! That bastard!"

Who better to blame than Farley? No one at the Institute knew Farley personally but doubtless they knew *of* him: an iconoclastic, hard-drinking rascal and presumably just the sort to be a pot-smoking corrupter of Canadian youth.

It made Farley furious to think he might have been accused of dark deeds by people who didn't know him and had never faced him with their accusations. Farley had never used drugs. In real life he did not drink nearly as much alcohol as he led people to believe. A couple of drinks were all he could handle if he was to get on with his work the next day.

The following morning he wrote a sharp letter to the director of the Institute demanding to know what, if anything, he had been accused of.

He never got a reply.

Chapter Sixteen

SEPTEMBER IS THE MONTH I WISH I had been a landscape painter. The evening light created colours and shadows I would have dearly loved to have captured in a painting. I had always intended to return to some form of visual art but in our busy life I could never find time for it. I could write or I could draw. I had made the decision to write. For some reason I felt more self-assured when I was writing. Drawing frustrated me, even though I had graduated from an art college; the pictures I drew never satisfied me. But reading over what I had written gave me a sense of accomplishment and enough conviction to continue.

My mother came for a visit that September. She had never said anything about it but she must have wondered why Farley and I chose to spend so much of our lives in out-of-the-way places like this—these islands she had never heard of until I pointed them out to her on a map. My mother thought of her summer cottage on Lake Muskoka as being distant and bucolic enough. Indeed, it was a pretty place. However, her friends and neighbours there were the same people she encountered in Toronto. For our own restless reasons, Farley and I were seeking other kinds of human society.

That autumn we got acquainted with Don and Sue Miller, new teachers at the Grosse Île school who had come from Montreal. They were living in an apartment inside the school. Sue didn't like it, being so close to the students all the time. They had been trying to find other accommodation but nothing was available. Farley suggested they might stay in our house through the coming winter. It was good to have someone occupying the place and it might be an advantage for them to be a half hour's drive away from the school. They moved in right after our departure at the end of the month.

The ominously named *Manic* landed us safely at Souris and we drove on westward. Although Prince Edward Island is the smallest province in Canada, we were always struck by its relative immensity and diversity as compared to the Magdalens. PEI had seemingly endless acres of farmland. There were even forests, albeit small ones. We could stop in any little town and buy a newspaper or magazine in English. In some ways it was a relief to be back among our own.

We drove aboard the car ferry at Borden to cross the Northumberland Strait and go on to New Brunswick, there to visit Chip and Lindee Climo, who now owned four acres of stony land and a barn on a ridge near the village of Anagance. Chip had constructed a one-room home for the two of them at the end of the barn. Lindee, the zealous farmer, had acquired a cow, some rabbits, and a few hens who occupied the other end of the barn. Their tiny home contained a wood stove, a table, two chairs, and a double bunk built into the wall.

They had also installed an abandoned, claw-footed, iron bathtub, which they had to fill from a well out in the yard. When not in use for bathing, a wooden cover over the tub provided Lindee with a place to draw and paint. Candles and kerosene lamps were the only sources of illumination. Chip had built an outhouse in the yard with a wooden drawer under the seat so he could rake out the offerings and put them in the mulch box to fertilize the garden they would plant in the spring. Nothing went to waste. Theirs was a classic counterculture abode. They had paid for this modest property with their gold bar, much to the amazement of the local real estate agent.

Although the coming winter would not be particularly comfortable I nevertheless envied them living their simple life with so few possessions. I was feeling bogged down by our two homes and everything in them and the tangle of schedules and appointments and lists of things to be done associated with them.

Soon we were back in Port Hope and a week later, Farley began another cross-Canada book-promotion tour, this time for *A Whale for the Killing*, the true story of the fin whale that had become trapped in a cove near our home in Newfoundland in 1967. She had swum in over a rocky reef at high "spring" tide but then was unable to swim back out again. She was discovered by local fishermen and the news quickly got around. A few men then fired hundreds of bullets into this defenceless creature for no reason we could fathom other than the hunter's lust for blood. There was no market for a dead whale in Burgeo and no one there would have ever considered eating whale meat. By the time Farley and I heard about what was happening the damage had been done.

One of our neighbours offered to take us in his trap boat to see the unlucky whale. On a cold January afternoon we drifted on the deep water of that sheltered cove and watched the whale swim round and round in her watery prison, surfacing every few minutes to breathe and, it seemed to me, to glance forlornly at us. I was spellbound at the sight of this gigantic animal, which was as long as a tennis court and weighed as much as seventy tons.

Neither of us had ever been that close to a whale before. At times we could almost have reached out and touched her but she never made any hostile move toward us, despite the scores of bullet wounds scarring her back and sides. Farley persuaded the local Mountie to stop the shooting but by then the whale had suffered serious injuries. As the days wore on, Farley's pleas for help for the whale became a national news event reported daily on radio and television and in the newspapers.

A television crew arrived from Toronto by chartered float plane. News photographers arrived on the coast boat. Never in the history of Burgeo had the outside world taken such an interest in anything happening in this isolated outport.

The opportunity to observe one of the great whales at close range was so unusual that a team of biologists and veterinarians from the United States headed for Newfoundland, hoping to be able to save the whale's life. The premier of Newfoundland, Joey Smallwood, chartered a herring seiner to sail to Burgeo to provide food for the whale. But stormy weather prevented any assistance from reaching her and by the time we got what Newfoundlanders call a "civil" day, in early February, the whale had died from massive infections of her wounds.

Accusations of barbarism and wanton cruelty were heaped on Burgeo from all over the world and naturally the inhabitants didn't like it one little bit. As Farley and I soon realized, the people of Burgeo were blaming him for the humiliation he had inadvertently brought upon them. Eight months later we moved away.

The Burgeo whale had been dead for five years by the time *A Whale for the Killing* was published in 1972. I had mixed feelings about that book. Its publication would seal our fate. Thereafter, I knew we could never return to live in Newfoundland, the island I had loved so much. Somehow it made the Magdalens feel like a place of exile rather than a sanctuary.

Farley's book tour began in Montreal. This would be the last time one of his epic cross-country publicity journeys started there because Toronto had by then become Canada's biggest book-marketing centre. I accompanied him to Montreal, which was a city more at peace with itself than it had been two years earlier when James Cross was being held captive by the FLQ.

Farley was almost unknown in francophone Quebec, as were most Canadian authors writing in English. It wasn't until 1980 that two of his young adult novels, *Owls in the Family* and *Curse of the Viking Grave*, would be published in translation in Quebec as *Deux Grand Ducs dans la Famille* and *La Malediction du Tombeau Viking* as part of a program to introduce young francophone readers to writing from the rest of Canada. However, it wasn't until twenty years after that, in the year 2000, that one of Farley's major books was published in French in Quebec: *The Farfarers* became *Les Hauturiers*.

On the other hand, Farley became a popular author in France during the 1970s with the publication of *Never Cry Wolf (Mes Amis les Loups)* and *The Boat Who Wouldn't Float (Le Bateau Qui ne Voulait pas Flotter)*. Over the years many of his books were published all over the world in more than twenty languages. It was a shame that Quebec French-language book publishers showed so little interest in English-Canadian writers. Francophone Quebec knew next to nothing about the rest of us and apparently didn't care to find out. There was even a widespread misconception among Quebecers that English Canada had no real culture of any kind.

After Montreal Farley headed for Toronto and was hurled into a media blitz there. Next he flew to Winnipeg and, after a hectic day of book promotion, crossed the prairie provinces one city per day until he reached Vancouver, where I joined him for a weekend.

Vancouver was fast becoming an important "book town" and Farley always got a hearty welcome there, which surprised me because he had never lived in British Columbia or written anything about the West Coast.

We stayed at the Georgia Hotel and, as it happened, were a few doors down the hall from Margaret Atwood, who was also in Vancouver, to promote her second novel, *Surfacing*. She was accompanied by the new man in her life, Graeme Gibson. Though all four of us were occupied with publicity events from morning till night, we did manage to get together briefly.

Graeme was then the author of two novels: *Five Legs* and *Communion*. He and Farley and Margaret (who was known to her family and friends as Peggy) talked about forming a Canadian writers' organization—a union perhaps—so authors would have some collective means of improving their lot and defending their rights. At that time there was no standard book-publishing contract and in some cases no guarantee that royalties would be paid on time. Government financial support was needed so that authors could make appearances and read from their work in libraries, schools, and arts festivals, for which they would be paid a standard fee. Graeme also advocated a fund to pay royalties to authors for the free circulation of their books in public libraries. Such a plan was already in effect in Britain and New Zealand. Surely Canada, a wealthy nation, could do the same for its authors. Farley and Graeme arranged to get together with several other authors in Toronto a few months later to launch the organization that would eventually become The Writers' Union of Canada.

It was in Vancouver that Farley had to work the hardest. There were a lot of open-line radio shows and several television interviews to do. All day he was escorted from one place to another by some tireless "book rep." At the time McClelland and Stewart had a sales and publicity representative in every large Canadian city. They were usually young, female, and attractive, and they had to work very hard. The job had some elements of glamour because of spin-offs like attending trendy parties, an occasional meal in a ritzy restaurant, and the chance to get acquainted with well-known authors. But it was a tough job with long hours. Very few people lasted more than a couple of years at it.

The king of the open-line radio shows in Vancouver was gruff, often-insulting, former Glaswegian Jack Webster. Jack's abrasive manner was legendary, but Farley was a match for him. Whenever they did a radio show together it sparked and bounced and the panel of lights on the console was ablaze with callers.

Webster's hour-long show with Farley was followed by yet anther phone-in program hosted by Dave Abbot. This turned out to be a spillover show for the callers who hadn't been able to reach the Webster show. Farley had to leave the radio station to appear on a television interview in another part of the city so Dave Abbot asked me to fill in. I protested that I was not a performer and couldn't imagine that anyone out there would be interested in talking to me. However, I agreed to stay and, as it turned out, lots of people who hadn't got through to Farley seemed content to ask me the same questions they would have asked him—about whales, about wolves, about Newfoundland. Some wanted to talk about the Soviet Union because it had only been two years since Farley had been in Vancouver to promote *Sibir*, his book about our travels in Siberia.

When the show was over, an hour later, I felt pleased with myself. I had actually survived an open-line show, something I had never imagined I could do.

One of Vancouver's biggest department stores, The Bay, had a book department on the fifth floor. Few department stores sell books now but in 1972 they all did. Farley was to appear at an autographing at The Bay but he predicted that few people would show up because anything taking place on the fifth floor was unlikely to draw a crowd. How wrong he was. When he arrived there were about a hundred people waiting patiently for him to autograph their copies of *A Whale for the Killing*.

On the evening of October 29 we had what was, for us, an odd experience watching the federal election returns on the television in our hotel room. What was so strange was that by the time the polls closed in British Columbia the votes in five other Canadian time zones had already been counted. In most federal elections the outcome would have been clear before the B.C. ballots were all tallied.

That night, at 8:00 p.m. Pacific time, the Liberals and the Progressive Conservatives were tied. Both parties had been elected or were leading in 109 ridings. The television cameras took us to Halifax, where a joyful celebration was taking place. It looked as if Robert Stanfield had a chance of forming a government and becoming the next prime minister. A former premier of Nova Scotia, he was an honourable, well-intentioned man but he lacked the flair and the personal style of Pierre Trudeau. Trudeau had swept to power like a prince on a white horse four and a half years earlier. Now, it appeared, a lot of Canadians wanted to see the last of him.

While the B.C. election results trickled in, the television coverage switched to Toronto and the headquarters of the New Democratic Party. Their leader, David Lewis, had been elected in his riding and the party had done surprisingly well, winning 31 seats.

After that the cameras focused on Pierre Trudeau in Ottawa. He looked anything but jubilant. Standing beside him was beautiful Margaret, looking equally solemn.

"The people have spoken," Pierre said philosophically. He looked chastened, like a clever child who had been too rambunctious and had tripped and hurt himself. I felt so sorry for him and for Margaret. I even felt I had betrayed them by voting for the New Democratic Party in an advance poll in Ontario.

"Shut the damn thing off. Come on to bed," said a weary Farley. He wasn't involved in the drama of this election to the extent that I was. "We've got a long day tomorrow," he reminded me as he crawled under the covers.

By the next morning, after some very close races had been counted, the Liberals had won 109 seats and the Progressive Conservatives held 107. The Trudeaumania of 1968 was dead in the water. However, the Trudeau Liberals were able to hold onto power with the support of the New Democratic Party. This minority government would last for two years, during which accommodations were made for the platform of the NDP. It was, I thought, the best possible outcome.

By nine o'clock we were heading for Victoria. The trip from Vancouver to Victoria on the ferry, or any ship, is one of the loveliest inter-city journeys in the world. Sailing past the misty Gulf Islands with the vista of distant mountains is unforgettable. Like innumerable other Canadians, Farley and I had sometimes considered moving to this spectacular coast, perhaps to Vancouver Island. Victoria is such a charming city with its Old English flavour and its balmy climate. It was tempting but we never succumbed. We felt the pull of the east—of family, old friends, and old associations—and, strange as it may seem, of the familiar rigours of a real winter.

Returning to Toronto we found ourselves on the same flight as Jack Davis, the federal Minister of Fisheries. He had just been re-elected in his Vancouver riding and was heading back to Ottawa. Farley, who had long been advocating the abolition of whaling in Canadian waters, had recently written to him asking him to put an end to the barbaric slaughter being conducted in Canada by two commercial whaling companies operated by Norwegians, one in Newfoundland and one in Nova Scotia.

Being on the same plane as the Minister of Fisheries for the next four hours was providential. Farley dared to approach Davis, expecting a polite brush-off. To his astonishment the Minister engaged in a long discussion of the matter and, at the end of it, agreed that commercial whale hunting off Canada's East Coast should cease. He would see to it that it did.

Within a few months the whaling stations at Port Blandford, Nova Scotia, and Dildo, Newfoundland, were shut down.

We returned to Port Hope exhausted but happy with the reception of Farley's book. A few days later Farley set off, by himself, on the train for Halifax. Halifax was seldom included in author tours. It had only two bookstores of any size and most smaller Maritime cities and towns had no bookstores at all.

More than once I had tried to persuade Jack McClelland to set up a mail-order book business in Canada, pointing out that there were millions of Canadians living in places far from bookstores. Jack always listened courteously, but he refused to consider the idea. He believed it would be unfair competition to the few existing bookstores that were the backbone of the retail book business.

Because Farley's tale of a doomed whale took place on the East Coast it was considered worthwhile sending him to Halifax for a day of interviews and book signings. However, the province in which the story took place—Newfoundland—was not on his schedule at all. It was economics that prevented him, and most other authors, from travelling further east than Halifax to promote a book. With only half a million people and, in 1972, only one bookstore, the cost of travelling to St. John's outweighed the sales potential.

Chapter Seventeen

OUR FRIEND FROM NEWFOUNDLAND, Harold Horwood, decided it would help his writing career if he spent some time in Ontario that year. Farley and I had stayed with him at his home near Beachy Cove in Conception Bay for a couple of months in 1962. Now, ten years later, we were able to offer him the use of a summer cottage named Indian Summer, which had been built by Farley's father in 1955. It stood on an acre of land near Carrying Place—between Brighton and Trenton—in eastern Ontario. After Angus and Helen separated it became difficult for Helen to use the place. She didn't drive, nor could she afford to keep the building in repair. No one had been in it for three years when, in the summer of 1968—a year after we had left Newfoundland—Farley bought it from her.

Indian Summer was the basic sort of summer cottage that many people owned years ago—before building codes and zoning regulations and the *House and Garden* attitude invaded the cottage world. It was a small frame building erected on the concrete foundation of what had once been a barn. The cottage was essentially one fairly large room containing a table and chairs, a couple of old chesterfields, and a double bed in one corner. At the back were two small bedrooms and a linen closet. At the front there was a kitchen the size of an average Canadian bathroom. An outhouse stood amid the trees at the back of the property. We did have the luxury of electricity, which made it possible to have an ancient electric stove on which only two burners worked, an equally old refrigerator, a radio, a toaster, and some lamps. All the furnishings were castoffs from Helen's friends.

Once we had purchased our Magdalen Island house in 1970 we no longer needed Indian Summer and were on the verge of listing it for sale when Harold showed up. Knowing that he was no slave to creature comforts (his rural Newfoundland house didn't even have electricity), we took him to see Indian Summer. He liked it and moved in at the beginning of June. He was still living there in November.

While Farley was in Halifax I drove to Indian Summer to see how Harold was doing and to meet a new lady friend who had recently arrived in her van from St. John's, where she ran a health-food store. Harold and Mary Jane were leaders in the alternative lifestyle that was fast gaining ground in Newfoundland. Harold had become the guru of a host of young nomads who hung around his Beachy Cove home. They wanted to write poems, play guitar, live off the land, and generally avoid the narrow social framework in which they had grown up. Harold's escape to Ontario that summer was necessary so that he would have some time for his own work.

During his stay at our cottage he finished writing the novel *White Eskimo*, a saga set in Labrador, a landscape he knew well since he had been the elected member for Labrador in 1949 in the first Newfoundland legislature after Confederation with Canada.

To make this drafty cottage habitable as the autumn weather grew colder, Harold had insulated the ceiling with slabs of white Styrofoam and he had also tacked large sheets of transparent plastic over the windows. He had chopped a pile of firewood from fallen trees on the property, which he burned in the Quebec heater. He had been living in the one main room, sleeping on a mattress on the floor. Sleeping on the floor was *de rigueur* for the hip crowd—but on a cold floor in a summer cottage in November it struck me as an act of masochism.

As I drove back to Port Hope after the visit I contemplated the back-to-the land life style that people like Harold and the Climos were undertaking. I admired them and even envied them, but knew perfectly well it wouldn't work for us. For one thing, it took too much time. Also Farley was, by then, a public figure. Journalists and photographers and television crews were often in our home. What would people think if they found us living in one room at the end of a barn?

When Farley returned from Nova Scotia, which was supposed to be the finale of his book tour, the Toronto media kept badgering him to appear on radio and television shows to talk about whales. Farley wanted to inform the world about whales but he wanted to do it by writing, not talking. A fascination with whales and a desire to help them was burgeoning in Canada. In Vancouver, activist Paul Watson was trying to get the Greenpeace movement, which he had helped to found, focused on whales worldwide.

When Greenpeace became too cautious an organization for him, Watson started the Sea Shepherd Society, of which Farley is now the international chairman.

An American group called Project Jonah was also organizing to save the whales and they asked Farley to establish a branch in Canada. Despite the fact that he is not, by nature, an administrator, he agreed.

All those people hoping to stop the killing of whales had a long struggle before them—one that hasn't ended yet. In the 1970s many nations, especially Norway and Japan, were still engaged in the massive commercial slaughter of whales in every ocean in the world. They had formed the International Whaling Commission to protect their interests and could muster massive political and financial support. The opposition had little money but lots of determination. It was one of the first real stirrings of the environmental movement we know today.

Farley threw himself into this crusade, with the result that we were inundated with phone calls, letters, and visitors. Normally Farley would have begun his next book in early December but the weeks rolled by and he hadn't written a word.

Meanwhile I was making a small protest of my own. As part of its attempt to diminish rail passenger services the CNR was about to remove the ticket agent from the Port Hope railway station. I objected. I knew that if the Port Hope station was left untended it would, in a very short time, be vandalized. That, in turn, would discourage passengers and give the railway the excuse it wanted to abandon the stop.

This mattered to me, as a matter of principle and personally, because the train was my main transport link to the world. Try as I might I never was comfortable driving at breakneck speed on highways and my fear of flying nearly paralyzed me.

I mailed a letter of complaint to the CNR and to my surprise soon got a phone call from a manager in Belleville, who said he would be in Port Hope later that week to talk to me. Even more surprising was the fact that he showed up as promised and was prepared to discuss the situation. Together we came up with a plan that would at least keep the station open part-time by hiring a retired section man to open the station at train time and generally keep the place clean.

It was satisfying that one person writing one letter could have such and immediate and positive effect on a government-owned transportation system. I saw it as a hopeful sign for those earnest people who were trying to save the whales, as well as the rest of the planet.

It was close to Christmas before Farley and I finally found a day free of obligations to drive to Indian Summer after Harold had returned to Newfoundland. It was a cold day with a light dusting of snow and almost no breeze. In winter there was very little traffic on the local roads in the vicinity south of Brighton. When I stepped out of the car I just stood there a minute, relishing the peace and the quiet.

Farley unlocked the door of the cold cottage and soon got a fire going in the small Quebec stove. Within twenty minutes and place was warm. Meanwhile, I had pumped several buckets of water from the well and lugged them into the tiny kitchen. I had brought a picnic lunch and we opened one of the bottles of homemade wine Harold had left behind. Food, wine, and warmth and no one distracting us. As we drove back to Port Hope that evening we agreed this had been the most tranquil day we had had in several months.

"All Indian Summer needs is a decent bed," Farley mused. "I'm damned if I'll sleep on that musty old mattress on the floor."

"You want to stay there...now?" I asked.

"Maybe. I just can't get any writing done at home. Yeah," he mumbled distractedly as he drove. "It could work. I could give it a try."

"For how long?"

"Until I get my book started anyway."

We agreed he should give it a try but before we could get back there another battle confronted us. The government of Ontario had begun amalgamating small towns, rural municipalities, and counties into large units called regions. Now, just seven days before Christmas, when people were distracted by other concerns, the province announced that the town of Port Hope was to be swallowed up by a huge region centred on Oshawa.

Very few people in Port Hope wanted to be absorbed by Oshawa, an industrial city thirty miles west of us with one hundred thousand people. Farley and I joined a hastily assembled group of protestors. First we requested that our Member of the Ontario Legislature, Alex Carruthers,

149

make our protest known to the provincial government. He wasn't exactly on our side. He accused us of being "emotional" about our town. Being emotional about your home, or anything else for that matter, was considered suspect by the bureaucrats and many elected politicians in charge of our municipal destiny. It still is.

Nevertheless, our protest was eventually successful and early in 1973 we did win our case. The eastern boundary of newly created Durham Region ended at a road five miles west of us. Port Hope remained a town within the county of Northumberland. We had resisted the worst intentions of the provincial planners and had come out the winners. Victory was sweet.

By January Farley had contracted a virus that left him with a hacking cough and in a depressed mood. He had had quite enough of meetings and intrusions, whether it was about whales or regional government. More than ever he wanted to hide away at Indian Summer, where the world couldn't get at him, so we decided to go there for a few days to see if it would work. On our way we stopped in Brighton and bought a brand-new bed.

I took my portable Smith-Corona typewriter with me so I could catch up on our correspondence. I set it on the sturdy old coffee table and went to work. Farley set up an "office" in the corner, just footsteps away from me, using a plywood slab door and four screw-on legs as his work table. It gave him enough room for all the papers and reference books and his indispensable Underwood typewriter. It felt familiar. He has never worked at a real desk.

He was then writing the third book in his trilogy about the European exploration of Canada's Arctic. It was to be titled *Tundra* and it required an enormous amount of research. He had to read the journals of Samuel Hearne, Alexander Mackenzie, John Franklin, George Back, the Tyrell brothers, Vilhjalmur Stefansson, Thierry Mallet, John Hornby, and Edgar Christian, as well as hundreds of reports from the RCMP and other men who had travelled overland in harsh conditions in unmapped northern Canada, some of them more than two centuries earlier.

Most days we set our work aside around four in the afternoon, dressed warmly, and headed outdoors for a walk—usually along the icy shore of Lake Ontario. We tramped past summer cottages boarded up for the winter and slid over frozen lawns where snowdrifts had replaced garden chairs.

Our two dogs trotted merrily alongside, relishing cottage life. We didn't care about the snow they tracked in. Nor did we shoo them off the collapsing old couch, where they like to sit and stare out the window at the birds dining at our feeder.

On days when the lake was stormy it reminded me of the home we had left behind in Newfoundland. Murray Township in Ontario lacked the drama and the isolation of the southwest coast of Newfoundland. It didn't sit alone in a great interior sea like the Magdalen Islands. Yet, in its own way, it served the same purpose for us. That winter, for the first time in many months, I felt that my life was under my control instead of being controlled by a host of interruptions.

Initially we had only planned to stay for three days but we were there for a week before returning to Port Hope. Farley made phone calls, visited his mother, enjoyed a nice warm bath, and packed up the clean clothes I had laid out for him. With a new pile of reference material he prepared to head back to the cottage with the dogs, leaving me to wallow in the creature comforts of our Port Hope house.

"Not on your life. I'm coming with you," I announced.

"Suit yourself," Farley said, "but it could get pretty boring. Just work, work, and more work."

"I'm never bored," I boasted, "unless I'm stuck in the company of someone who's boring."

"You'll be stuck with me. And two dogs."

"Sounds okay."

"What are you going to do all day?"

"I'll write a book too."

"You could do that," Farley agreed, as if I had just told him I was going to paint the bedroom or take a course in cake decorating.

Ever since we had moved away from Newfoundland it had been in the back of my mind that I might write an account of our life there. This was the era of the "Newfie" joke, the kind of put-down that is often visited upon recent newcomers trying to incorporate themselves into an unfamiliar society. I personally felt insulted when I heard one of those racist jokes. I knew what people in outport Newfoundland were really like and comic insinuations that they were dim or lazy rankled me.

The more I thought about it the more I felt I should at least try to describe them as they actually were. So few people, unless they had lived in an outport, knew anything about these extraordinary people. I wanted to tell the world.

So we established a new routine. We would go to the cottage on Thursday mornings and stay until the following Tuesday afternoon. Then we would spend a day and a half in Port Hope dealing with life's red tape, and enjoy some simple pleasures like a bath and a change of clothes. Anyone who wanted to talk to Farley about business matters or protests or saving whales could see him on Wednesdays or not at all. By Thursday we would again be incommunicado for five days.

We stuck with this routine all through the winter. Our only diversion was a couple of visits with Angus and Barbara, who lived only half an hour's drive east.

Angus was always glad to see us, but we never knew where we stood with Barbara. Sometimes she appeared pleased we had come. At other times she would make snide remarks about the way we lived, coupled with a bundle of unwanted advice. At that time Angus was rebuilding a 1910 Lake Ontario fishing boat, duplicating the remains of a rotting old vessel he had discovered on the shore. Plank by plank he was constructing what was likely the last boat of its kind in existence. He had been familiar with them when he was a child in Trenton and this project was a labour of love that would take him several years to complete.

Farley used to join his father in the workshop to discuss progress on the boat and that left me alone in the house with Barbara. I had begun to dread these occasions because she used them to tell *me* all the things she wanted to say to Farley—but didn't dare. Several times she told me that Farley was "turning into the media image of himself," whatever that meant. Farley did have a media image but it was just that: an image. His private persona was another matter that they should surely have been able to recognize.

I had hoped Angus and Barbara would be impressed with the Spartan life we were living that winter, particularly as it was in the cottage Angus had built eighteen years earlier, but there were no compliments. I thought they might be interested that I was attempting to write a book, but they weren't. They probably believed that I wasn't smart enough to write anything serious because I had not read the complete works of William Faulkner, Joseph Conrad, or John Galsworthy and that branded me, in their opinion, as barely literate.

Possibly because she had no children of her own, Barbara, as a quasi-step-mother, tried to exert her influence over Angus's family. She should have known her efforts would not be gladly received. These weren't children she was dealing with. Farley was fifty-one years old with an established reputation as an author. John and Mary were in their late twenties, with jobs, spouses, and families of their own. None of them reacted kindly to direction from this woman who had not been part of their earlier lives And whenever she talked to Farley and me about John or Mary, or their families, she made a point of describing their shortcomings, real or imagined. We suspected, and later found out, that she did the same thing when talking about us to them. Whether it was intentionally malicious or not, it did not promote harmony in the family.

Sensibly, I did not convey Barbara's criticism to Farley. But once, when we were driving back to Indian Summer, I did burst out with "I never want to see that woman again as long as I live"—even though I knew I would likely have to put up with her again for the sake of Angus. We concluded that she was a compulsive manipulator of other people and that she was never content unless that was what she was doing.

By March the snow had begun to melt. In April we heard the peeping of the frogs in the wetlands around us. Bright yellow marsh marigolds could be seen blooming in the ditch below our front window. But it was the return of the birds that made our rural spring so joyful. We were only a couple of miles, as the crow flies, from Presqu'ile Provincial Park, which hosts one of Ontario's prime concentrations of migrating birds. That spring we saw everything from robins to Canada geese without leaving our own little acre.

However, the return of human neighbours marked the end of our idyll. The nearby cottages became a lot nearer once we had to listen to loud gatherings around the barbeque and a motor bike that a twelve-year-old boy delighted in roaring back and forth all day. Before long there would be power lawnmowers and outboard motorboats to shatter our solitude. It was time to go.

By the end of April Farley had finished *Tundra*, the final book in his Top of the World Trilogy. Although the content of the book was not essentially his own work, he enjoyed writing the accompanying essays of this rather scholarly epic, as well as arranging all those nineteenth-century excerpts in a way that would engage the readers.

Usually I was the first reader of Farley's manuscripts, slowly perusing his work as I looked for repetitious words or for sentences or paragraphs where the meaning might be unclear. Writing a book, I concluded, was somewhat akin to painting a mural. An artist working on a large project for many months—or maybe even years—can become too engrossed to see the whole thing in perspective. Commentary by someone else viewing the picture with fresh eyes is invaluable. I had begun doing this at the start of our life together in the winter when Farley completed the manuscript for *Never Cry Wolf*.

Farley had always written on a standard Underwood typewriter that dated from about 1950. Electric typewriters had been available for years but he never felt comfortable using one. And he never really learned how to type. His entire literary output has been written with his two index fingers pounding away on one of his several standard typewriters, amplified by countless scribbled notes in the margins. His finished manuscripts always have to be re-typed by someone else.

I also did my writing directly on a typewriter, but I knew how to touch type using all my fingers, so my work was relatively neat. I had had the good fortune to be part of a generation of Ontario students who, in grade nine, had to learn to type. Boys as well as girls—whether we were headed for technical schools or university, or dropping out at age sixteen—we all had three compulsory typing classes a week for one school year on typewriters with blank keys. Our eyes were on our text books, or the blackboard, as we progressed through a series of lessons in which our fingers memorized where the letters were.

Typing classes for every student were dropped a few years after I completed grade nine in 1948. It became an optional subject and was compulsory only for students in commercial high schools. I think it was a stupid decision. Learning to touch type was the most useful skill I acquired in my entire five years of high school. The irregular verbs of Latin, the laws of physics, and the rules of girls' field hockey have all disappeared from my brain but the ability to type has served me well in whatever goals I have pursued.

Farley became my coach, my mentor, during that winter as I stumbled along trying to write my own book. No one can actually teach another person to write; the spark has to come from within. But without Farley's encouragement I doubt that I would ever have continued beyond Chapter 2. I had made a worthy start, he insisted, though we both knew I had a long way to go.

Chapter Eighteen

THOSE QUIET WINTER MONTHS had been our salvation. Once we got back to Port Hope, our telephone never stopped ringing. Farley was getting invitations from all over Canada to come and be the keynote speaker. He turned almost all of them down. He turned fifty-two in May and no longer wanted to spend time and energy on public appearances. To give a speech in a distant location, he calculated, took four days out of his life: one day to write the speech, one day to travel to the destination, one day to attend the event and give the talk, then another day to return home. He had, over the years, given many talks for causes that were dear to his heart but by 1973 he didn't want to do it any more.

However, that year the whales just wouldn't leave him alone. A group at the University of Guelph had persuaded him, as the founder of the Canadian Project Jonah, to come and speak to two thousand students on the subject of the world's oceans and the wondrous creatures who lived in them. I went with him, as did Joan McIntyre, an energetic activist who headed the American Project Jonah, and Lynn Cunningham, the director of the project in Canada. Farley gave a rousing speech to an attentive audience who were very excited to have him there.

One of the few other invitations Farley accepted that spring was to receive an honorary doctorate from the University of Lethbridge in southern Alberta. This would be his second honorary degree, the first having been awarded in 1970 by Laurentian University in Sudbury. Neither Farley nor I had ever been to Lethbridge and we looked forward to a weekend in a corner of Canada that was new to us. However, another whale tale entered our lives before we got as far west as Lethbridge.

Farley read in *The Globe and Mail* that the manager of a tourist lodge in Churchill, Manitoba, had organized a new experience for "sportsmen" that summer. They could roar out into the estuary of the Churchill River on

Hudson Bay in powered canoes and have the dubious pleasure of shooting and killing (or possibly only injuring) beluga whales.

"For God's sake, why?" he exploded. "They can't take a dead whale home and mount it on the wall. This is just wanton, bloody slaughter!"

Beluga, or white whales, are fairly small members of the whale clan, less than twenty feet long. They live in large pods, or extended families. They had survived the general butchery of whales up to now because they lived mostly in high arctic waters.

Farley was appalled that they were to be made targets for sport hunters. He was determined to prevent it. Since we were heading to western Canada anyway, we would make a stop at Winnipeg, where he hoped to convince the cabinet minister in charge of Manitoba's northern resources to stop the slaughter before it got started.

Winnipeg was sunny and welcoming the day in May when we arrived. We had looked forward to staying at the Fort Garry, one of the fine old railway hotels that used to make travel such a pleasure. Alas, it was booked solid so our travel agent could only find us a room in a grotty downtown motel. We checked in, deposited our luggage, and set off for the Manitoba Legislature.

It is a very impressive Edwardian building with a large interior rotunda and a broad staircase watched over by two statues of immense, hairy bison. Farley had hoped to meet the Minister of Northern Development, but to his surprise was told the premier wanted to meet him. The premier, no less—and we had only been in Manitoba for an hour! We, of course, had long wanted to meet Ed Schreyer, who, in 1969, had formed the first New Democratic Party provincial government in Canada.

Ten minutes later Premier Schreyer came striding into the room, shook hands, and invited us into his office. A photographer followed, to take photos of the premier and Farley. After that the three of us sat in a circle of comfortable chairs upholstered in dark blue velvet. It was an elegant, large room with a broad mahogany desk, a thick rug on the floor, and wide windows overlooking the leafy park that surrounds the legislative building. I was astonished that we were sitting in that well-appointed space with the premier of the province. It had happened so quickly and we had not even come to Manitoba to invest in a business or promise anyone jobs. Farley had come to complain.

First, Premier Schreyer wanted to talk about Siberia and about Farley's book *Sibir*. He had never been to Siberia himself but that huge region of the USSR was of interest to him because there were so many similarities with northern Canada in general and northern Manitoba in particular. He loved the north, he told us, and wanted it to prosper. Having read *Sibir*, he hoped to import reindeer into northern Manitoba to start a herding operation very much like those Farley had described in the book. However, Premier Schreyer's experts and advisors kept telling him it wouldn't work. Why not? Wasn't Canadian tundra as good as Siberian tundra? he wanted to know.

The two men were on the same wavelength from the outset, no matter where the discussion led. When the subject of the imperilled beluga whales came up the premier sent for the minister in charge, Sid Green. Since the tourist lodge in Churchill was operating with regional development funding, the province had some direct say in its activities. Premier Schreyer suggested a meeting be called the following day, including qualified people from the Department of Biology at the University of Manitoba. Within minutes the whole thing was organized. Then the premier said that, though he must leave for another appointment, he still had a lot of things he wanted to discuss with Farley. He asked where we were staying and could he drop by around, say, five-thirty when his day's work was over.

"Join us for a drink," Farley offered hospitably, naming our motel.

"Wouldn't you know it?" I laughed. "The crummiest place we've stayed in in years and the Premier of Manitoba is coming to visit."

"Well, he'll see we're not the sort of people who try to keep up with the Joneses. We are social democrats, after all."

"Yes, but I like to think I'm a social democrat with style."

Ed—and he asked us to call him that—did arrive shortly after five-thirty. We sat on the cheap plastic and metal-tubing chairs in our room while the two men had a drink of rum and talked about the north and also the forthcoming provincial election. Ed told us NDP support was strong in the north and in half of the city of Winnipeg. In the agricultural south people tended to vote for the Conservatives.

My initial nervousness at having a premier in our hotel room soon wore off. This man was approachable in a way that Pierre Trudeau was not. Tall, good-looking, with dark hair and blue eyes, Ed talked to us as if we were neighbours with shared concerns about getting the road graded.

The only other provincial premier I had ever met, back in 1965 and in 1966, had been Joe Smallwood of Newfoundland. Smallwood was an ego-centric raconteur, a man who seldom stopped talking long enough for anyone else to say anything. He was an engaging leader of a unique province, but he was not a good listener. Ed Schreyer was.

He stayed for about an hour and then invited us to join him that evening at a city candidate's nomination meeting. We attended the meeting and a small party afterward, where we met Lily Schreyer, the premier's wife. We had seen her photo in various newspapers so we knew that she had long, red hair, but that night, as a joke on her husband, she had attended the meeting dressed in someone else's clothes with her hair hidden under a curly blonde wig. Ed, sitting on the platform with the candidate, failed to recognize her. It was only when she greeted him at the party that he realized who she was. The laugh was on him. I liked Lily's sense of humour and she seemed to like us, because she invited us to spend the weekend with them at their home in the northern suburbs of Winnipeg. We would gladly have gone there but Farley had to be in Lethbridge by then.

Next day Farley and I attended a meeting at the University of Manitoba. We were amazed at the speed with which things happened in Manitoba! Even the hunting lodge owner had been flown in from Churchill a thousand miles north. He turned out to be a former Newfoundlander nicknamed Newfy. It had been his idea to commercialize the "sport hunting" of whales. He rationalized his venture as being good for the local economy because he would employ native people to operate the canoes. He even brought some brochures with him.

Within a couple of hours the whole project had been turned around. Even Newfy accepted the new concept. Tourists would still be encouraged to come to the resort at Manitoba's northern port. Native people would still be hired to take them out in canoes. But instead of shooting whales with guns the tourists could do so with cameras. What's more, each canoe would carry a biology student from the University of Manitoba to explain the life of the beluga whale and answer questions. Ten native men would be hired and several students would get summer jobs. And the lives of countless whales would be spared.

The premier invited Farley to return to Manitoba as soon as he could and tour the northern part of the province with him in a government-owned float plane. Farley was delighted at the prospect. We regretted having to leave Manitoba so soon. The next morning we took a flight to Calgary, where we rented a car and drove south to Lethbridge.

Chapter Nineteen

To the eye of an eastern Canadian, downtown Lethbridge was hardly an attractive streetscape. The roads were too wide, the buildings looked flimsy, and there was a car dealership on every corner. On the positive side, the city had an uncomplicated layout and on that sunny Friday we easily found our way around.

The University of Lethbridge was like no other university I had ever seen. It was a long, low, horizontal structure nestled into a steep-sided coulee. There were no other buildings nearby. There were no trees. From a distance there didn't appear to be any windows in the building nor any people. This buff-coloured edifice had been designed by the celebrated Canadian architect Arthur Erickson in such a way as to blend subtly into the tawny surrounding landscape instead of intruding on it in the monumental way of most older halls of academe.

There *were* windows, lots of them in fact, and they overlooked the coulee and the river. I had never seen a coulee before our visit to Lethbridge. Essentially they are deep, canyon-like ravines carved by prairie rivers, in this case by the Oldman River.

Having parked the car, the challenge was to find the main door. I suffer from a mild attack of panic whenever I enter an unfamiliar school. It could date from the day I first entered grade one and felt overwhelmed by what, to a six-year-old, was a huge, terrifying building full of large people hurrying from one place to another. Whatever the cause, I still have to muster a degree of courage to enter a strange school and even more to ask anyone for directions once inside.

Fortunately Farley does not share this phobia. He strode boldly down a broad corridor in the direction of a distant babble of voices and soon located a group of people enjoying a sherry party. Farley was recognized; we were greeted; and from then on we were treated royally by a hospitable group of academics and members of the board of governors. Honorary degrees do not bring much prestige in the literary world, nor do they generate any money. Universities frequently bestow them on people who have donated a lot of money to their institution but they attempt to balance this by awarding degrees to notable people in such fields as science, education, government, and the arts.

A young professor named Ian Wishaw escorted us in to dinner. His scholarly specialty was animal behaviour and it had been he who had nominated Farley for the honorary degree. Farley, he told us, had been his favourite author since childhood and it had been Farley's writing that had influenced Ian to choose his particular field of academic study.

It wasn't the first time that Farley had encountered someone who told him this, nor would it be the last. I was always thrilled to hear it but Farley tended to be vaguely uncomfortable with the fact that one, or more, of his books had influenced the direction of someone's life. Perhaps he was bothered by the responsibility, in case things turned out badly for that person; but I believe he was secretly delighted all the same. Writing, as I was discovering for myself, is an insecure, solitary activity. You wonder if anyone is ever going to read your words, let alone be uplifted or changed by what you have said.

At dinner I sat beside the chancellor of the university, Dr. Jim Oshiro, who had grown up in Kenora, Ontario, and then studied medicine at the University of Manitoba. His had been the only Japanese-Canadian family in Kenora at the time—a legacy of the diaspora that Canada imposed on people of Japanese ancestry after the bombing of Pearl Harbor in December 1941. When they were finally released from an internment camp in British Columbia, the Oshiros, like all Japanese-Canadians at the time, had been permitted to resettle in Canada—anywhere east of the Rocky Mountains but *not* in coastal British Columbia, where most of them had previously lived.

After graduation Dr. Oshiro had married a British woman and settled in Coaldale in southern Alberta, where he practiced medicine and became such an important part of the community that he was eventually chosen to be the chancellor of this fledgling university.

The convocation ceremony the next day was terribly long, a hot afternoon spent in a building that had been designed as a gymnasium. The saving grace of that torrid experience was the presence of the Lethbridge Symphony Orchestra. I might have expected to hear country music in Lethbridge, but certainly not live classical music. Lo and behold, here was a small but well-trained symphony orchestra adding a much-appreciated dimension to the occasion.

Farley had begged off giving a convocation speech. However, later, at a dinner honouring the graduates, he did give a talk about the environment, stressing the responsibility of these young men and women as custodians of this planet, our home. In conclusion, he told his audience that, in this era of the liberation of women, he would now shut up and let his wife do the talking.

This was his idea of a joke. He knew I was too shy to stand up and say anything in front of an audience. I merely smiled an acknowledgement. The audience clapped and, to me, the incident was closed. But later, as we were leaving the banquet hall, two humourless young women confronted us. They scolded Farley for embarrassing me, and then admonished me for not leaping to my feet, seizing the microphone, and putting in my two cents' worth.

I have always been content to play second fiddle in our marriage and I didn't see it any differently then, or now, than playing second violin in an orchestra or acting in a supporting role in a play. Not destined to be a star performer myself, I was glad that Farley was one.

For a long time afterwards I kept thinking about what those two young graduates had said to me. I had just turned forty. They were barely into their twenties. For the first time it dawned on me that being a wife was going out of fashion—at least, the sort of wife I was: one who stayed home, helped her husband in his work, raised kids, hosted dinner parties, and seldom pursued anything more daring than refinishing old furniture. And yet I *did* have my aspirations. I was writing a book, but I couldn't really call myself a writer until something I had written had been published and taken seriously.

The truth was I loved staying home. Sharing a life with Farley had liberated me from being subservient to a job I hated in downtown Toronto. But now I wondered if my image was being challenged or even mocked by the new generation of women. I felt as antiquated as a one-door Frigidaire.

On Sunday morning Farley and I were invited to a gathering at a farm belonging to one of the professors. Several Lethbridge academics had built their homes outside the city on forty acres of land—which was the maximum amount of land that could be purchased for non-agrarian use in that part of Alberta. We accepted the invitation but declined offers of a ride. We would take our rented car so we could escape if need be. In the past we had accepted invitations from people we didn't know who, it turned out, wanted a celebrity in their midst to impress their friends and colleagues. Too often we had been surrounded by a crowd of well-meaning strangers with whom we had little in common and to whom we had little to say.

However, this Sunday proved to be a happy exception. The gathering was outdoors and we had a chance to enjoy a lush stretch of grassland down at the river's edge, far from the windswept prairie above us. The grass was dense and dotted with wildflowers. Farley had happy memories of this kind of oasis from his boyhood in and around Saskatoon. He told me there were lots of snakes in these river valleys, but luckily I didn't see any that day.

The one thing our hosts and their guests had in common was that none had originally come from this region. Some were from western Canadian cities. A few were from the western United States. One couple had come from England and another pair from Holland.

I listened to the chitchat of a group of academic wives, some of them academics themselves. Most of their conversation revolved around possible moves to other universities. Professors had a lot of mobility in the 1970s, when new universities were popping up all over the place. One woman said she had applied to the University of Alaska. Another was hoping to go to a new department in an Australian university. They seemed oddly adrift, uncertain whether they wanted to stay where they were or move on. Their predicament was not unlike ours. We too had a huge range of choices open to us, but just where could we happily settle down?

Later that day we did meet a group of people who knew where they belonged. We were taken to a Hutterite colony near Cardston, close to the southern border of Alberta with Montana. Ian Wishaw and his wife, Susan, offered us the chance to visit this colony, where they had made friends among the elders.

I had long wanted to see a Hutterite colony, having read quite a bit about their communal life. At a time when getting back to the land was the chief goal for the counter-culture, the Hutterites looked like an excellent role model.

Hutterites first settled in western Canada in 1918—spilling over from colonies in the northwestern United States that they had settled fifty years earlier. Long before that they had been expelled from Russia, Ukraine, and Moravia, as well as from Transylvania, where Jacob Hutter and his followers had originated their agrarian, religious life in the sixteenth century. A peaceable sect, they had been driven from their homelands largely because they chose a cooperative, rather than competitive, way of life and because they were adamantly opposed to taking part in war in any of its guises. These qualities had not endeared them to people in power in Europe and did not sit well with those in power in the United States or Canada.

Hutterites do not seek publicity and usually only appear in the news when they get into disputes with governments. In Alberta there had been frequent disagreements about schooling. The province insisted that Hutterite children, like all other children, must attend accredited schools until the age of sixteen. The Hutterites insisted on having their own schools within the colony. They feared that their way of life would be seriously at risk if their children were forced into the public system and educated away from the colony. The colony we visited had their own school but had to accept the Alberta school curriculum taught by a licensed teacher from outside the colony. However, when the official school day ended an additional hour was devoted to the study of German and religion, taught by a member of the colony.

The Cardston colony was a collection of tidy, efficient buildings. As soon as we parked the car in the shade of a big, modern barn a couple of teenage girls wandered over to welcome us. Apart from their old-fashioned clothes, they reminded me of Newfoundland outport children: unabashedly curious to see the strangers in their midst. The girls were dressed in ankle-length, floral-printed cotton skirts, dark-blue blouses, and patterned kerchiefs over their braided hair. Susan Wishaw's friend Rachel welcomed us, dressed in an adult version of the same sort of clothes. Her bearded husband, Wally, dressed in the traditional men's garb of white shirt, black trousers, and black, broad-brimmed hat, also came to greet us.

They were smiling people who spoke softly with a slight German accent. They seemed pleased that we had come to visit, but explained that, since this was Sunday, all the adults would soon be on their way to church. On Sundays they attended church in the morning for two hours, then in the afternoon there was another one-hour service. It seemed excessive to me yet I remember that my own mother, who grew up in England in the early twentieth century, had also attended church twice every Sunday: Matins at eleven and Evensong at seven.

Wally told us the two girls, Sara and Elizabeth, would be pleased to show us around. They were both fourteen—just one year away from joining their elders. They first took us to see the church, an unadorned wooden building that served both as church and school. Inside were forty school desks and at the back of the room were several rows of benches, which was where everyone over the age of fifteen sat for church services. At that age a Hutterite boy or girl ceases to attend school, is baptized into the church, and takes his or her place in the shared work of the colony.

Sara and Elizabeth were self-possessed as they described for us what life was like here. They showed us the songbooks, in German, that every Hutterite child must make before entering adult society. The books were hand lettered in Old German script with colourful, illuminated capital letters in the manner of a medieval Bible. The crafting of these books continued a tradition going back to a time before the printing press was widely used. Making the book was considered a practical as well as symbolic way of connecting children with their Hutterite culture. If they hadn't finished the book by school-leaving time they were expected to do so in their spare time afterwards. Sara giggled and told us that the boys were not as good at printing as were the girls.

The two girls asked us if we would like to hear them sing one of the songs. We certainly would, so they sang a hymn of many verses in German in two-part harmony, so innocently and perfectly that I would have given a lot to have had a tape recorder with me.

Adults began arriving for the church service so we left the building, noting that women sat on one side and men on the other. The same separation of the sexes applied in their community dining room. Although a small home was provided for each family, in which they could enjoy some privacy, the largest part of their day was spent working in the company of other members of the colony.

We went to see the spotless kitchen, bakery, butchery, and dining hall, accompanied by a growing crowd of younger children, who found us to be an entertainment on this quiet Sunday afternoon. Sara and Elizabeth explained that the pots and pans in the kitchen were made by their own tinsmith. The plain wooden furniture was constructed by their carpenter. The women sewed all their own, their husbands', and their children's clothes. Although the colony purchased fabric, shoes, underwear, eye glasses, and farm machinery in nearby towns, it bought very little else—a fact that did not endear the Hutterites to local merchants.

The girls answered our questions with a quiet certainty that very few fourteen-year-olds who live in our cultural stew possess. Sara and Elizabeth did not appear to be distracted by a flurry of adolescent excitement. These girls knew they would not be marrying any of the boys from their own colony. Young, single men from other Hutterite colonies, who came to help with the farm work, would be their suitors and eventually their husbands. Similarly young, single men from this colony were sent to help in some other colony and would find brides there.

Ideally, a Hutterite colony would number about one hundred people. When the numbers grew much beyond that size the colony would split and a new colony would be established somewhere else. In 1973 there were about seventy Hutterite colonies in Alberta, extending from north of Edmonton all the way down to the American border.

The one commodity on which Hutterites spent money lavishly was farm machinery. We were shown the newest combines, tractors, and trucks. While they abided by sixteenth-century principles and practices that had been established by their founder, they had no reservations about making use of the latest developments in farming technology.

This colony had a tanner—though not every colony did. The tannery was full of beautifully tanned sheepskins and cowhides. Some were for Hutterite use, especially for winter coats and mitts. However, much was for sale to the public. I bought two sheepskins to use as rugs and I have them to this day.

I was reluctant to leave the colony. I would have relished staying there for days or weeks to discover how these people managed to work and live together in harmony. Was it real, or only apparent? Well, very few Hutterites desert their communal lives to live the way we do. And anyone who does leave is always welcome to come back to regain the familiar rhythm of the life they had known since birth.

As we drove away I turned and looked back to see the two girls waving goodbye. The land was lush and verdant, irrigated by a reservoir of deep-blue water. In the distance we could see the snowcapped Rocky Mountains. It looked utterly serene and beautiful.

"I wish I was younger," I lamented. "If I was twenty instead of forty I'll bet I could find a way to fit in there. Maybe as a schoolteacher..."

"Or a chicken-plucker," Farley suggested.

"Maybe a baker," I sighed.

"Or a swine herder," Farley added.

"Whatever. Wouldn't it be wonderful to be fourteen and to know what you were supposed to be doing with your life? I wish I'd had a clear idea of my destiny when I was fourteen."

"Don't you think you would have rebelled against all those rules and regulations?" Farley asked me.

I thought about that but concluded most likely I would not have rebelled because I would have been embedded in a community where everyone shared the same convictions and expectations. I would have felt secure and accepted and been regarded as a full-fledged adult when I reached the age of fifteen. Would I truly have missed high school, the hit parade, lipstick, movies, and television—all prohibited in a Hutterite colony? I doubt it.

We still don't hear much about the Hutterites. Living communally, growing one's own food, and producing most everything else that's needed is not part of the vision our leaders have for the Western world. A life of shared goals and communal activity—whether it's under a totalitarian regime overseas or in a religious community on the Canadian prairies—is at odds with the principle of self-interest that governs the lives of most of us.

When we flew back to Ontario Farley was still basking in the glow of the warm reception he had received in Manitoba, still slightly incredulous that his defence of the beluga had been taken seriously and acted upon so quickly.

He was intrigued by Ed Schreyer's invitation to travel with him into the northern part of the province. A provincial election had been called for late June and Schreyer and his entourage would be all over Manitoba. Farley didn't have to surmount any philosophical hurdles to join the Schreyer bandwagon. The political left, which he had supported all his life, had never looked more appealing. And while I dreamed of belonging somewhere— anywhere—Farley dreamed about northern landscapes, northern people, and the possibility that he might be able to improve their lives.

Manitoba had not seen the last of my husband.

Chapter Twenty

FARLEY WAS AWARDED yet another honorary degree that spring but receiving this one didn't require a long journey. In June the University of Toronto, from which he had graduated in 1949 with a Bachelor of Arts degree, bestowed on him his second Doctor of Law degree that year.

This convocation was in Toronto so we were able to invite both our mothers. My mother's apartment on Bloor Street was within walking distance of Convocation Hall. We drove Helen Mowat in with us from Port Hope, then the four of us strolled along Philosopher's Walk, a park-like passage that extends south from Bloor Street into the green and leafy university campus.

Neither of our mothers had ever attended a university convocation before. My mother's education, in England, had ended when she finished grade eight. Helen, in her teens, had attended a convent school in eastern Ontario for a couple of years, where she studied music, embroidery, and etiquette. She would have gone to Farley's graduation from university except for the fact that Farley had been too busy, and too indifferent, to be there himself. My mother had been present at my graduation from the Ontario College of Art, but that had been a lacklustre event compared to the pomp and tradition that attends a convocation at the University of Toronto.

As the sonorous pipe organ sounded a rousing march and the parade of academics proceeded down the aisle, along came Farley, garbed in a red-and-pink academic gown, a red-and-white hood, and a black mortarboard hat. He looked for all the world like some exotic bird because he was wearing all this over his multi-coloured kilt. His kilt attire, which he had purchased in Scotland a few years earlier, was the only formal suit of clothes he owned. In his kilt and short tweed jacket he could be well dressed while sharing an identity with his stalwart—or maybe even wild—Scottish ancestors. However, there was one real disadvantage to this Celtic costume. It had been designed for a cooler climate. In Toronto, in June, with the addition of the academic regalia, it was stifling.

The best part for me was that I had been assigned to sit beside Robertson Davies at luncheon, which meant I could talk for more than a minute or two with the celebrated author and playwright who was then the Master of Massey College.

I can't recall why, but we got onto the subject of variety theatre in England in the early twentieth century. This had always interested me because of my mother's stories, her clear recollections of how much she had enjoyed it. As a teenaged store clerk in London during the First World War, she and her girlfriends had gone to the theatre every Wednesday afternoon (when the shops were closed) to watch live performances. She often told me how much she missed it after moving to dour Toronto in 1920 in order to marry my father.

I had recently read the novel *Lost Empires* by J.B. Priestly, a story that revolved around theatre performers in London at the very time my mother had seen them. I asked Davies if he had read it. He certainly had, he told me. What's more, he knew J.B. Priestly personally. This was the only one of Priestley's novels I had ever read but our shared love of that book sustained a lively conversation that lasted throughout the meal.

We also shared an intense dislike of Richard Nixon, then the president of the United States. Davies had his own perspective on that country. He said it was hidebound by eighteenth-century conservative ideas, locked into a system of government that hadn't changed significantly since the 1780s. Consequently it lacked the flexibility of ours, of the UK, of most western European nations. That Davies was right can hardly be argued. The predicament persists to this day.

When the disruptions had died down, Farley and I returned to Port Hope and some semblance of a normal life. We spent three days at Indian Summer, mainly to clean the place because we were going to lend it to a friend, Diane Woodman, for the summer. Diane was the publicity director of McClelland and Stewart, a single mother of four who had recently moved from Edmonton to Toronto to take on the daunting job of promoting the latest books of Jack McClelland's stable of authors. If anyone needed a weekend getaway place in the country, she did.

We had only been at Indian Summer for a day when we had an unexpected visit from Farley's father and Barbara. Farley had earlier written Angus to tell him Helen needed more money to cope with her needs. Barbara insisted Helen actually had lots of money stashed away in a bank account somewhere but was too miserly to spend it. Where Barbara got this notion I could not imagine. Throughout her marriage to Angus, the only money Helen received had been a fixed, minimal allowance from Angus with which to run the home. She had never had a paying job. She had not inherited any money. She was then living on two hundred dollars a month, which Angus provided, along with her Old Age Pension.

Farley did his best to distance himself from his parents' money squabbles. He suggested that Helen's finances be turned over to a lawyer. He anticipated this would infuriate Barbara, which is why, when he saw Angus's Volkswagen pull into the yard, he said to me, "Oh-oh, she's with him. Here's trouble."

For the first little while it seemed he was wrong. Barbara's most exasperating behaviour was her ability to be coldly critical, and even insulting; then she'd switch to being as friendly as a puppy. We never knew which it would be but we had figured out that when she was in a chummy mood she was after something. On this occasion there were none of the usual sly digs about Farley's name popping up in the vulgar media too often. There was no sermonette about how we should be living our lives. There was even a compliment about Farley's book *A Whale for the Killing*, which was still on the best-seller list eight months after it had been published.

Barbara's sweetness that day was unsettling. So many of our recent visits with her had an undercurrent of sour criticism. Now, as she tried to persuade us there was no need to increase Helen's allowance, or bring in a financial intermediary, Barbara couldn't have been nicer.

Farley did his best to argue on his mother's behalf, but in the end nothing changed very much. Angus did agree to pay for having her snow shovelled next winter, but when he said he would also pay for plumbing repairs, Barbara insisted he do so only if we got at least two prior estimates of the cost.

"Two estimates!" I snorted, after they had gone. "For the cost of replacing a washer in a tap?"

A month earlier a plumber had charged the reasonable sum of three dollars for fixing a dripping tap in Helen's bathroom, a charge that Barbara insisted was outrageous.

"Your mother," I declared angrily, "is the least extravagant woman I know. Sometimes Barbara makes me...want to throw up!"

Actually, I was angry with myself for having been cordial to her. She knew how to play on my weaknesses. When people treat me in a friendly manner I can be counted on to be friendly in return. Although I had vowed never to speak to her again, or even be in the same room with her, I had succumbed. I had made a pot of tea and offered Barbara and Angus homemade cookies. On a lovely June day, with the fragrance of lilacs wafting across the lawn, it was difficult to stay angry at anyone. In spite of everything I cared about Angus; but now I was furious at having allowed myself to be a pawn in Barbara's cunning family chess game.

The fact was that I had never encountered anyone quite like her before. We should have been pals—we had many shared interests—but Barbara simply had to control the people around her. I had once worked under an office manager who had the same tendencies, but she had not been part of my family circle and at the end of the day I could go home and forget about her. Eventually I quit that job. I couldn't dispose of Barbara so easily.

Farley concluded she was Machiavellian, and that she rehearsed the mood she would project and what she was going to say before every encounter with us. Maybe she did this with everyone. One possible explanation for her behaviour was that her mother had exercised the same sort of control over all of her eight children, a lament I had heard from Barbara several times. In fact, Barbara was seeing a psychiatrist once a week to try and exorcise the demons from her own childhood; but there was no indication that she recognized the same behaviour in herself.

I found it frightening to see the influence she had over Angus. Part of his failure to confront her was likely due to his age. Perhaps he no longer had the energy to resist her constant meddling in his relationships with family and friends. More and more he tended to lose himself in his beloved carpentry work during the day and in the evenings retreated into the world of books.

The following week Farley boarded a flight to Winnipeg to help in the campaign to re-elect the Manitoba New Democrats for a second term. He phoned me from time to time and sounded elated about his participation. Things were going well and the prediction was the NDP would win. Farley was meeting all sorts of interesting people. Flying around in a light aircraft with the premier and his team was exhilarating. They had even been to Brochet in the extreme north of the province, a Cree settlement where Farley had lived for several months in 1948 and where he began writing the narrative that eventually became his first book, *People of the Deer*.

While he was away I stayed in Port Hope, weary from all our travels. Without Farley, there was more time to make decisions about all the clothes and books we would need during the coming months on the Magdalen Islands. When Farley was home in Port Hope I rarely found the time to write anything longer than a letter. On my own I could find two or three hours a day to write seriously, to add another chapter to the book I was determined to finish. Still, I was plagued with doubt, wondering if I was wasting my time, unsure that anything I wrote would ever be worth publishing.

On June 28 the Manitoba NDP elected their second majority government. Farley returned home very tired but satisfied he had been able to make a contribution. He set aside one frantic day in which to deal with the bank, the post office, his accountant, and his mother. I washed his clothes and repacked them. The next day we set off on the one-thousand-mile drive to Cape Tormentine, New Brunswick; the ferry to Prince Edward Island; and finally the ferry to the Magdalens. We were in a hurry. We had to get to Prince Edward Island before the Queen did.

Chapter Twenty-one

QUEEN ELIZABETH WAS due to arrive in Charlottetown on July 1 to preside at the celebration of the centenary of Prince Edward Island's entry into the Canadian Confederation. Farley and I were afraid there might be multitudes from off the island driving to this royal event, resulting in long line-ups for the car ferry at Cape Tormentine. As it turned out we only had to wait half an hour before driving aboard the *John Hamilton Gray* to cross Northumberland Strait.

After landing at Borden it took us a couple of hours to reach our next destination, the Lord Rollo Motel near Souris. Hordes of people were invading Charlottetown but no one in Souris appeared to be caught up in the celebration. There were plenty of rooms to rent, even at 10:30 at night.

We rose early the next morning and prepared to board the *Manic* for the five-hour voyage to the Magdalens. Run by a private company, the Magdalen Islands service did not operate with the same brisk efficiency as the Marine Division of Canadian National, which ran the car ferries elsewhere in the Atlantic provinces. At Souris there was no advance reservation system so we had to park at the loading dock several hours ahead of departure time. There we bought a ticket from a glum fellow and were assigned a boarding number that bore no relationship to our place in the line-up. Although ours was the third car in line that morning our reservation number was 14. Somewhere, in and around this loading dock, there were at least eleven other motor vehicles whose drivers had made more satisfactory, if more expensive, arrangements with the sullen ticket seller.

We were the only English-speaking people waiting to get out to the islands that day. All around us was a cheery babble in French among couples, families, and friends.

I couldn't help but wonder if the number the ticket seller had given us reflected disdain for *les Anglais*. Our car had Ontario licence plates. Who were we anyway? If some vehicle had to be bumped and wait an extra day to cross, would it be ours? I tried not to be paranoid but at the ferry dock the two of us represented a minority with little bargaining power.

The parking area soon filled up and our compact station wagon was hemmed in. We faced a long and tedious morning. We had each brought a book to read, although I could not read seriously amid the heat, the flies, the distractions, and the uncertainty of our departure. I have never been able to read in airports either. Farley, like most men, could close off the rest of the world when he wanted and immerse himself in a good book.

Lunch came from the canvas picnic bag we always carried with us when we travelled by car in rural Atlantic Canada. In those days, with only a few exceptions such as the Marshlands Inn in Sackville, New Brunswick, good restaurants were few and far between. Our picnic bag was stocked with a chunk of cheddar cheese, canned sardines, canned pâté, a jar of butter, a jar of jam, biscuits, small cans of fruit juice, and a package of cookies. It was surprising how good everything tasted, especially as we usually found a quiet place to eat by a stream or a lake. That day we dined in a grassy field uphill from the wharf. The sun shone, the breeze was gentle, and pastoral Prince Edward Island had never looked lovelier. As I observed the growing line-up of cars and trucks awaiting the ferry I wished we had found a home somewhere on PEI, where we didn't have to cope with the vagaries of travelling to those seductive, but faraway, islands.

My angst at the prospect of being left behind turned out to be unfounded and we did drive aboard the ferry early that afternoon. By evening we were once again sailing past the sculptured hills of Entry Island and into the aptly named Baie de Plaisance—or Pleasant Bay, depending which map you looked at.

Before the sun set we had reached our other home, at the northeast end of the islands. As always we were infatuated with the beauty of the place. Our rapture was short-lived. Isaac LaPierre, who had offered to open up the house for us, greeted us with the news that our hot-water heater had once again burned out. Isaac and his father had been trying to fix it but, as ever, the part they needed was not to be found on the islands and we would have to wait for one to be sent over from Moncton. Isaac was a treasure, one of those gifted men with the ability to figure out how anything worked and, when it didn't, how to put it back in working order. He was our salvation because something was always out of order in that house—the freezer, the furnace, the plumbing.

I resigned myself to living without hot tap water for an indeterminate period. After all, we had managed to live without it at Indian Summer in the winter. So did the hardy backpackers who invaded the islands every summer.

The first pair arrived only a few days after we did. Ian and Marie lived in Jonquière in the Saguenay region of Quebec. He taught English at a community college and she worked in the college office. Ian was a rarity, a Toronto-born Anglophone who had immersed himself in the hinterland of Quebec. He told us he loved it there and never intended to return to Ontario. He now lived his life totally in French and only spoke English when he was teaching it to his French-speaking students. Marie, who wore faded jeans and a tie-dyed T-shirt, spoke very little English.

They were a thoughtful couple who asked permission to camp on "our" beach, which, of course, wasn't ours since beaches are Crown land up to the highest tide mark. They had a small tent and basic camping gear. They gathered driftwood to build a fire to cook their meals. They generously invited Farley and me to join them one evening for a lobster supper. They bought the lobsters from a fisherman and boiled them in a galvanized bucket. We supplied potato salad and a bottle of wine. We had a lovely time.

There was a rather reclusive man named Benoit from our village whose favourite pastime was roaming the beaches. That evening, observing our little party, he stopped to chat. He was curious about this young couple and asked them where they came from. Marie told him and described the life she and Ian lived, which must have been an existence that Benoit could hardly imagine since he had never left these islands. She saw that he was a bit perplexed and added, *"Mais, je suis Québécois, comme vous."*

He nodded, smiled, and said something amicable to her and then continued on his way. But her words had struck a nerve inside me.

I was so obviously not a Québécois. Nor was Farley, although it didn't bother him as much.

That night I slept fitfully, and I was downcast all the next day. What was I doing in this place where I would never be accepted: an outsider to both the French and the English? The question plagued me.

In July our friends Arnold and Vi Warren returned to the Magdalens, to the same rented house in Old Harry. They were still keen to buy a place of their own here. We told them the Gibson house, across the field from ours, had just been listed for sale.

We got the key from Morris McQuaid, our ship-building neighbour, and let ourselves in. It was a solid, two-storey frame house built in the 1920s, the same vintage as ours. There was the usual large, welcoming kitchen. The parlour was small with a stiff brown chesterfield. Upstairs were three bedrooms and a bathroom. What was most noteworthy about the house was the outlook. From the windows on the south and west sides one had a sweeping view of the Gulf, bordered by a long, curving beach that rose to a commanding red sandstone cape. It was a vista to die for. The Warrens decided to buy it.

The prospect of having two good friends next door enormously lightened my feeling of being isolated in an alien place. However, there was a downside. I worried that if the Warrens settled here we would somehow feel obligated to stay on, too, well into the foreseeable future. The thought roused an unease that I shared with Farley, who was also beginning to have doubts about the choice of the Magdalens as a home. We decided to level with the Warrens and tell them we were uncertain about how long we would be staying here. Farley had already arranged to buy a small travel trailer—a "caravan" he called it—from a company in New Brunswick and, later in the summer, we intended to drive to Manitoba to visit the Schreyers and see if we might find the haven we were looking for in the west instead of the east.

Undismayed, the Warrens made an offer on the house and it was accepted. To celebrate the occasion they invited us to Old Harry for dinner. We parked our car and paused to chat with Rhoda and Wesley next door. Rhoda was weeding her flower bed. Wesley was standing at the door of the garden shed. They had just returned from a trip to Charlottetown to visit their son and his family.

"Hey Farley, buddy..." Wesley called. "Seen ya on the TV when I was in PEI."

"So what was I going on about?"

"Y'er out there gettin' that fella elected in Manitoba. That communist. We figgered all along you were some kind of pinko," he snorted. Wesley had been drinking, perhaps all day.

Rhoda glanced disapprovingly at Wesley's back, then complained that the weeds were taking over. She smiled and enquired how our garden was doing. It was a safer subject.

This wasn't the first time Farley had been accused of being a communist. On these islands, as in many other places, the term "communist" could apply to almost anyone who didn't live, and think, much the same way the locals did. Hippie campers—like Ian and Marie—had been branded as "communists" by the local children. The children, and probably their parents too, had no idea what a communist was but suspected that people who didn't dress or talk or sleep in houses as they did must have heretical ideas.

Wesley was a hard-working man in his sixties who clung to his prejudices. I tried to fathom people like him who, despite their labours, never got their share of the nation's wealth yet unquestionably swallowed the dogma of right-wing capitalism. Why didn't he smarten up? Farley was more tolerant. He said most people formed their political views from information fed to them by their parents, by the media, and by vested interests like big business, and they shouldn't be blamed for their narrow focus or one-sided conclusions.

Arnold and Vi were full of plans for renovating the Gibson house. I wondered if they were doing the right thing. Neither spoke a word of French. However, they were a very self-reliant pair and they regarded this move to the Magdalens as one big adventure. We had thought of it that way too, initially. Nevertheless, it was their decision so I kept my doubts to myself.

For the rest of the summer I resolved to enjoy myself, despite the disturbing undercurrents in the community that I could feel but couldn't exactly define. Every morning I would work at my writing. In midsummer I planned to pick wild strawberries every afternoon. On sunny days I would pack a picnic and Farley and I would climb our grassy hill, then clamber down the cliff to the beach, where we could spend lazy hours soaking up the sun and swimming in the surf.

From time to time Arnold and Vi joined us on the beach as we sipped iced tea from our thermos, gazed at the sea, and felt sorry for everyone who wasn't there that day to enjoy such a wondrous place. The Warrens had formed a strong friendship with their landlady, Rhoda, and one day they brought her to the beach with them. Rhoda didn't swim. It seemed odd to us how few local people, other than children, spent time on these dazzling beaches that so enchanted us.

David Mowat, by then seventeen, arrived unexpectedly at the end of July. Once again he had hitchhiked all the way from Ontario and, again, it had taken him several days to do it. We still had reservations about his mode of travel but at seventeen he did seem able to take care of himself. He had also lost interest in tagging along with us. He and his two chums, the Agnew brothers up the road, pursued an agenda of their own and, apart from meals and bedtime, we didn't see him all that often. Luckily none of them had a driver's licence or a car—the line of demarcation between mere mischief and genuine trouble.

The Magdalen Islands had an alarming rate of traffic accidents. The kind of discipline required to drive on mainland superhighways was not present here. The weekends, when some people partied and drank—and then attempted to drive home—were particularly bad and we avoided driving on Friday nights or Saturday nights if at all possible. There weren't nearly enough police officers to patrol the roads—a fact that was well known to drinking drivers.

In August one of Stuart Richards's colleagues, Lyndon Bechervaise, the director of adult education in the English system for the Gaspé region, came to spend a few days in the Magdalens. He had not come for a holiday. He had the distasteful task of explaining to the embattled people of Grosse Île what the provincial government had in store for them.

Some witless bureaucrat in Quebec City was proposing that the people of Grosse Île should all be moved to Grande Entrée, which would then become a single community requiring one school instead of the two existing schools that served two communities ten miles apart, one in English and one in French.

When Lyndon told us of this plan we were incredulous that anyone with a grain of common sense would consider uprooting an entire village in the name of cutting the cost of education. Apart from the fact that there wasn't enough vacant land in Grande Entrée on which to house the ninety Anglo families from Grosse Île, the result of moving an English-speaking community into the midst of a French one would be utter chaos.

Farley thought this was a cunning plot to absorb the Magdalens' English minority into the French majority. More likely it was because the *fonction-naires* eight hundred miles away in the capital had no idea that the habitable land in Grande Entrée was nearly fully occupied, and it was even possible they didn't know that the people of Grosse Île spoke only English.

We should all be wary of government planners. They tend to be self-absorbed people armed with charts and maps and degrees in business administration. They know a lot about money but not very much about human nature. I believe they should all be required in to live in a small rural community for at least three years before they are given the authority to make decisions affecting the lives of other people.

Lyndon told us he was not looking forward to presenting this proposal to the fractious people of Grosse Île, especially since he knew about Farley's earlier attempts to persuade them of the merits of a marine park at East Point. Plenty of people still believed this was a sinister plot to confis-cate their land.

"They'll figure I'm behind this one too," Farley laughed as he wished Lyndon the best of luck.

The people of Grosse Île were understandably furious when they heard about Quebec's totalitarian scheme to move them. Eventually the whole plan was abandoned, but not before it had added more fuel to the smolder-ing fires of suspicion and anxiety.

A horrible accident occurred in the middle of August. An eighteen-year-old man from Grosse Île was driving his car far too fast through Grande Entrée in the evening. He swerved to avoid hitting what he thought was a pedestrian walking on the paved road, only to hit several others who were walking on the narrow shoulder. He killed three girls aged thirteen and fourteen and seriously injured a fourth. Two of the dead were sisters and the third was their cousin. They were French. The driver was English. No one knew for sure, but most suspected he had been drinking.

The two-lane blacktop road that meandered through the three-mile lin-ear village of Grande Entrée looked unremarkable but was extremely dangerous. Like most rural roads it had evolved over time from a bumpy trail into a gravel road. When, eventually, there was enough government money to pave it, the contractors hadn't bothered to iron out the rises and falls, or to straighten the curves or widen the shoulders. As a result there were several blind spots and treacherous curves. This narrow road was the only stretch of pavement in the east end of the archipelago so it was all too tempting for drivers to ignore the speed limit.

Teenagers roamed the road on summer evenings. Since there were no sidewalks they strolled along, side by side in the dark, heedless of the peril as they chatted and giggled and fell in and out of love. Now three girls were dead, one was disabled, and a host of parents, grandparents, and friends were brokenhearted.

And one young man, over in the English community, was left to live with the consequences of his carelessness for the rest of his life.

Chapter Twenty-two

LATE IN AUGUST WE CLOSED our Magdalen Islands home and headed for Woodstock, New Brunswick, to collect our Cygnet—a compact British trailer with large windows. It was small—about the same length as our Volvo station wagon—yet contained a table and two benches that converted into a double bed, a basic kitchen with a sink, a two-burner stove, and a refrigerator the size of a television set. There was a narrow couch that could also be used as an additional bed, a tiny fold-out desk, a clothes closet, and another little closet with a portable toilet. Everything ran on propane gas—the lights, the stove, the fridge, and a space heater. Independent of the need for electricity, we could camp almost anywhere. This compact little home was a lot easier to tow across the country than the recreational vehicles that were even then beginning to hog the highways in the summer.

In fits and starts we hauled the Cygnet to our home in Port Hope, from where, a few days later, we set off for Winnipeg. We took our time travelling through the wilds of northern Ontario. By early September we had already travelled 1700 miles and had yet to reach Kenora.

During our journey we listened to the car radio and heard the news of the overthrow of the Salvador Allende government in Chile. Was Allende alive or dead? For days no one knew. The radio news told us that a coup d'état had been carried out by the Chilean military under General Pinochet to rid the country of the Marxist government of Allende. However, it was pretty obvious to us that the bloodbath had been instigated by the United States.

"Goddam CIA," Farley muttered every time it was mentioned on the news.

On September 11 we pulled into a provincial campsite just east of Dryden to spend the night. The place was officially closed for the season so there were no attendants, no electricity or running water, and no fees, but in our self-contained little home we were perfectly comfortable.

Travelling with a trailer—or caravan, as Farley insisted on describing it—was a new experience for me. We had begun our life together sailing in Farley's rough-and-ready schooner in Newfoundland coastal waters. Driving on busy highways pulling our household behind us was not quite the same thing. However, for Farley it held echoes of his boyhood.

In 1933, in the depths of the Great Depression, Angus Mowat had been hired to take charge of the Saskatoon library. He decided to drive there with his wife and son from Windsor, Ontario, in the family's Model A Ford, hauling a caravan he would build himself. Constructed on a four-wheel truck chassis, this turned out to be a huge green box fitted out like the cabin of a ship. Under ideal conditions it could be towed at thirty miles per hour, but conditions were seldom ideal.

There was no Canadian road linking Ontario and western Canada at the time so the Mowats had to travel south through the United States. During their slow and dusty rambles they encountered genuine pioneers and witnessed some terrible poverty. They also met with a lot of curiosity about the bizarre caravan they were towing.

Forty years later no one was particularly interested in what *we* were doing. Cars towing campers and trailers were everywhere and for those impatient drivers who couldn't wait to get past us we were a nuisance, plain and simple.

That night I fried a couple of pork chops on our propane stove, tossed a salad, and warmed up a can of peas for supper while Farley took the dogs for a walk around the campsite. He stopped to chat with the driver of a Volvo similar to ours. She was a young American who, unencumbered by a trailer or even camping gear, slept in a sleeping bag in the reclining front seat of her car. She bought her meals in local restaurants. Farley invited her to join us for a drink.

She told us she lived in the suburbs of New York and was studying architecture at a university in Olympia, Washington. She loved to travel. The previous year she had driven across the United States and back, not once but *twice*. This year she had decided to see Canada. This wasn't the only time we would encounter one of these wandering Americans determined to see the world. At times it seemed as if all America was on the road.

Farley asked her what she thought of the overthrow of Allende. She didn't reply right away and after a thoughtful pause said that she had heard Perón was going to take over. Perón? She was talking about Argentina. It turned out she knew nothing about what was happening in Chile. Farley remarked that Allende was the first Marxist ever to be elected as a head of state in South America. It didn't register. Apparently she didn't listen to news broadcasts or read newspapers.

We mentioned that we had three provincial social-democrat governments in Canada but that didn't sink in either. Whatever impressions she would get of Canada on her long, long drive would be limited to vignettes of campsites, take-out food, forests, prairies, mountains, and the endless highway.

We woke next morning to a cool but bright and sunny sky. Farley ignited our little propane space heater and in a matter of minutes our miniature home was warm.

We packed up and headed west and by lunchtime we had driven, on a nearly empty highway, past the pulp-and-paper town of Dryden, with its tall chimneys belching God-knows-what kind of pollutants into the air. We continued on past Kenora and the Lake of the Woods to cross the boundary between Ontario and Manitoba.

Nearby Whiteshell Provincial Park seemed an ideal place to stop for lunch. It turned out we were the only occupants. There are not a lot of people in the rural regions of the Prairie provinces. Those who do live there are mostly busy farmers with something more pressing to do than visit a park in the middle of the week. Fresh from the embattled Magdalens, we relished this uncrowded land.

I realized how deceptive maps can be. On a map the Magdalens—adrift in the middle of the Gulf of St. Lawrence—looked to be nearly abandoned, yet were full of people arguing over property lines. On the other hand, our map of southern Manitoba, with a complex spider web of secondary roads, gave the false impression of being densely populated.

Further west the bush country of Whiteshell Park elided into the flat, lush prairie under that enormous western sky. We drove past the town of Beausejour, where Ed Schreyer had grown up on a farm. Nearby we stopped at a gas station. All the other vehicles in sight bore licence plates that said "Friendly Manitoba." There was a vegetable stand across the road so I walked over and bought some tomatoes and cucumbers. I tried to chat with the old couple who were selling their farm produce but they spoke almost no English. I tried French, since I knew there were pockets of French-speaking people in Manitoba, but they didn't understand me. I guessed they were Polish or Ukrainian—languages of which I knew not a word.

As we drove away Farley remarked that the service station attendant had indeed been friendly, just as the licence plates proclaimed, and not like some of his indifferent counterparts we had encountered in gas stations in parts of Ontario. But Farley has a bias against Ontario, his birthplace and home to at least six generations of his ancestors. As a boy he fell in love with the prairies. Later in life he became infatuated with the Atlantic provinces. Ontario always seemed to disappoint him.

Following Highway 44, we drove through Winnipeg, a remarkably well-planned city. We had directions to the Schreyers' house on Henderson Highway on the northern edge of the city, and we found it easily. Their modest ranch-style house was on a four-acre wooded lot that felt almost rural. There was plenty of room for us to park our caravan beside a grove of oak trees.

Anyone wanting to learn about a hitherto-unknown province of Canada could hardly do better than to get acquainted with its premier. They travel to every corner of their domain in order to get elected. They know the best places and the places to avoid. They know who the interesting people are. Ed Schreyer had a passion for local history and we were looking forward to Manitoba rambles under his tutelage.

Ed was at work in the legislature that afternoon, but Lily was at home awaiting our arrival. Farley unhitched the trailer from the car and made sure it was level and secure, and then we invited Lily into our travelling home for a cup of tea. Soon after that their children arrived home from school: eleven-year-old Lisa, nine-year-old Karmel, and Jason, who was six. They were bright, friendly kids and were naturally curious about the new people whose household had just been deposited in their yard. They came to the door to view the interior of our dollhouse-sized home.

That evening Lily invited us over to their house for one of her extraordinary dinners. She called the main dish Bessarabian borscht in a tribute to her origins. Lily had been born and raised on a farm near Grandview in western Manitoba, but her parents had immigrated to Canada from Bessarabia, which was swallowed up by the Soviet Republic of Moldavia (now called Moldova). I had never heard of Bessarabia until I became friends with Lily. It stands as a reminder to me that all the nations of the world are forever in a state of flux. Small countries are often eclipsed by bigger ones and disappear for generations or forever.

We had planned to stay with the Schreyers only two or three days, time enough to pore over the map of Manitoba with Ed and find out about interesting places to visit. However, a week later we were still camped in their backyard, enjoying their unstinting western hospitality. Almost every evening there were guests for dinner at their house, usually people from other parts of Manitoba who were involved with the government and who savoured Lily's marvellous meals. It surprised us to find the premier of a province so accessible.

Part of my enjoyment stemmed from not being at the centre of the household. Instead of coping with all the details that surrounded me in my own home, here I was a mere spectator. I helped Lily whenever I could but I wasn't in charge. I didn't have to make decisions about everything from dentist appointments to dinner parties.

On the weekend Ed drove us to the family farm to meet his parents. They were retired by then but still living in the comfortable home where they had raised one daughter and five sons. They were friendly but undemonstrative people. I wondered if they were bursting with pride that their youngest son had become the premier of Manitoba. Or, conversely, did they, and Ed's siblings, resent his success? I don't believe they did. They were a political family and Ed's progress in public life from Member of the Manitoba Legislature when he was only twenty-two, followed by his years as a Member of Parliament in Ottawa, and then finally Premier of Manitoba was most likely what they had expected of him.

Like many other retired farmers, the elder Schreyers were renting their land to a neighbour, who was growing wheat and flax and pasturing cattle on it. This neighbour, Clarence Baker, was farming the equivalent of six family farms. The prototypical hundred-acre family farm had already become a thing of the past.

Ed had enjoyed his boyhood on the farm but had never wanted to be a farmer. "You have to have an ear for it," he remarked, as if he were describing a career in music and, indeed, farmers and artists have a lot in common. They do work they love but very few become wealthy doing it.

There was always something going on in the Schreyer family. One day we attended an NDP pancake breakfast in Heidelberg Park, north of Winnipeg. Another day a neighbour who owned a motor launch took us all for a cruise on the Red River. It was tempting to hang around and be part of the premier's busy life but we finally broke away and headed west to explore Manitoba on our own. We had a lot more to see before it became too cold for our gypsy existence.

The uncrowded Trans-Canada Highway led us to Neepawa, the hometown of novelist Margaret Laurence. The first thing I did was to buy a postcard at a gas station and mail it to her. A cherished friend, she was then living in Lakefield, Ontario. We drove around this drab-looking little town, which hardly looked like the passionate place Margaret described in her novels. Yet every community has love, hate, envy, generosity, kindness, sex, betrayal, and death within it. It only takes a gifted author to bring it out.

We headed north to Riding Mountain National Park—called Galloping Mountain in Margaret Laurence's books. It was not a mountain in the sense that the Rockies are; it is a plateau that is elevated only a few hundred feet from the land below it. Tens of thousands of years earlier it had been an island in an ancient inland sea called Lake Agassiz, which covered most of what is now southern and central Manitoba. From this high ground we overlooked a vast sweep of prairie stretching to the horizon. I realized why the first European explorers had called the prairie an ocean of grass, for it seemed to have no limits.

We continued north until we reached a pretty campsite beside Moon Lake. Unlike northern Ontario, the Manitoba campsites were staffed throughout September. As we paid the park attendant a fifty-cent fee, he said he had seen Farley on television the day before talking about whales.

There was only one other vehicle in the campsite that evening, an old school bus that had been converted into a motor home. As he was always curious to meet other travellers, Farley went over for a chat while I pre-

Claire in Manitoba, 1973

pared supper. The occupants, a young couple named Derek and Patsy, had lived in this vehicle in the Yukon all the previous winter, together with three dogs and a cat. Then they had added a son— now four months old— to the entourage. Derek was a forester by profession and was looking for work in Manitoba or northern Ontario.

Later that evening we joined them around their campfire. The baby dozed in his carry cot. Their dogs were tied to a tree and ours remained in our car because we could hear elk bugling to one another and none of us wanted our dogs heading into the bush to investigate.

Sitting by the fire I could imagine how indigenous people had thrived here for centuries before settlers came along. The resonant cries of the bull elk and the crackling fire were the background as we talked of the travels that had brought us together from opposite directions. Our companions were younger than we were, in their mid-twenties and unafraid to take on the world. I admired their simple household and their optimism.

Next day, on a gorgeous fall morning, the lake was full of gabbling ducks. Canada jays were tame enough to eat biscuits out of our dogs' dishes. I could have stayed on at Moon Lake happily for a long time but we had to move on.

Highway 10 took us north to the town with the aristocratic French name of Dauphin. I thought it odd that this town, which was famous for its lively festival of Ukrainian music and dance, should bear the title of the eldest son of the King of France. Much later I learned that the name was in place long before the Ukrainian settlers arrived. The explorer Pierre La Vérendrye had established a trading post here in the 1770s and, being the patriot that he was, had named the post for the king's son. The name stuck, though no one from France had stayed there very long.

We drove on north to Duck Mountain, which, again, was not a mountain but a plateau. It was also a beautiful provincial park but it was crawling with hunters—grim-faced, macho guys wearing fluorescent caps and jackets. The season for elk hunting had begun. The presence of these "sportsmen" sent us back out to the highway with Farley muttering there should be some way the elk could turn the tables on their killers.

I realize that human beings could never have survived in northern latitudes had it not been for their ability to slay animals for food and for clothing. But I am still mystified by the motivation of modern people who can readily obtain meat from domestic animals but still want to kill some unlucky moose, elk, or deer.

In Saskatchewan, on the western side of Duck Mountain there is also a provincial campground and this is where we ended up spending the night. Again, a park attendant recognized Farley and he advised us in a friendly manner not to go roaming about because we or our dogs might easily get shot. We would have preferred a safer campsite but were told this was the only one open this late in the season—kept open for the benefit of hunters. We were the only non-hunters there that evening.

Located beside a small lake, it was a pretty place and had the added benefit of clean public washrooms and running water. While Farley got the trailer in place, I took the dogs for a walk along the shore of the shallow lake. Walking back in the dusk the dogs darted off ahead of me. I found them sniffing energetically at the foot of a tall tree. Then I saw a huge cloven hoof dangling right in front of my face. I looked up to see the leg and then the body of an enormous, dead elk. It was chained to a scaffold high up in the tree from which it hung like a monstrous puppet. It had been disemboweled and the dogs were searching for bits of entrails. I hustled them out of there and back to the caravan.

The hunters all returned after dark. I only spoke to one of them: a pleasant, grey-haired man who was getting a pail of water at the same time I was. He asked me if I wasn't afraid of being shot. He went on to say that a bear had been shot the day before only a hundred yards from where we were. I took my pail back to our trailer and vowed neither Farley nor I nor the dogs would stick our heads outdoors that night.

The next morning cold rain drummed on the metal roof. The only other sound was that of the trucks belonging to the hunters driving off. We had had enough of them. We washed and dressed, bolted down some breakfast, and left as soon as we could.

On a dull, overcast day we made our longest single journey: all the way from the Saskatchewan-Manitoba border to the Interlake region of Manitoba. On the way we passed through Ste. Rose du Lac, the region about which Gabrielle Roy wrote her first book, *Where Nests the Water Hen*. Roy was born and raised in St. Boniface, a French-Canadian community adjacent to Winnipeg. However, she had come to the Ste. Rose community as a schoolteacher and so had no first-hand experience with French-speaking Prairie settlers. I would have enjoyed exploring this area but it was still raining and Farley was eager to reach our destination and get settled for the night.

The land lying between Lake Manitoba and Lake Winnipeg is as flat as the prairie but not as lush. Here and there we saw stands of bush and stunted trees. Scraggy cattle appeared to be the only crop in this somewhat impoverished landscape.

Our destination was the western shore of Lake Winnipeg, a region of Manitoba settled by Icelanders in the late-nineteenth century. Bringing Icelanders to Manitoba had been the brainchild of Lord Dufferin, then Governor General of Canada. At the time, Iceland was plagued by volcanic eruptions that left hundreds of families homeless. The newly created Province of Manitoba needed settlers, and Lord Dufferin presumed Icelandic farmers were accustomed to cold winters and so would do well in central Manitoba. What he didn't know is that Iceland is not particularly cold in winter, when the temperature usually hovers just above and just below the freezing mark. The first Icelandic immigrants nearly perished in the intensely cold Manitoba winters. Since the land was poor many of them turned to fishing rather than to farming and to this day the majority of commercial fishermen on Lake Winnipeg are of Icelandic descent.

The towns in the region were Arborg, Hnausa, Arnes, and Gimli. There was even one called Reykjavik after the capital of Iceland. We had long wanted to visit that city in Iceland but, alas, when we reached the Canadian Reykjavik it was to find virtually nothing—no post office, store, church, school, or gas station. There were only a few scattered, and mostly abandoned, farms. No people were anywhere to be seen.

Farley, always eager to talk to some local person, knocked on the door of a small farmhouse. A shy young woman with curlers in her hair came to the door and asked if we were lost. No, Farley replied, we were just looking around and could she tell us about the place? She shook her head rather sadly and said she had only recently come here as the bride of a local man and knew nothing about the region except that it was "awful lonely." I could feel the loneliness myself and felt sorry for her.

Driving on, we eventually came to a gas station and a convenience store. The fair-haired man who filled our tank spoke with an accent that I took to be Icelandic.

I bought a few groceries and when I paid for them the young sales girl tried to give me change in American currency. I asked for Canadian money, which, after a search of the cash drawer, she finally found. It was duck-hunting season in that part of Manitoba and apparently the only outsiders who shopped there were American hunters.

At nightfall we reached Hnausa, a small fishing port on Lake Winnipeg with a public campground beside a sandy beach. Large bodies of water are not usually associated in the public mind with the Prairie provinces but it is those vast interior lakes, especially Lake Winnipeg, that make Manitoba unique. The rain finally stopped and from our campsite that night we could imagine ourselves on the shore of an ocean while we watched the distant horizon lighten as the storm gradually moved away to the east.

There was one other trailer on the site but no sign of any occupants. Farley positioned our caravan and then set up the barbeque and grilled a steak for our supper. The dogs ran and splashed in the surf. That night we were lulled to sleep by the sound of waves pounding on the beach.

Next day we left our wheeled home at the campsite and went for a drive through Hecla Provincial Park, which is located on a series of peninsulas and islands jutting out into Lake Winnipeg. The park was in the process of being developed. People who had homes there could stay as long as they wanted but when it came time to sell, they could only sell to the province. It was a more humane process than the bullying tactics that had recently been used in the assembly of land for national parks in eastern Quebec and in New Brunswick.

The town of Hecla, we learned, had once been home to more than five hundred people; but there were now many unoccupied houses. There was, however, a fully occupied cemetery surrounding a small Lutheran Church. Two men were working at a grave there and Farley went over to talk to them while I, who love exploring cemeteries, wandered among the headstones. All the early ones were inscribed in Icelandic: Olafson, Benjamsdottir, Sigurdson, Thomason, Jonnson, Stefanson, Stefansdottir—many of them people who had died generations earlier and who had been born in Iceland. The first women buried here were still using the traditional Icelandic system of taking their father's first name, with *dottir* added to it as their surname for life, whether they married or not.

The two men working there that morning turned out to be the owners of the other trailer at the Hnausa campground. They were professional grave restorers. Both were Manitobans, one of Cree ancestry and the other of Scots. They made a living by searching out old cemeteries with crumbling gravestones; then they contacted the families who had relatives buried there. For a modest fee they would repair broken headstones. Usually this involved pouring a concrete base and implanting what was left of the original marker in it. They would inscribe the name of the dead person and the dates of birth and death in the concrete.

What they produced was not exactly a work of art but it was, as they pointed out, far less expensive than buying a new granite headstone, and it ensured that the dead would not be forgotten at least for a while longer. Business was good, they said. They had all the work they could handle. One of them had recently prospected the situation in Newfoundland and told us there was ten times as much work there as he and his partner could ever take on. Yes, I thought, Newfoundland was awash in cemeteries where old stone or wooden markers were fast disappearing.

We were full of admiration for the initiative of these two men. They were making a living in dwindling communities like this one, but if work ran out here they were prepared to move to Newfoundland—a province that, at the time, did not attract many people looking for work.

Later that day we hitched up our caravan and headed south. We stopped at the town of Arnes to see the park and the monument commemorating the life of Vilhjalmur Stefansson, Canada's foremost Arctic explorer, who had been born there in 1879. He eventually moved to the United States, and the Americans now claim him as one of theirs but it was here in this small village that he was born to parents who had recently emigrated from Iceland.

Further south on Highway 9 we drove through the busy, prosperous-looking town of Gimli (whose name translates as *Paradise* in Icelandic). The town had something of the look of a summer resort, which was not surprising since it was located on the lakeshore a little over an hour's drive north of Winnipeg. We were now in cottage country, where city people had been vacationing for generations. We drove past a lot of old-fashioned cottages, with names like Lotsa Rest, Dunrovin, and Dew Drop Inn. The region reminded me of Lake Simcoe, a similar distance north of Toronto, which had provided a summer respite for Torontonians ever since there was a Toronto. Winnipeggers were similarly blessed.

Chapter Twenty-three

OUR MUD-SPATTERED CARAVAN was once again parked in a familiar corner of the Schreyers' yard. The following day Farley joined the premier and a couple of his staff, who were flying five hundred miles north to visit South Indian Lake. The land surrounding that lake was home to a small population of Cree and some of their hunting grounds were due to be flooded by a hydro-electric dam.

There had already been protests about this dam in Winnipeg by environmental groups concerned about the fate of the native people, as well as the wildlife. Farley now found himself in a real dilemma because preserving natural habitats had long been a priority for him. On the other hand, he was concerned about the effects on the world's environment of our enormous use of fossil fuels for energy. He felt that more water-generated power would help reduce that problem. Ed Schreyer believed the dam was necessary to ensure the economic independence of the province. Like it or not, Farley was faced with making a political compromise.

It rained most of the time he was away, which kept me inside our damp little home. It was a time to catch up on paperwork, to answer our mail, and to make notes about our recent travels. I had, by then, taken over the job of journal-keeping. Farley was too busy to do it and I found that I enjoyed it. My Smith-Corona portable typewriter clickety-clacked all morning as the rain drummed noisily and wet autumn leaves plastered our aluminum roof.

Lily invited me over to the house for lunch. I always enjoyed her company. The two of us had a bond insofar as our lives were closely linked to our husbands' careers. Another thing Lily shared with me was the pressure she often felt from some feminists, who regarded her life as a cop-out from the real world.

Lily had two unfulfilled ambitions. She hoped to have one more child. She also wanted to pursue her love of drawing and painting. In high school she had daydreamed of becoming a commercial artist—which was something I had actually done.

What surprised me about Lily's day-to-day life was that she had more time to herself than I did. Once Ed had departed for the legislature each morning and the kids had boarded the bus for school, she had the day pretty well to herself until they all returned. I envied her relatively quiet weekdays. Ed, as a provincial premier, and before that as a federal member of parliament, had a staff to cope with the administrative details of his life. Farley, at that point in his life, had only me.

Our husbands returned from the north convinced that the proposed flooding around South Indian Lake would be minimal and not nearly as damaging to the lifestyle of the Cree as the protestors claimed. They were also full of talk about building supplies. Ed didn't believe it made sense to transport building materials into the north, at considerable cost, from southern Manitoba when there was an abundance of timber in the north. He believed sawmills should be set up on building sites. His advisors insisted it wouldn't work. Capital and operating costs would be prohibitive, they claimed.

Farley believed Ed was right and so he volunteered to spend some time researching the possibilities for establishing small, cooperative sawmills in native communities. People could then mill their own lumber at little cost other than their labour. We didn't know it at the time but this was the beginning of Farley's one venture into the labyrinth of government bureaucracy.

Early in October we set off to continue our exploration of Manitoba—this time to the southwest. Following Highway 3, we made our first stop in the town of Carman. This region had been settled by people from Ontario about a hundred years earlier. I found it a novelty that Ontarians constituted an ethnic minority amid the patchwork quilt of all the other nationalities who had settled Manitoba: French, Scots, Germans, Ukrainians, Mennonites, Icelanders—to name a few. In Ontario I knew people whose families had lived there for generations but insisted on identifying themselves as Irish, Scottish, or United Empire Loyalists.

The small town of Carman actually felt like an Ontario town of the same size. Only the broad main street advertised that we were in the west.

The houses and shops reminded me of Port Hope. Even the trees appeared to have come from Ontario: tall oaks and maples.

On the way out of town Farley asked an elderly fellow for directions to Highway 245. The man said he didn't know the roads by numbers but would point us in the right direction. He asked us if we were "just passing through" the province. We said no, we were exploring Manitoba. He looked surprised, as if he had never heard of anyone doing such a thing. Manitobans are accustomed to travellers hurrying through en route from one side of Canada to the other. They are also familiar with strangers, mostly from the United States, who come to hunt and fish; but wanderers like us, especially in the fall of the year, were rare birds indeed.

As we drove further south and west the land looked more and more like southern Ontario: small, gently contoured hills and ploughed fields. Our destination was a campsite at Rock Lake, which we had noted on the map not far from the town of Pilot Mound. The campground was on a spectacular promontory overlooking a long, narrow, silver-rippled lake. The leaves on the surrounding trees had turned incandescent orange and yellow. On a warm, hazy evening we were the only occupants of this perfect place. Hordes of honking Canada geese out on the lake serenaded us as we settled in for the night. At dusk their music was replaced by the distant howls of coyotes. If there were any hunters in the vicinity we didn't see or hear them.

The Rock Lake campsite turned out to be so idyllic that we stayed for three days. It was the sort of place where I could imagine putting down roots. Farley unhitched the trailer from our car and we drove all around the district. This charming corner of the province was full of winding rivers, pastoral valleys, deep lakes, and prosperous-looking farms. A mere hundred and fifty miles from Winnipeg, it appeared to be undiscovered by other Manitobans.

We stopped in the town of Killarney, a few miles west of Rock Lake, to buy groceries and mail some letters. We liked this region so much that we also visited a local real estate office to inquire if there was any land for sale on the shores of Rock Lake. The cordial salesman didn't think there was. "Mostly it's good farm land," he explained apologetically. "Farmers don't like to give it up to cottagers and the like." He did say there were several building lots on Pelican Lake, a few miles further south. Farley perked up at the mention of the name. He knew that white pelicans bred on an island in Pelican Lake and they were something of a rarity in the world of birds. However, the land for sale there turned out to be a development of thirty cottage sites side-by-side, which didn't appeal to us. The salesman said he would inquire if any of the farmers whose land extended to the shore of Rock Lake would be willing to sell a few acres, but we never did hear from him again.

Back at the campsite someone had discovered our presence. A teenaged girl and her younger brother knocked on our door and asked Farley to autograph her copy of *Never Cry Wolf*. The word was out that Farley Mowat was in the vicinity. They were charming, shy kids and we invited them into our caravan for a visit. Their last name was Avery and their parents ran a small resort that we had noticed further up the road. We soon got acquainted with the Avery clan: Bill and his family, who operated a nearby farm, and Bob and his wife, who ran the resort.

They told us that their grandfather had moved to Manitoba in 1900 from Port Perry, Ontario. He farmed for a few years but in 1912 decided to set up a duck-hunting lodge, mainly for Americans from nearby North Dakota. The lodge changed over time. By the 1930s cars and better roads were bringing summer visitors, not just hunters, from the parched Dakotas, and they had kept this comfortable old resort in business ever since, through three generations of the same family.

It was a family kind of place, a rambling wooden building to which several additions had been made over the years, along with a number of outlying cabins, all with a view of serene Rock Lake. Avery's Resort offered boat rentals, fishing, hunting, trailer sites, bird watching, and "modern and semi-modern" accommodation. We wondered what they meant by "semi-modern" but never did find out.

The Averys had a large collection of flint arrowheads and stone tools, collected over many years. They told us their land had once been the home of "mound dwellers," indigenous people who constructed huge mounds wherever they lived. There was one such mysterious mound on the Avery property, an artificial hill about twenty feet high and a hundred feet in diameter. No one had dug into it, whether out of respect for the spirits of the departed Mound People or from unacknowledged dread of what might result.

We were sorry to leave Rock Lake. If we hadn't been invited to join the NDP caucus for a three-day cruise on Lake Winnipeg we would have stayed several more days, content to watch the endless flocks of migrating ducks and geese and hoping to catch sight of a whistling swan as we day-dreamed of building a house overlooking this tranquil scene.

On Saturday morning of the Thanksgiving weekend we boarded the passenger ship *Lord Selkirk* for her final voyage of the season. She was roughly the same size as the coastal boats that serviced the south coast of Newfoundland but had a few more frills—notably a large dining room, a well-stocked bar, and a small dance floor. She set sail from a wharf near the mouth of the Red River and for the first hour or so we were in very shallow water—a vast marshy bay where wild rice grew. A carefully buoyed channel eventually led us to deeper water and the open lake.

After twenty-four hours "at sea" our ship docked at the village of Berens River on the east coast. Originally a Hudson's Bay Company trading post, it was now home to a few hundred people, chiefly Cree and Métis and some "whites" who had moved here from "the south." This was Canadian Shield country, primordial rock overlaid with boreal forest of pine and spruce—a land unfit for any kind of agriculture. Until recently the lake had yielded a prosperous fishery, but the discovery of high mercury levels in the fish had led to a ban on all commercial fishing for two years. The source had been traced to a pulp-and-paper mill in northwestern Ontario, hundreds of miles distant from Lake Winnipeg.

As unwelcome as it was, the mercury poisoning had some benefits. Lake Winnipeg had been overfished for years, and the two-year moratorium was allowing the stocks of many species to make a spectacular recovery.

Everyone went ashore at Berens River, although there wasn't much to see. A cluster of local children and dogs took a keen interest in looking at us. There was no road into or out of this community. Boats brought the few visitors and the year's supplies during the brief season of navigation. Otherwise, a small airstrip was the only connection to the wider world.

There was *one* tourist attraction: a dilapidated wooden hotel, the home of Ma Kemp, who was then ninety-one years old and living in a nursing home in Winnipeg. She had been a celebrated pioneer in this part of Manitoba and now her son was making a meagre living charging visitors a dollar to look around at what had once been her cheery home and hotel. There were hand-hooked rugs on the floor, crocheted doilies on the chairs, and old sepia photographs on the walls. The Kemp family had been the first white family to settle in this remote place.

"At sea" once again, we found ourselves seated at the captain's table at dinner, along with the premier and his wife. Captain Allan was a jovial, sixty-four-year-old Scotsman who had spent most of his career on northern oceans, sailing to such places as Murmansk during the Second World War and, more recently, commanding Canadian Coast Guard vessels in the Arctic. He said he liked his present job because it had a lively social side, a change from lonely years aboard an icebreaker.

By the time the cruise was over there was frost in the air. Winter was coming and we had not yet found a new home in Manitoba. Hoping to continue the search the following year, we parked our caravan for the winter in a trucking garage owned by a friend of Ed's. Then we drove back to Ontario in our car.

I was more than ready for a period of stability. We owned a perfectly nice house in a pleasant town but Farley didn't feel he belonged there, nor anywhere else, so we had been on the move since the previous spring. I longed to stay in one place for a while.

On our return trip we listened to news reports that a worldwide shortage of oil appeared to be looming. There were accounts of long lineups at gas stations in the United States and, according to all the experts, the same fate would soon afflict Canadians. There was talk of gas rationing of the kind we had had thirty years earlier during the Second World War.

I began to picture empty highways. There might be no more journeys of the kind we had just made. "I want to get the hell out of it," Farley declared when, two and a half days later, we found ourselves in the traffic frenzy of Ontario's Highway 401.

"But where *can* we go?" I asked wearily.

"Anywhere except here!" he proclaimed stubbornly.

Anywhere isn't a destination. I sighed and said no more.

Chapter Twenty-four

WE ARRIVED BACK IN PORT HOPE at the end of October. For months we had been out of the three-ring circus that swirled around Farley whenever he stood still long enough. After a week of dinner parties, overnight guests, and ringing phones, I felt utterly weary and longed to drive right back to Manitoba.

Farley's mother needed to consult us about her ongoing difficulties with house repairs. Her seventy-five-year-old sister, Frances, was retiring from a job in Toronto and planned on moving in with Helen—a prospect fraught with rue because the two sisters were as different as night and day and had never been able to tolerate one another's company for more than a few days. My mother phoned from Toronto, glad that I was back in Ontario. She gave me the unhappy news that my brother had separated from his second wife.

One of our house guests was Alan Cooke, a friend and colleague who was an archivist at Laval University. His area of scholastic expertise lay in the history of arctic exploration and he had been a great help during the years Farley had been researching and writing *Ordeal by Ice*, *The Polar Passion*, and *Tundra*. During Alan's visit the conversation was not entirely about nineteenth-century polar explorers. Alan, the father of a nine-year-old son, had recently separated from *his* wife. As well, he had come out of the closet and acknowledged his homosexuality—an anguishing event that he wanted to share with us.

A few days later we had a brief visit from another friend, John de Visser, whose haunting photographs had captured outport life in *This Rock Within the Sea*, a book that Farley had written. John's marriage, too, was coming unstuck, though not for the same reason as Alan's. John had fallen in love with another woman and wasn't sure just where his life was going.

It always unsettled me to learn of the failed marriages of friends and relatives. They would be enduring pain and upheaval, but I would be losing something too. When couples split, one of them usually disappeared from my life; it is rare for anyone to remain friends with both parties after a divorce. Perhaps I was anxious that our own marriage might fall apart somewhere down the road. I was certainly worried about losing friends, my substitute kinfolk who, it seemed to me, had a way of disappearing.

Farley's ex-wife, Fran, phoned him one evening in a state of agitation because she had found a joint of marijuana in the pocket of David's shirt. She told Farley that she believed David's entire personality had changed as a result of smoking marijuana.

That autumn, every time we turned around it was to find some minor or major disaster in the lives of our family and friends. I was glad they felt they could confide in us, that they regarded us as sympathetic people. But it was sometimes overwhelming.

In November we travelled to Ottawa to attend the first meeting of The Writers' Union of Canada. Farley was one of the founders and although I was not yet a member I went along, pleased to have a weekend respite. In a hotel I could always withdraw to our room if I was tired—something I found much more difficult to do at home.

All of us were booked into the Lord Nelson Hotel in downtown Ottawa, a far-from-glamorous place but its modest rates and out-of-date décor suited our purpose—to establish a union—although obviously a union of book writers was not going to be of the same sort as that which served teachers or autoworkers. Canadian writers would not, for example, be going on strike. However, they were extremely vulnerable to certain aspects of publishing, such as unfair contracts, dishonest accounting, low royalties, and other cutthroat business practices. It was also felt that there should be more government interests in, and support for, writers who were, after all, as much primary producers as farmers or fishermen. These, and other matters, resulted in the founding of our union, which, though small at first (initially it had less than a hundred members) gave us a feeling of solidarity and allowed us to work together to figure out ways to survive in what was, and still is, a very precarious profession.

A few la-di-da members had snobbishly advocated that membership be restricted to novelists; but they were outvoted by the majority, who realized that strength lay in numbers. Writers of cookbooks, travel guides, memoirs, children's books, poetry, and how-to books were all to be encouraged to join.

Harold Horwood, fellow author and longtime friend, had travelled to the meeting from his home in Newfoundland. A fifty-year-old bachelor, he surprised us all by announcing his impending marriage. For me this was positive news after hearing about so many break-ups and divorces.

That weekend we became acquainted with Edna Staebler, who lived near Waterloo, Ontario, and who, in addition to a career as a journalist, had written a charming memoir of life in a village in Cape Breton Island, as well as a couple of cookbooks. We also met Silver Donald Cameron, an author and former professor, who was living in a small village in Cape Breton, having turned his back on a university career. Marian Engel, a promising new novelist from Toronto, joined us for drinks, along with Peggy Atwood and Graeme Gibson. Everyone wanted to talk to Margaret Laurence, den mother to a lot of people in the writing community. I marvelled at how she found time to listen to the many writers who wanted to share their sorrows and ambitions with her. Almost all of us hoped Margaret would become the first chairman of the Union but she wisely declined to take on more than she could handle.

While Union members were earnestly drawing up a constitution I spent most of a day browsing in the National Gallery of Canada. It was then housed in a charmless glass-and-steel office building, but the art inside was well worth viewing. I dallied in front of paintings by Alex Colville, Emily Carr, and the Group of Seven—treasures I had only previously seen reproduced in books.

By evening Marian Engel had been elected first chairman of the Union, along with two vice-presidents: Rudy Wiebe, from Alberta, representing western Canada and our pal Harold Horwood, representing eastern Canada.

All of us were taken by chartered bus to Aylmer, Quebec, to a club unimaginatively named the Country Club, there to be wined and dined. We were treated to a classic Canadian banquet: smoked salmon from Newfoundland, clam chowder from the Maritimes, beet borscht from the Prairies, scallops from British Columbia, a tourtière pork pie from Quebec, a green salad from Ontario, and maple mousse for dessert. At the time there were many who doubted that Canada had a cuisine. I never doubted it after savouring such a feast.

The Canada Council paid for our dinner, our hotel accommodations, and our transportation to Ottawa from wherever we lived. Members of the federal government at the time (Pierre Trudeau's Liberals) wanted to be seen as patrons and supporters of the arts. They made it possible for us to make history by bringing a group of professional Canadian authors together for the first time.

On Sunday, with the meetings and festivities behind us, Farley and I took a taxi to the Ottawa railway station to board our train for home. Fellow passengers included Alice Munro and Audrey Thomas, two fiction writers who were heading to Toronto for a few days. Although I was not familiar with Audrey's work then, I had read Alice's superb collection of short stories *Dance of the Happy Shades*, which won the Governor General's Award for Fiction in 1968. Alice grew up in the Ontario town of Wingham and I grew up at the same time in the Toronto suburb of East York, yet I sensed that we had to some degree lived parallel childhoods. It was an inspiration to talk to such a brilliant yet thoroughly unpretentious writer.

Alice had separated from her husband, Jim Munro (who owned a bookstore in Victoria), about a year earlier and had moved to London, Ontario. She said she couldn't think of anywhere else to go and wasn't sure if she was going to stay. Her youngest daughter had come with her, while the other two remained in Victoria. She was, as we were, searching for a suitable place in which to live her life. She had a position teaching creative writing at the University of Western Ontario, although she didn't like it very much. It took a great deal of time to read everything her students had written and then comment on it, leaving little time for her own writing.

Audrey Thomas was also separated or divorced from her husband and was, like Alice, the mother of three young daughters. Her life, on British Columbia's Galiano Island, sounded more settled and peaceful than the lives the rest of us were living. Audrey's problem was a lack of money. At that point she had published four novels, none of which had sold in sufficient quantities to provide her with an adequate income. Alice, with a teaching job, was at least able to make ends meet.

Farley and I got off the train at Cobourg, the nearest stop to Port Hope. As we trudged up the aisle to the exit I noticed a fellow sitting two seats ahead of us who was reading from a copy of *The Boat Who Wouldn't Float*. I wondered if he knew that the author had been sitting close behind him.

Next morning Farley left Port Hope for Toronto and the usual enervating round of radio talk shows, television shows, and interviews with newspaper reporters. We were in the season leading up to Christmas, which was, and still is, the prime time to promote and sell books. *Tundra*, Farley's newest book, had been published in the spring of that year but he hadn't had time to do any promotion until November.

After the promotion tour, Jack McClelland wanted to get together with Farley to discuss future writing plans. Jack and Farley were more than publisher and author; they were buddies, guys who liked to sit around for hours, drinking and smoking far too much, as they bounced book ideas back and forth. They often did this at Jack's cottage in Muskoka, at any season. It had been at the Foote's Bay cottage, back in 1962, that the two of them had come up with the concept for one of Farley's most popular books, *Never Cry Wolf*.

Jack McClelland had a close personal relationship with many of his authors, the kind of bond that is rare in the world of book publishing now. Jack often wrote long, thoughtful letters to his authors. He travelled extensively to keep in touch with writers such as Thomas B. Raddall in Nova Scotia, Gabrielle Roy in rural eastern Quebec, Mordecai Richler in Montreal, Earle Birney in British Columbia, and Margaret Laurence wherever she happened to be living. Because of this rapport most of his authors were singularly loyal to him and to the company. Once they became part of the team very few of them jumped ship, despite the ongoing financial difficulties the firm faced.

When Farley returned to Port Hope a week later he looked wretched and he felt sick. A boozy weekend with Jack following a hard-hitting week in the city had just about finished him off. The intensity with which he hurled himself into public appearances had drained him totally. He stayed in bed, grumpily, for several days, and when he finally saw our doctor he was told he had pneumonia.

A young Toronto journalist had been assigned to interview him for the February issue of *En Route*, the magazine Air Canada places in the pocket in front of each seat. Her name was Joanne Kates and when she learned that Farley was ill she said she would be glad to interview him at his home. Furthermore, she brought along a container of her homemade chicken soup, which she said was sure to help him recover. She has since gone on to become Toronto's most celebrated restaurant reviewer. Food and the written word were obviously her métier.

Her interview with Farley occurred on the same day as the marriage, in England, of Princess Anne and Captain Mark Phillips, and I had risen very early to watch their London wedding—live—on television. Farley was not the least bit interested but I love pageantry and history, which is why, in part, I take an interest in the British royal family. The royals have another attraction for me. They offer more continuity and class than do the usual icons on this side of the water: Hollywood stars and the excessively wealthy.

The wedding of Princess Anne, the first of the Queen's four children to be married, was a resplendent ceremony with all the pomp and theatre the royal family and the Church of England could project. As I watched the couple make their solemn vows I truly felt it would be forever, not like the crumbled marriages of so many of our friends. Surely such a thing could never happen to ethereal Princess Anne and dashing Captain Phillips.

Several weeks later, on Christmas Day, Margaret Trudeau gave birth to the Trudeaus' second son. Two baby boys, two years apart, and both born on December 25. There was something slightly miraculous about it. Ah, there was another fairy-tale marriage: Pierre, our philosopher-king with his gorgeous flower-child wife, Margaret, and now two little sons. A perfect family—or so I thought.

By New Year's Eve Farley still hadn't totally recovered. We had been invited to a party but we decided to celebrate the first day of 1974 by ourselves in Indian Summer, that ramshackle cottage that I dearly loved.

We remained there for nine days. In the mornings Farley was busy making notes for a book he intended to write—one of these days. He was becoming discouraged with writing books. For all the crusading he had done using the printed word, he believed that nothing much had changed.

Wolves were still being wantonly killed no matter how many copies of *Never Cry Wolf* had been read. Whales were still being slaughtered on the high seas despite all his protests. He felt it was time to get more directly involved, to accept some challenge that would make a direct difference in the lives of people and animals, and he believed he saw a chance to do this in northern Manitoba.

Our brief sojourn at the old cottage did us a world of good. There was enough snow that we headed back into the woods on our snowshoes every afternoon. Snowshoeing was the winter sport we both liked. We got to be very good at it and sometimes travelled for hours without seeing another soul, in a wooded area north of the lakeshore cottages and south of the farms along Highway 2. In the evenings we usually read or listened to CBC radio. At the time I was working my way through the novels of Hugh Hood, a Montreal writer and professor. I would gladly have spent the rest of the winter there, but it wasn't possible because of Farley's decision to become an activist in Manitoba.

There was only one sour note in our short, happy holiday. One afternoon we drove over to Prince Edward County to visit Angus and Barbara. We hadn't been to see them since September and although we kept in touch through letters, we felt it was time to wish them a happy new year in person. I might have guessed it wouldn't be all that happy.

Barbara was lying on the chesterfield wearing her dressing gown, covered with a plaid blanket. More and more she was "feeling poorly" with one of a host of non-specific ailments. It was never anything as straightforward as a cold or the flu. She claimed to be allergic to just about everything, although her medical tests were always inconclusive. This time, she told us, she had worms—some peculiar kind of worm that was crawling around in her stomach. It made her very tired.

"What did the doctor say?" I asked her.

"Doctors!" she snorted. "What do they know?" And she lit another cigarette.

Angus, who was then eighty-one, was left in charge of the household: a woman's task that he considered beneath him. His only culinary skill was cooking oatmeal porridge. Men of Angus's generation rarely knew how to cook.

I didn't relish the prospect of eating porridge for my evening meal, no matter how much brown sugar was sprinkled on it, so Farley drove to Napanee and bought some pork chops and vegetables and I cooked a square meal for the four of us.

I thought that a sense of family unity would have buried disagreements between us that day but no such luck. At supper we got into a heated argument about, of all things, the etchings of David Blackwood. Blackwood, originally from Newfoundland, had recently bought a house in Port Hope. Farley and I admired his work, which depicted Newfoundland outport life, and we mentioned that we had purchased two prints.

Barbara thereupon declared she had a brilliant artist friend who was utterly disdainful of Blackwood's work, describing it as sentimental and colourless. Barbara always claimed to know someone who was an authority on just about any subject, and they were always at variance with any opinion or passion of ours.

I couldn't figure her out. Why didn't she like us? Or even pretend to like us? Did she believe that by constantly disagreeing with us it proved she was smarter or better informed than we were? Did she want to create tension between Farley and his father for some perverse reason of her own?

Afterward Farley shrugged and told me not to let it get to me. But it always did. I had begun to feel that during our visits someone was kicking my shins under the table, then feigning surprise when I yelped in pain.

Angus, unwilling or unable to take a stand, always let her get away with it.

I didn't yelp. I gave up the argument and washed the dishes in grim silence. As we drove back to our cottage, I tried to dispel the taste of ashes.

Chapter Twenty-five

My relationship with Angus's lady was not improving, but with Farley's son Sandy it was. Sandy turned twenty that year. He was a student at the Erindale campus of the University of Toronto. He commuted to university in his red Mazda truck and he could now drive to Port Hope to visit us. Somewhere along the way he had begun to see me as a human being and not as the scarlet lady who had stolen his father.

Farley's two sons visited us separately. They never liked one another and the situation didn't get any better as they reached maturity. Sandy remained a bright, conscientious student who sailed through university with high marks. He always found summer employment. In his final university year his fellow students elected him president of the Erindale College Students' Union. We wondered if he, like his great-great-uncle, Oliver Mowat—the Premier of Ontario for twenty-three years—was headed for a life in politics. He said he wasn't. His abiding passion was CBC radio and he hoped someday to have a career there.

All our attempts to keep David Mowat in school were unsuccessful. After David failed Grade Nine at Orangeville High School, Farley arranged to send him to an Outward Bound residential school near Edmonton. St. John's was the sort of school where physical challenges such as canoe trips and cross-country skiing might have engaged him in a way that the sedentary curriculum in a high school had not. It didn't work. He ran away from school more than once.

After a year and a half he dropped out and hitchhiked from Alberta back to live with his mother near Palgrave. He re-entered Orangeville High School, but this attempt was no more successful than the first. Half the time his worried mother had no idea where this seventeen-year-old was, nor what he was doing. We didn't see much of him either.

The events of that winter didn't follow our usual pattern. For a change Farley was not writing a book. He was spending one week every month in

Manitoba as an unpaid advisor to the cabinet on subjects ranging from environmental protection to programs to encourage the arts. When he was at home he spent much of his time working on plans and proposals. He joked that he had become a "dollar-a-year man," a designation used during the Second World War for people who made a full-time contribution to the war effort but were paid only a token fee.

Farley was under far less pressure than if he had been writing a book, which was why, when he was asked to join a group of Port Hope towns people who had something to protest, he joined, and so did I. It was all about Kentucky Fried Chicken.

Colonel Sanders and "his boys"—the executives who managed the Ontario division of the fried chicken empire—proposed to build one of their franchises at Port Hope's main intersection, the junction of Walton and Mill Streets. This was a focal point where, in an Italian town, there would have been a splashing fountain or a classic statue.

Port Hope's principal retail street, Walton Street, is bordered by an impressive array of nineteenth-century architecture. By the 1970s some of these buildings had been "modernized" with ugly signs and incongruous windows, but most of these splendid old brick buildings had remained intact. This unique street was a major part of the town's considerable charm, a feature that set it apart from more "progressive" towns where old buildings had been neglected and then demolished to make way for parking lots and franchised food outlets.

About a dozen of us banded together to protest the Colonel's plans for our town. We called ourselves the Friends of Port Hope. We didn't object to fried chicken but we did object to that big bucket with the caricature Kentucky colonel on it dominating our main street.

Nowadays, most towns and cities have architectural heritage districts and such a protest wouldn't be necessary; but in 1974 trying to convince the Port Hope town council and the entrepreneurs of the Colonel Sanders corporation that we had a valid complaint was next to impossible. The council held the view that any new business was a good thing, providing jobs and bringing in revenue. What did it matter where it was located so long as customers could easily reach it? The possibility that the historic atmosphere of Port Hope might itself attract both customers and new residents who would contribute to the financial well-being of the town was a concept that had evidently never crossed the minds of our elected representatives.

Only the mayor, a dedicated man named Mike Wladyka who loved and appreciated the character of this old town, was on our side. However, he had only one vote in council meetings. The six councillors dismissed our group as a bunch of elitists. Jobs and money were what mattered and why would anyone give a hoot about saving those old-fashioned buildings anyway? I'm sure most of them believed it was high time they were either modernized or demolished. In their view anyone who opposed a fried-chicken franchise was against progress.

We thought we would lose the battle. There was no groundswell of support for us among the townsfolk. In the end we were saved by a technicality. Mayor Wladyka, who had been involved in town politics most of his life, unearthed a little-known by-law regulating the proximity of driveways to intersections. The half-acre that was needed for the franchise and its adjoining parking lot proved to be far too close to the intersection for safety. Some weeks later an alternate location was found further down the road, where "finger lickin' good" chicken could be sold profitably, but not quite so visibly.

This small victory made me feel better about Port Hope. Until then I had imagined the town getting uglier and uglier as gracious old buildings fell into disuse or were wrecked. Tearing the core out of the old downtowns had been the fashion all over Canada since the end of the Second World War. Now there appeared to be at least a chance that our dignified downtown could be saved. All it took was a handful of concerned people and a mayor whose vision extended beyond the quick buck.

By spring Farley's forays into Manitoba had made him realize that bureaucracy was an almost insurmountable obstacle, a slow-moving, entrenched body that, though its members may have listened to him and even sometimes agreed with him, in the end resisted any change to its established ways. Farley was an impatient visionary and it became clear to him that the nitty-gritty of trying to make things happen in government was going to take far more time than he was prepared to contribute.

We were back to square one in our search for a home.

Scanning the map of the Atlantic provinces I suggested that we hadn't given Prince Edward Island much consideration. We had been driving through part of it for four years to get to the ferry to the Magdalen Islands but apart from some hasty, last-minute shopping, we had never taken the time to really look around.

With his usual zeal for getting things done right away, Farley proposed taking a trip there in April to look at possibilities. He was feeling fidgety and unfulfilled because he hadn't done any real writing that winter. He finally acknowledged that he was a writer first and always and he was not going to spend another year dilly-dallying with other pursuits.

He took his son Sandy, who had completed his university year but not yet begun his summer job, with him for a reconnaissance of PEI. It was an ideal opportunity for father and son to share a small adventure. The downside was that April in Prince Edward Island—or that particular April anyway—did not provide the sort of weather celebrated in brochures of Canada's picture province. There was snow. There was rain. The wind howled. That famous red soil turned to a gummy mess as frost left the rural roads while rain and drizzle filled the puddles and the ditches.

Sandy stayed for a week, then flew back to Ontario. I joined Farley for the second week of the search. Travelling by train to Amherst, Nova Scotia, I boarded the bus heading for PEI. As we drove closer to the Strait of Northumberland a light fall of snow turned into a blinding blizzard. I fully expected the ferry crossing to be cancelled but somehow the captain made his way to the other side.

Farley was waiting for me in snowbound Charlottetown with his rented car. He had not had any luck in his search the previous week. A real estate salesman named Mel was doing his best but there were obstacles. PEI had recently passed legislation imposing restrictions on the sale of land to non-residents. In a small province there had to be a limit to how much land could be taken away from agriculture by summer people. We learned we would be limited to no more than twelve acres unless the land we bought was to be used for farming.

This did not deter Farley. In fact, it fitted in with his prognosis for the future of the world. He was sure there would be a doomsday war between capitalism and communism not too far into the future and that, in the chaos that followed, most of the world was going to run short of food. He figured we would all be heading for starvation unless we could become self-sustaining. The best plan would be to start farming in some relatively uncrowded place in company with a few like-minded souls. While we had been visiting Chip and Lindee Climo the previous autumn, Farley had talked to them about the way he saw the future and what we should be doing about it. They said they would like to join in. Farley concluded that a farm in PEI might be the answer, where, if the worse came to the worst, we could survive on our own efforts.

We were somewhat familiar with the countryside near Souris and I hoped we might find something there. The problem was that a provincial park was then on the drawing board for the east end of the island and the possibility of expropriation had frozen all land sales.

Shopping for real estate in an unfamiliar place was a bewildering experience for me. We drove and drove. At the end of each day I tried to sort out where we had been and what we had seen. Was that big white house we liked near Murray River? Or was it near Georgetown? That other place, the one with the long farm lane, was that near Belfast or Flat River? I couldn't remember. I kept hoping we would suddenly come upon the perfect place and I would fall in love with it, the way I had in the Magdalens a few years before; but as our time was drawing to a close no such magical place had appeared.

Then, on the second-to-last day, we did find a possibility. Its owner was a sixty-year-old bachelor, the last of a large family, who for years had been living in just the kitchen of what was a rundown, four-bedroom, two-storey farmhouse. The hundred-acre farm, now partly covered by trees, still had about fifty cleared acres. There was a large barn in fairly good repair. The owner was ready to sell. We settled on a price. The farm would be ours in two months.

Farley felt sure the place had a good future. Chip and Lindee could camp initially in the large kitchen. They were, after all, currently living in one room that was even smaller. We could live temporarily in our caravan, once we had retrieved it from Manitoba. Bit by bit we could repair and open up the rest of the house, install a heating system, do some decorating. There was enough land to pasture some cattle and a flock of sheep. The sturdy old barn would shelter them in winter. The woodlot at the back of the property promised many years of firewood.

Farley phoned the Climos that evening and they sounded delighted. If all went well they could move in early summer. When we returned to Ontario the next day, Farley felt satisfied he had accomplished what he had set out to do—ensure a rural retreat where we could be self-sufficient.

There was only one problem with our latest acquisition. I really didn't like the place at all.

Chapter Twenty-six

WHEN WE RETURNED to the Magdalens in June and told our friends the Warrens about the purchase of our new farm, they must have wondered, as I did, why we had done such a thing. Although they didn't exactly say so, I was sure they thought Farley's plans for surviving the impending cataclysm were farfetched. I, too, was skeptical but I wasn't going to rain on his parade.

How could we make a home on the farm we had just bought? It was rough, scrubby land with no view of the ocean. The landscape was not nearly as appealing as the fields of waving grass on our eleven acres at Grande Entrée and there was no enticing sandy beach just over the hill.

It was time to rethink my attitude toward the Magdalens. We did have a pleasing house. We had enough land so we could grow more food or even pasture a cow if we needed to. Besides, we had two of our dearest friends living next door. All I had to do was narrow my focus to this little corner of the islands. I would simply ignore all the local squabbling, the drinking and the hostile phone calls. I would busy myself with fundamental pleasures such as swimming, gardening, and reading. And I would keep on with my writing and, maybe, even get back to drawing again. If Farley saw that I was happy at Grande Entrée he would change his mind about the farm on PEI, list it for sale, and be content to stay where we were.

I arranged my life so that only rarely would I have to go beyond our own property or the adjoining acres belonging to the Warrens. I made a deal with Farley: I would weed the vegetable garden if he would do our grocery shopping. Trying to shop on these islands had resulted in a kind of paranoia I just couldn't shake. In my rational mind I knew I wasn't in any danger but I couldn't quell the panic I felt when I had to enter a store. More than once I had had to leave, feeling defeated. As the years went by, I had hoped that I would develop a thicker skin, that I could fade into the crowd and not be the object of anyone's attention, but it hadn't happened.

Our few local friends were a consolation. Stuart and Joan Richards were glad to see us return that spring. They had recently returned as well, having spent the academic year in Lennoxville, Quebec, where Stuart was upgrading his academic qualifications at Bishop's University. Because his studies concluded at the end of April it also gave him one final spring season to join his father in lobster fishing. Being a school principal carried more prestige in the outer world than doing the work his father and grandfather had done, but Stuart said he could never feel quite the same attachment to teaching as he felt for the lobster fishery.

His feisty wife, Joan, was not as pleased to be back on these islands after eight months in a relatively harmonious university town in Quebec's Eastern Townships. It wasn't long before she resumed her embattled state with certain people in Grosse Île. She couldn't wall herself off from them as I was attempting to do in Grande Entrée. She was the mother of two daughters and the wife of the school principal. Like it or not she had to be involved in the community.

Isaac and Jacquie LaPierre invited us to a party at their home to celebrate Isaac's thirty-first birthday on August the eighth. Jacquie was another wife who was not content living in the Magdalens, even though she had been born there. She wanted Isaac to move their family to Sept-Îles, on the north shore of the Gulf. It was an industrial town with a future, she believed. Grande Entrée wasn't.

Richard Nixon resigned as President of the United States on the same day we celebrated Isaac's birthday. Nixon had been caught in the Watergate scandal. I imagine a lot of Americans were celebrating Nixon's departure, because every American we had encountered in Canada said they hated him. That evening, at Isaac's house, we watched a televised message from an American president being delivered in French—dubbed in by an announcer at the CBC French-language headquarters in Montreal. It was a strange experience to watch a US president resign, but even stranger, for us, to hear it in French.

Our gate, at the end of the lane, remained closed to discourage unwanted visitors. We kept to ourselves as much as possible. However, when I learned the disturbing fate of Morris McQuaid's boat I could no longer leave my head buried in the sand.

The fifty-four-foot boat had been completed and launched in the spring. The buyer, a Madelinôt from Cap-aux-Meules, had paid Morris the agreed-upon sum of ten thousand dollars, then had immediately sold the vessel to someone over in the Gaspé region for forty thousand.

Because of the rampant inflation of the 1970s the boat had cost Morris nearly seven thousand dollars for building materials alone, so his three years' work had only earned him three thousand dollars. However, being a man of his word he had charged the price he had quoted at the outset and not a penny more.

We thought it was a disgrace to take such advantage of a man who kept religiously to his word, a man who spoke no French and was out of touch with the shrewd world of business. Cunning business deals like that happened all over the world every day, but having it happen right next door, to a decent man from the minority here, really upset me. I had thought I could live a cloistered life at the end of the road, ignoring the world beyond our gate; but now I knew I couldn't.

"I guess I've learned my lesson," was Morris's only comment when he told us about it. There was no display of anger, no hint of vengeance; just quiet resignation.

A new person appeared in Morris's mostly solitary life that year: a young, energetic, and very attractive woman named Norma. Her parents were from Grosse Île but her father had joined the army, so Norma and her two sisters had grown up on military bases all across Canada.

Norma had embraced the counter-culture—those idealists who were heading out of the cities looking for a simpler, purer life—and had decided to practise it in the Magdalens. She had the advantage of roots and relatives in this out-of-the-way place. She had studied to be a potter and intended to set up a home and a studio, and had set her sights on the empty schoolhouse owned by Morris McQuaid. She was, she pointed out to him, distantly related to his late wife, if they traced their ancestry back four generations.

Morris had refused several offers to sell the schoolhouse. He sometimes rented the building in the summer, but was reluctant to let it go. Apart from the fact the school had been the honeymoon cottage for his ill-fated and brief marriage, Morris did not want to sell any portion of his land on these finite islands. However, Norma's charms and persistence were more than

Farley with Jack McClelland, Grande Entrée, 1974

he could resist. Perhaps he was hoping Norma might eventually marry him. In any case, he sold her the old school and its half-acre of land, and Norma moved in.

The end of August brought us an unexpected visit from Jack McClelland, who had travelled first to Liverpool, on the eastern shore of Nova Scotia, to visit author Tom Raddall. I always enjoyed visits with Jack. He was an ideal house guest, just as Peter Davison was. Both men always had something important to do—a manuscript to read. Jack slept in late in the mornings so there was no rush to serve him breakfast. He didn't get in my way in the kitchen. He was charming and funny, and full of anecdotes about people we all knew. His presence always reassured Farley that his writing was going in the right direction.

I had no intention of talking to him about my own writing. I knew I still had a long way to go before I had written anything that might be considered a book. When—and if—I finished my opus I would summon my courage and then show it to him.

Surprisingly he wanted to talk about it.

"I suppose," he began, "you've been wondering why I haven't asked you how your writing is going."

"No," I replied. "It's nowhere near completion."

"The fact is…" he paused for an awkward few seconds, "that's not what I think you should be doing."

For a moment I was too stunned to say anything.

"There are so many options out there," he went on. "It just isn't advisable…sensible…to get into the same field as your husband. You mentioned you had a friend here—Father What's-his-name—who's starting a museum. Well, you could get involved with that; maybe fund-raising, that kind of thing."

My surprise turned to anger. Jack had known me for fourteen years, yet he seemed to think of me as a bored housewife who didn't have enough to do; a potential committee lady and nothing more. Or worse, he may have thought I might produce something so slipshod it would be embarrassing and reflect badly on Farley's reputation. Either way, I felt insulted to the core by a man I liked and admired.

"Well, Jack," I finally managed to say, "that's your opinion; but I plan to continue writing anyway."

He shrugged and gave me that familiar half-grin of his, as if to say that it was my decision, even if it was the wrong one.

I was so angry I could have thrown my drink at him. How could he have understood so little about me? The only careers I had ever longed for had all been in the arts: acting, music, painting, and writing. Furthermore, I had no talent for things like committees or management. I was too shy to be a fund-raiser. I was happiest when I worked alone.

Farley took me aside and calmed me down, explaining that Jack had surely meant no harm. It was, he believed, that Jack could only understand two kinds of women. There were those who were like his mother and like his wife, Elizabeth: ladies whose lives centred on their homes and families and who contributed to the community by volunteering their time for worthy causes. The other kind of women Jack encountered were fiercely ambitious people whose work was their first priority and for whom husbands and families were incidental, if they existed at all. Most of them were divorced and, to do him justice, Jack didn't want to see Farley and me split up.

Nor did we, but I was sure there was room in our marriage for me to write a book. Farley always encouraged me. We weren't competitors. We were companions.

Not another word was said about my endeavours that weekend. The three of us left the islands together on the same flight on Sunday night. Jack was returning to Toronto, to his never-ending struggle to keep book publishing alive in Canada. Despite the many best-sellers written by Farley and by Pierre Berton, Margaret Laurence, Peter Newman, Mordecai Richler, Margaret Atwood, and a host of other authors, the firm of McClelland and Stewart was still teetering on the edge of bankruptcy.

Farley and I were heading for an adventure that would be far more entertaining than the travails of the book business. We were off to Greenland.

Ed Schreyer had phoned us from Winnipeg earlier in August to tell us he was going to Greenland on a fact-finding mission connected with northern economics and development. He would be hiring a plane belonging to the government of the Northwest Territories. It had lots of space, so did we want to come along?

Did we! As far back as we could remember we had both wanted to visit Greenland. I could recall singing a hymn called "From Greenland's Icy Mountains" when I was in Sunday school and picturing all that ice in my mind. I still don't know why I wanted to see those icy mountains or why they appealed to me more than "India's coral strand," which was the second line of the hymn. Farley, always intrigued by the ancient migrations of people from northern Europe to northern Canada, knew how vital the historic link with Greenland had been. The reason we had never been there was that Greenland, Canada's eastern next-door neighbour, was then one of the least accessible countries in the world.

Farley and I were to fly from Montreal north to the community of Frobisher Bay (now named Iqaluit) to await the arrival of the plane bearing Ed and Lily Schreyer from Winnipeg. Our Nordair flight for the twelve-hundred-mile journey from Montreal to Frobisher Bay was full—mostly with men carrying parkas over their arms. We learned they were going to Frobisher to a conference on the implications of European law and punishment on native people. They included delegates from Canada, Alaska, and Greenland.

Since there were then no scheduled flights between Canada and Greenland, the Greenland delegates had had to fly from Greenland to Denmark, then from Copenhagen to Montreal, and finally from Montreal to Frobisher. It must have taken them several days. We were lucky indeed to have the rare chance of flying directly from Canada to Greenland.

Four and a half hours after leaving Montreal we landed at Frobisher. It was not a welcoming place. The temperature was 43°F, thirty degrees cooler than it had been in Montreal, and rain was pelting down.

This town had originally been hastily assembled by the US military during the Second World War. Along with an immense airstrip, the Americans had built a huge building known locally as The Complex, a monstrous grey edifice dominating the whole community and housing a hotel, a restaurant, apartments, a Hudson's Bay store, and various offices. We spent a day and a night there and I had to hand it to the engineers who had figured out a way to erect such a structure in a hostile climate where all building materials had to be imported. However, no designer of prisons could have conceived of anything quite so dismal. The ground floor had no windows in it at all. The corridors were painted battleship grey and were devoid of any form of decoration. There wasn't a trace of the Eskimo art that was then taking the world by storm. Mostly we saw young Inuit children loitering, begging, and smoking cigarettes.

We stayed in a tiny apartment on the second floor, which did, at least, have a window. Our view was restricted to a square, flat, gravel roof, and all we could see was the rain forming puddles on it.

Next morning it was still raining and I looked out the window at the same puddles as the day before. I wanted to see rocks and hills and the great bay, and especially people. It occurred to me that this same space had been occupied thirty years earlier by American servicemen who would have had just as little sense as I did of where in the world they were.

We ate an undistinguished breakfast of greasy bacon and eggs, which cost twice as much as it would have in Montreal. Any food that cannot be raised in the Arctic has to be flown in at considerable expense. Later that morning we met the two men who would be travelling with the Schreyers and us to Greenland.

Ewan Cotterill, the assistant commissioner of the Northwest Territories, was a thirty-six-year-old who had spent the past eighteen years in various communities in the Canadian North. He told us he had chosen to leave the "south" and head north after reading Farley's first book, *People of the Deer*, in 1952. I was always dumbfounded to think that any one book could so profoundly affect a reader's destiny, yet that one had for Ewan. At the age of twenty he had married an Inuit woman with whom he had a daughter and a son. Tragically, his wife had died of cancer while still in her twenties. Ewan's fourteen-year-old son would be travelling with us. The boy lived in Regina with Ewan's parents, but whenever there was a chance, Ewan brought his children north to keep them connected to their heritage.

Our other travelling companion was Bob Pilot, also an administrator in the Northwest Territories government. Bob had originally come north as an RCMP officer. After fourteen years in the Arctic he had left the Mounties to join the civil service. Bob had been to Greenland several times, having served in Canada's northernmost outpost, at Grise Fiord, and from there his travels had taken him even further north. It was possible, he pointed out, to *walk* from Canada to Greenland in winter across the frozen channel that separates the two countries at their northern extremities. He did not recommend the journey to us.

When we headed out to the airport that afternoon the rain had finally stopped and I could at last see something of the landscape. At low tide Frobisher Bay itself was shallow and dotted with thousands of boulders. Rocky islands rose in the distance and beyond them a horizon, where the inky blue of the Arctic Ocean met a slate-grey sky. Not a tree or a bush was to be seen anywhere. The terrain was not unlike the southwest coast of Newfoundland and it dawned on me why many Newfoundlanders were able to move to the Arctic and feel more or less at home there.

The twin-engined Gulf Stream aircraft bearing Ed and Lily was already at the airport terminal. This was the Schreyers' first visit to Frobisher Bay and Ed, true to his inquiring nature, was full of questions about how things worked. Ewan and Bob had all the answers. Ewan mentioned that the settlements still further north depended on only one ship a year, usually in September, for their basic supplies.

"Imagine," I said to Lily, "trying to plan your grocery list a whole year in advance."

We agreed that neither of us would know where to begin.

Soon we were on board the plane, flying east to a land I had never expected to see.

It turned out to be love at first sight.

Chapter Twenty-seven

IT WAS TWILIGHT when we touched down at the surprisingly vast airport at Söndre Strömfjord in western Greenland. Built in the 1940s by the US military on one of the few level stretches of ice-free land in the entire country, it had served as a refuelling stop for aircraft crossing the North Atlantic during the war. After the war it had been enlarged to accommodate the US Air Force's B-52 bombers threatening the Soviet Union. Now it was also serving as Greenland's international airport. Located in relative shelter at the head of a fjord that reaches a hundred miles into the interior, it was one of the very few places in all of Greenland where large airplanes on wheels could land at all.

The airport manager, a tall, fair-haired fellow named Steen Malmquist, greeted our delegation. We were shepherded into a mini-bus and driven to the modern terminal building, where we were treated to a welcome snack: open-faced Danish sandwiches, platters of Greenland shrimp, and as much Danish beer as we cared to drink.

Almost all the people in the airport—ticket agents, baggage handlers, waitresses, and security guards—were Inuit; essentially the same people as those who lived across Davis Strait in Canada, but whose presence in the Frobisher Bay airport had been far less evident. Canadian Inuit, then called Eskimos, had been colonized by the British in the nineteenth century but were now governed by Ottawa. Modern Greenland Inuit had been colonized by the Danes, beginning with the arrival of the Danish missionary Hans Egede in 1721. Which had fared the best? With any luck I hoped to find out.

Across the tarmac from the airport was the sprawling American military base, but there was no civilian settlement anywhere in sight. Our overnight accommodation was in a hotel upstairs in the airport terminal, where Farley and I were allotted a compact little room similar to the stateroom in a ship. It had an upper and lower bunk, a couple of teak chairs, a mirror, and a slim closet. The bathroom was across the hall. Unlike our room-without-a-view in Frobisher Bay, this one had a wide window over-looking the airstrip. There were double drapes: patterned cotton facing the room, backed by black cotton facing the window. At latitude 65° North, where summer daylight lasts for twenty-four hours, this was the most appropriate window treatment I had seen in the north.

We were jolted awake early the next morning by the roar of an aircraft. I pushed back the double drapes to see a huge US military transport about to take off. It resembled a pregnant elephant with wings; a clumsy-looking monster that looked as if it couldn't possibly leave the ground. However, two minutes later it did, ponderously and noisily, to be followed in quick succession by three fighter airplanes. The cumbersome transport could have been full of tanks or trucks or platoons of soldiers. Had war been declared somewhere? I hoped they were just practicing.

As the commotion of the departing planes subsided, we dressed and packed and headed down to the restaurant for breakfast. We were ready for the next stage of our journey—a helicopter flight to Greenland's capital—then called Godthåb but now renamed Nuuk. As things turned out we needn't have hurried. We spent two days at Söndre Strömfjord awaiting the arrival of one of Groenlandair's huge Sikorsky helicopters, which were the principal means of internal transportation for the entire island, a land mass slightly larger than all of Mexico. Greenland is actually the third-largest country in continental North America, after Canada and the United States.

Waiting around in an airport becomes very boring very quickly, although this one was more interesting than most. For one thing the food was superb: salmon, shrimp, pickled herring, rye bread, Danish cheeses, Danish pastries, and, of course, that effervescent Danish beer. Once in a while a trans-polar airliner would land for refuelling, usually en route between northern Europe and the West Coast of the United States. It was a diversion to observe the passengers as they straggled into the terminal. There was an intriguing gift shop that drew Lily and me like a magnet. It sold exquisite Danish crystal and china and interesting Greenland crafts: bright, beaded mats, bone jewellery and strange-looking soapstone carvings of some mythical animal with its head on backwards.

To lure us away from the gift shop, Farley suggested that we four go for a walk. Ed is a traveller who likes to keep moving and he was becoming impatient with this delay. Farley and I, having spent so many years on the often-fog-bound, stormy East Coast of Canada, were more accustomed to waiting.

This time the delay was not about the weather. Ed discovered that, of the six helicopters that normally served all of Greenland, only three were in service. The others all had mechanical problems. We also learned that several inbound passengers had already been waiting in the terminal four days for their helicopter to arrive.

On a sunny day that was just cool enough for a lightweight jacket, we set off along a roughly gravelled road that led further into the interior. Uphill from the terminal buildings was a small, plastic-sheathed greenhouse where someone was growing lettuce and nasturtiums, an admirable effort in this subarctic climate. Not far from the edge of the airstrip we met three buck caribou nonchalantly feeding on lichens—as carefree as three cows in a pasture. As we walked on I saw plants that were familiar from Newfoundland, including Arctic cotton, bluebells, and Labrador tea.

We followed the road through rolling tundra for nearly an hour, eventually reaching a very small lake where we were surprised to see a cluster of shiny new outboard motorboats moored to a wharf. We guessed, correctly, that this lake was used for recreation by US military personnel from the base, people who, like ourselves, probably wanted to get away from the confines of an airport.

In the afternoon Steen Malmquist took us for a drive in a Land Rover on the longest paved road in all of Greenland: twelve miles between the airport and a US naval dock at the head of the fjord. From the fjord valley we could glimpse a distant edge of the ice cap that covers most of this, the largest island in the world. The weight of this mile-thick ice is so great that the land that bears it has, in many places, been depressed below sea level.

One of my ancestors must have come from fjord country because I always feel drawn to places like this: deep, dark water dotted with icebergs, stony mountains, implacable glaciers, and, on the ground, a carpet of tiny subarctic flowers. Ed Schreyer may have been impatient to move on, but I was quite content to linger.

None of us moved on that day. The ever-helpful Steen suggested that, since we had a spare evening, we might enjoy a visit to the US base. At the officers' club, we were greeted by the commanding officer, a colonel named Swartz, and by a petite army captain whose name tag told us she was Mary Lou McAlister. We learned that this base was considered an isolation posting, which meant that personnel who served here could not bring their wives, husbands, or children.

We told the colonel we were from Canada, which didn't appear to interest him. Farley and I, and then Bob Pilot, made a point of the fact that we had the premier of Manitoba with us, but this didn't rouse his curiosity either. It wasn't until I explained that a premier was the equivalent of a governor of a state, and that Manitoba was a province of Canada right next door to North Dakota, that he remarked, "Well, well now...why didn't somebody tell me?"

Our hearty meal consisted of grilled sirloin steak, a tossed salad made with lettuce flown in from California, and California red wine. Colonel Swartz and Mary Lou had collected their steaks raw and took them away somewhere to grill privately on a barbeque.

We six Canadians dined with Steen, whose Danish parents had immigrated to northern Greenland in the 1930s as schoolteachers. He had grown up in a home heated with seal oil. His boyhood friends were all native Greenlanders, so he became fluent in Inuktitut. In his teens he had signed on as a crew member on a Greenland freighter and, for some reason, ended up staying in the United States for several months, where he learned English. At the age of eighteen he joined the Danish army and was eventually posted to the lonely task of patrolling northeastern Greenland. This was in the 1950s, when all countries, including Canada, whose territory extended into the Arctic, were nervous about infiltration or an attack from the Soviet Union, which was figuratively just a hop, skip, and a jump away across the North Pole. For four years Steen, and two other men, patrolled the region around Scoresby Sound, one of the remotest, uninhabited, and coldest places in the world. Bob Pilot, during his career as an RCMP officer, had done much the same job in Canada on Ellesmere Island.

After dinner Steen invited us back to his apartment for a nightcap. The building in which he lived was grey and institutional outside but inside it was warm and bright. The furniture was teak, the rugs Persian, and the artwork Eskimo—the living room wouldn't have looked out of place in a home decorating magazine. During the summer months his wife and two teenagers had been here with him but had recently departed for Denmark so the children could continue their education. Steen missed them very much.

Later the following afternoon we finally got away in a huge Sikorsky chopper, full to capacity with twenty-one passengers and all their baggage. We first flew west above the long fjord, following it as if it were a meandering road beneath us. The Sikorsky flew lower and slower than an airplane, which gave us a spectacular view. On both sides of the fjord rose the sheer rock of ice-scoured mountains. Occasionally we flew a shortcut above the land and over glaciers that, from the air, looked like broad, fossilized rivers heading down toward the ocean. This grey rock landscape had random patches of subtle colour: bronze, pale green, and a shade of dark blue—the colours of lichens, those earthly forms of life that are the first to appear after the glacial ice has moved, ever so slowly, on.

The vista of glaciers and that ultramarine fjord dotted with small icebergs was stunning. The only setback was that I was too paralyzed by fear to really enjoy it. The realization that only the huge propeller overhead was keeping us in the air, without any wings, was terrifying. Knowing that only a few months earlier one of these monsters had stalled and dropped straight into a fjord, drowning everyone on board, didn't help. I spent most of that journey looking for relatively level places where we might hope to land if there was an emergency. I couldn't find even one.

Farley, Ed, Ewan, and Bob had something else on which to focus. When we reached the mouth of the long fjord they prepared to test one of Farley's theories. In his 1965 book *Westviking* he had proposed that the "loom" of high land in Baffin Island, nearly two hundred miles west, could be seen from the mountains of western Greenland and that this would, sooner or later, have led early Viking settlers in Greenland to set sail and discover the rest of North America.

As the chopper headed south, along the west coast, we all stared intently at the horizon. And sure enough, we could see a distant "loom"—a cloudy presence above the horizon that would have indicated to some intrepid Norse mariner who had climbed a mountain a very long time ago, that there was land somewhere far to the west. Farley's theory was confirmed. He was delighted.

The heliport where we landed at Godthåb was right in the middle of this administrative town, the largest community in Greenland, which in 1974 was home to about eight thousand people. It did not resemble any North American town I had ever seen, in that it had very few single-family houses. Instead, there were rows of enormous, low-rise apartment buildings, some as long as a city block.

We were greeted at the heliport by a charming young Danish woman who introduced herself as Dortë, secretary to Greenland's governor, who would have been there to meet us himself had he not been away in a distant part of the island. Like most Danes, Dortë spoke English perfectly.

We were booked into the Greenland Hotel, which was quintessentially modern in design and furnishings. The Danes, who number only about five million people in a country whose land mass is smaller than Nova Scotia, are masters of design and their visual imprint on Greenland communities was unmistakable.

Farley and I went for a walk before dinner. It was then around five o'clock when people were heading home, mostly on foot, carrying groceries in plastic bags. A few were on motor scooters or in cars or trucks. We took a close look at one of the four-storey, sprawling apartment blocks. It reminded us of the massive apartment buildings we had seen in Siberia, whose landscape and climate also made construction of individual houses prohibitively expensive. As in Siberia some of these structures had been built on bedrock foundations, while others were on pilings driven deep into the permafrost. The significant external difference between Siberian apartments and these was that in Godthåb every one had a balcony. Some balconies sported lines of laundry, others a string of split fish drying in the sun and wind. Several were draped with uncured sealskins or caribou hides. These apartment dwellers were, at least some of the time, still hunter-gatherers, people who had previously lived in tents and igloos widely dispersed around the coasts of this enormous land. I wondered how well they were adapting to life in that jammed, concrete village. They were in transition from their old way of life into a radically new one—which tends to be an unhappy situation anywhere in the world.

Deputy Governor John Kronborg invited us Canadians to his home that evening for an informal reception and briefing about present-day

Greenland. Greenlanders, he began, had one of the world's highest birth rates, without which they could not have survived in times past because the harsh conditions of the far north had resulted in a high rate of child mortality. Now, however, as the risks diminished with modern medical care and social services, a population explosion had occurred and the number of Greenlanders had actually doubled between 1949 and 1965.

The deputy governor and his gracious wife, Ellen, lived in one of the few single-family houses in Godthåb. It was furnished in the Danish modern style but decorated with Canadian Inuit art, the Kronborgs having spent several months the previous year in Yellowknife, where they had bought many prints and carvings. Although I wouldn't have dreamed of saying so, these had far more artistic merit than most of the Greenland carvings we had seen. The Danes may have been able to build more elegant hotels in the Arctic, but in Canada the Inuit had become more accomplished artists.

Ed had come to Greenland in search of facts and figures and the deputy governor was a fountain of information. He told us that almost all Greenlanders had once made their living from sea mammals—mostly seals—but by the 1930s the ocean climate had warmed so much that many kinds of sea mammals had moved further north. At the same time cod and some other fishes began appearing off the coasts of south and west-central Greenland. The Danes were quick to capitalize on this and to introduce modern commercial fishing, including offshore draggers and efficient fish-packing and freezing plants. Furthermore, they trained the native people to operate the new industry, which had been very successful in helping bring the people into "modern times." Unfortunately the cod fishery was now in decline—which the deputy governor blamed more on climate changes than on the overfishing that, in a few more years, would virtually bring to an end the commercial cod stocks in the entire North Atlantic Ocean. He was optimistic and went on to add that a northern shrimp fishery was thriving.

Kronborg talked at some length about the warming and cooling cycles in Greenland over the past thousand years and how these had affected human history. Navigation from Iceland had been a fairly straightforward matter around A.D. 982, when Europeans from Iceland first settled in southwestern Greenland. Their descendants had been able to prosper for nearly four hundred years, mainly as farmers. Then the climate grew much colder, until it was no longer possible to pasture sheep and cattle. Pack ice increased and navigation to and from Europe became more and more difficult and dangerous and, finally, impossible. Then the Greenland Norse farmer-settlers vanished. What happened to them remains a matter that historians, and others, have been debating for a long time.

We learned that Greenland was officially bilingual in Danish and Inuktitut. The Danes had started training native Greenlanders as schoolteachers back in the 1920s to ensure that children would be educated in both languages. Greenlanders were encouraged to attend university in Denmark at government expense, and many had done so.

The Danes were certainly one up on us in the field of education. In the 1970s we had only just begun to train the Inuit to become teachers and very few had gone south to study at Canadian universities.

Walking back to our hotel we encountered more than a few drunks wandering around. Prostitutes could be seen dallying on street corners—small, dark women in slacks and nylon jackets. Back at the hotel, the bar was teeming with loud, inebriated Greenlanders. I put all this down to the fact that it was Friday night, which is traditionally a time for partying in our towns and cities too. But we were to witness the same scene every evening we were in Godthåb.

This didn't surprise Farley, who had found the same behaviour in every large settlement in the Canadian north, including Yellowknife, Churchill, and Frobisher Bay. Later that evening, when we Canadians had gathered in the Schreyers' room for a nightcap, we got talking about why this was so. Why is there such an upsurge of social problems when people are uprooted from one culture and find themselves living in another?

Farley's theory was that when any people are collectively divorced from the realities that sustained them for thousands of years, they become hopelessly disoriented and the wonder is that more of them don't go completely around the bend. Ed Schreyer had a theory that it was the most recent arrivals from another culture who had to endure a generation of upheaval, but the second generation fitted in more comfortably. Though this might be true among European settlers in Canada, it didn't explain the despair in some of the communities of indigenous people.

Next day we all dined with Governor Hans Lassen. He and I got into a discussion about the growing independence movement known as Home Rule for Greenland. The governor believed it would eventually happen, but not for a long time. There were simply not enough people in Greenland to support it, he said. Iceland, which had been a Danish territory until 1944, had been able to become independent only because it had reached a population of 250,000. Greenland had just 50,000. The best procedure, he believed, was to transfer government authority to Greenland very gradually over a period of years. However, many Greenlanders were impatient with this concept. They wanted a referendum now, and early severance of Danish control, with a few exceptions such as foreign affairs and defence.

This had a familiar ring to my Canadian ears. It sounded like sovereignty-association, a governing arrangement that quite a few Quebecers were advocating in order to be free of control by the rest of Canada.

Denmark was in no hurry to drop the reins. The Danes we had been meeting appeared content to remain in Greenland indefinitely and a surprising number of them had married Greenlanders and made this their permanent home. The blending of races had been taking place for centuries, which explained why many native surnames were Danish, while first names were Inuit. Only in the very far north, in the vicinity of Thule, could the people still be classified as essentially Inuit, rather than the vigorous mix that constitutes the race known as Greenlanders.

Godthåb was interesting, but we were delighted to be invited to make a boat voyage into the fjords that penetrate deep into the interior country beyond the town. We were to be among the very first guests to stay at a remote and most unusual hotel that had opened only a few weeks earlier.

We made the voyage in a sturdy, double-ended vessel of the same general shape and size as the Viking ships that had come this way so long before. The major difference was that our boat was propelled by a diesel engine and not by sail.

The waters under our keel were as still as a millpond. As we chugged deeper and deeper into the maze of fjords, we were flanked on all sides by stony mountains ground down by the glaciers that had covered them until only six or seven thousand years earlier. Sharing the waterways with us were hundreds of miniature blue-and-white icebergs that had been

Claire with Lily and Ed Schreyer, Greenland, 1974

"calved" by the great interior ice cap. At times we sailed so close to these convoluted, floating sculptures we could almost reach out and touch them.

It was an other-worldly voyage, during which we spoke very little to one another. We were too enthralled by the magnitude of the scene. Late in the day we rounded the base of a sweeping conical mountain and dropped anchor at the foot of a stunningly green valley. Not far from a small sandy beach stood a low, unobtrusive wooden structure: the Hotel Qorqot, the first evidence we had seen of any other human life in this lonely landscape. A crystalline brook of ice water tumbled down the slope behind the hotel, coursing through tundra meadows where a few dozen sheep were pasturing. We could see at a glance why, a thousand years earlier, Norse settlers from Iceland had chosen to homestead here in what came to be known as the Western Settlement. Despite all the changes in the climate, sheep farming had survived on this spot until a generation earlier and was now being revived by the owners of the newly built hotel, Lars and Kirsten Rasmussen.

This young couple was waiting to welcome us. Lars was the son of Greenland's most famous explorer, Knud Rasmussen, an intrepid traveller who, early in the twentieth century, had made a dog-sled journey from Greenland to Alaska. His son, Lars, had dreamed of a life that would combine the best of Inuit ways with the best of the Old Norse. Hotel Qorqot was his attempt at bringing the dream to life. He and his wife believed they could introduce visitors from other lands to the magnificent reality of Greenland.

The food they served was local and delicious. They fed us caribou, trout, wild berries, ptarmigan, and all sorts of vegetables that they grew in their own small greenhouse. However, it was not the food or the cozy rooms that impressed us most. It was the land.

Farley and I walked way up the long slope of the valley toward the far wall of glacial ice. A herd of caribou noticed us and came close to investigate before they snorted indifferently and cantered away. We were startled by a giant arctic hare as big as a spaniel, which popped out from a clump of dwarf birch. We listened to the cackling of ptarmigan on the rocky slopes above us. A magnificent white-tailed sea eagle screamed past our heads and landed on a rock a mere hundred feet from us, the first time I had ever seen such a bird.

It was a scene of primordial grandeur. When we told our hosts, Lars and Kirsten, how much pleasure this place had given us, Lars said, "Then we have succeeded with what we hope to do. We want this place to be a serene retreat from the world, a haven for those who want to experience the old reality." Learning that Farley was a writer of books, he went on to offer us the hospitality of this hotel for the winter, at rates that would barely cover his costs.

It certainly was tempting: winter in Greenland with nothing more pressing to do than write a book and take a daily hike in the stupendous countryside. If only Farley and I could have stayed. But our life was too complicated for that. In a few days we had to return to Canada. At least, that was the plan.

Our excursion to Qorqot made the perfect finale to our journey. On Monday morning we were back in Godthåb ready to board a helicopter to take us to the airport at Söndre Strömfjord. However, due to delays the previous day, all helicopter flights were fully booked and we would have to wait yet another day.

The next morning we were at the terminal by 7:30. Soon afterwards John and Ellen Kronborg arrived, along with Dortë, the governor's secretary, all of whom had come to bid us goodbye. Our flight was called (it was the only flight scheduled for that day) and we climbed on board the mighty Sikorsky. The blades whirled faster and faster…then slower and slower, until they stopped. We were told to get off because Sukkertoppen, our refuelling stop, was fogged in.

Our Greenland friends, who were obviously used to this sort of thing, had lingered in the terminal, so we joined them for some excellent coffee and chatted for an hour or so before again boarding the helicopter. The engines roared. The blades whirled faster and faster…and then slower and slower, until they stopped. The pilot announced that a "mechanical adjustment" was necessary.

It was then nearly noon so we insisted our hosts go about their own business, which they did. It was anyone's guess how long we would have to wait this time.

We found a café, where we bought sandwiches. I also bought a Danish women's magazine full of decorating ideas; then we returned to the terminal to wait and wait. Farley got into a conversation with a young Greenlander. He was from Holsteinsborg, a community further north, but he had spent several years at a university in Denmark and graduated with a degree in social work. He was a strong advocate of Home Rule for Greenland. He and "many more people," he declared emphatically, were fed up with the Danish administration and the "stupid way they had ruled Greenland for centuries." He believed the Greenlanders alone, in an elected parliament, were far better qualified to govern Greenland. "Danes," he stated loudly, "do not understand Greenland. The time has come to kick them out!"

This was a shock to me. All the Danes we had met were, I thought, kind people with the best interests of Greenlanders at heart. But I wasn't a Greenlander. I hadn't lived my life under the colonial administration of a completely alien people.

Finally, in mid-afternoon, we re-boarded the helicopter and, after a couple of heart-stopping, faltering attempts at taking off, managed to stay up in the air all the way to Sukkertoppen and then on to Söndre Strömfjord. By the time we got there I was a total wreck, cursing whoever it was who had invented the helicopter. I can't describe how reassuring it was to see our own, unassuming Canadian plane on the tarmac, waiting to take us home.

Ed, whose curiosity is insatiable, had spent some time checking the hotel registers in both Godthåb and Söndre Strömfjord. He discovered that the main foreign clients in both places were from the Sikorsky Corporation, an American helicopter manufacturer. He guessed they were mechanics and engineers trying to keep the Greenland fleet flying.

"They'd be so much better off flying Beavers and Otters," Ed remarked. "Canadian bush planes They can land almost anywhere on floats, skis, or big wheels, and can get along without airports if they have to. Real Canadian work horses. And safe ones too They're sold all over the world. Why not here?"

Ewan had the answer. "It's simple, Ed. Salesmanship. The Americans have a military presence in Greenland. They lean on the Danes to buy their products. *C'est la vie.*"

I felt very tired by the time we boarded the plane for our return flight to Frobisher Bay. We all were weary, and most of us hoped to doze off on the two-hour flight. And we did, but not before we were served a depressingly Canadian meal: a sandwich made with stale bread, with instant coffee and a sticky dessert covered with artificial whipped cream. When it came to cuisine in the far north, the Greenlanders won hands down.

I was so happy to have been able to see Greenland with my own eyes. How was I to know that over the next twenty-five years I would visit Greenland five more times?

Chapter Twenty-eight

BY 1974 I HAD BEGUN to dread Christmas. The season I had adored in my childhood had lost its magic. Even into my twenties I still loved all the little rituals like wrapping gifts and decorating the tree. When Farley and I moved to Newfoundland, where they actually celebrated the Twelve Days of Christmas (something I had only sung about but never seen), I was fascinated. Those masquerading mummers who visited from house to house gave me a sense that I had fallen through the looking glass and landed in a nicer place, where people entertained one another rather than silently staring at a television screen.

Once we moved back to Ontario I was confronted by a season that was neither nostalgic nor merry. For over a month, stores played Christmas pop tunes. Homeowners competed with one another for the gaudiest display of coloured lights. Children told their parents what gifts they wanted—and expected to get. It was all about money, not fun. But worse than all this was our personal juggling act. Would we spend the big day with Farley's mother (inviting my mother as well) or would we spend it with Farley's father and Barbara? We tried to alternate each year but it was never that simple. Would anyone invite Helen for Christmas dinner if we were away at Angus's place? And when could Farley fit in a Christmas visit with his two sons, who stayed with their mother on Christmas Day? Whatever we decided to do meant a lot of driving in winter weather and a double load of preparations.

At Christmas I was responsible for everything except the driving. Baking, shopping, gift-wrapping, decorating the house and the tree, and sending out about a hundred cards were all mine to do. Farley just shrugged and delivered mini sermons to the effect that the hyped-up, consumer Christmas was a lot of nonsense and I, and everyone else, should ignore it.

But I couldn't. Christmas is a season of giving. Everyone else in our extended family was either too old, too far away, or living in quarters that were too small to cope with it all, so I was stuck.

David Mowat, then eighteen, had come to live with us that winter because of conflict with his mother and brother; but he wasn't happy living with us either. He continued to indulge in the unsettling habit of disappearing—often for days at a time. He had given up on high school and was in no hurry to find a job, spending most of his time at our house sleeping or raiding the refrigerator late at night. His presence did not lighten my Christmas overload and his lack of motivation was a constant irritant to his industrious, self-disciplined father.

That year we had been invited to spend Christmas Day with Angus and Barbara. Despite my feelings about her I was pleased to be going somewhere, even for a day. The tension in our house was getting me down.

As she usually did, my mother had arrived a few days prior to Christmas. By then she knew about Angus's relationship with Barbara and they had invited her for Christmas as well, along with David.

On December 23 Barbara phoned to say that Angus had had emergency dental work. He was in pain. It would be too much for him to have the four of us for a visit on Christmas Day. I said we were sorry to hear about it and we would visit them some other time.

That left me with one day to produce Christmas dinner at home. After a hurried visit to the supermarket I spent December 24 in the kitchen. Luckily my mother and David had discovered they both like to play cribbage, so that kept them out of my way. I invited Farley's mother, Helen, and her sister, Frances, to join us as well, since they would otherwise only have had one another for company for Christmas. In the end our festive day wasn't all that bad. Even David had bought gifts for everyone.

The next day, Angus phoned to say he had gone skating on the frozen Bay of Quinte on Christmas Day. At the age of 82 he was pleased with himself to be able to do such a thing. I asked him about his teeth. "Oh, fine, fine. No trouble at all," he replied.

Had Barbara invented this tale of a toothache simply because she was too lazy to prepare a holiday dinner for Angus's family, or was this just another subterfuge to keep us apart on a day when we had anticipated a family get-together? I wondered what she had told Angus about our absence. Were we somehow being blamed for not being there? I couldn't give her the benefit of the doubt any more. Despite my charitable inclinations I had really begun to loathe her.

The generally unloved month of January was emerging as my favourite month of the year, mainly because the work and anguish of Christmas were over. But January didn't turn out very well that year.

Farley's brother, John, had a friend—an electrician who needed a helper—who hired David. Soon after that we found a local family with whom he could board. There now seemed to be a semblance of order in his life—as well as in ours. We felt we could once again resume our winter routine: five days a week at the Indian Summer cottage and two days in Port Hope.

We had only been at the cottage for a couple of days when our dog Albert died. Born in LaPoile, Newfoundland, Albert had been our first dog. He was unique: a dauntless creature who had charged through life with bravura and style. Early in January he was stricken by a series of seizures that left him dazed and disoriented. Farley took him to a veterinarian and a drug was prescribed to help his ailing heart; but in the end nothing could save this beloved old friend.

We buried him in a grove of cedar trees on a moonless, snowless night. January 1975 had been a season of rain and freezing drizzle—a depressing, grey month but sufficiently frost-free to allow us to bury a dead dog on the twenty-seventh of January.

Although well aware that he had been growing old, we weren't prepared for how much we would miss him. In a way he was the child I never had, this twelve-year-old creature who was at the end of his long life and not at the beginning, as a child would have been. We had shared so many adventures with Albert. It felt as if, without him, there wouldn't be any more fun in our lives.

We still had Edward, Albert's son, a good dog but not the heroic fellow his father had been. Deaf since birth, Edward had always lived with other dogs, including, at various times, his mother and sister as well as his father, and he had learned to follow them. Now that his father was dead and there were no other dogs in our household, he was bewildered. It took him a while to learn to watch us more carefully for clues as to what might be happening next.

We stayed at the cottage for a few more days but neither of us had the heart to buckle down to the discipline needed to write effectively. We decided we needed a break and remembered several long-standing invitations from friends around Ontario. February might not be the best time for travelling but Farley made some phone calls and arrangements and a few days later we were on our way to stay with distant cousins of his who lived on their family farm not far from London, Ontario.

Tom Bedggood was descended from the Farley family that had settled in St. Thomas, Ontario, in the 1840s. So, too, was Farley Mowat, on his mother's side. For many years Tom had kept in touch with Farley's mother and her sister, and with us, always urging us to come for a visit.

Tom and his wife, Helen, were just the right sort of people to cheer us up. Hospitable and generous, and secure in their own lives, they quickly made us feel at home. Tom was about to retire from Ontario Hydro and looked forward to spending more time on his hobbies: making his own wine and refinishing furniture. They had a perky little dachshund who immediately made friends with our Edward.

One day we asked the Bedggoods if we might invite Alice Munro, who was then living in London, over to their cozy house, explaining that she was another writer who was going through a rather lonely time. Generous to a fault, they insisted Alice, and her eight-year-old daughter, come for supper. We all got along together very well, partly because the Bedggoods were the kind of people Alice wrote about in her enchanting short stories set in rural Ontario.

Alice was still teaching creative writing to university students "who had never heard of me," she told us dryly. Her reputation was soaring in both Canada and the United States, as we well knew, but Canadian literature as a university subject in Canada had just barely taken hold.

After the visit, we drove Alice and her daughter, Andrea, back to her apartment on Oxford Street and she invited us in for a nightcap. What I liked about her as a person, as well as a writer, was that there was no trace of feminist militancy. She recognized the inequity of women's status without being overtly angry about it... unlike many women writers at the time, who hammered the point until the reader became sick and tired of being lectured.

Claire with Max and Aileen Braithwaite, Port Carling, Ontario, 1975

After Andrea had gone to bed Alice confided that there was a new man in her life and, sometime in the not-too-distant future, they planned to marry; but her daughter didn't like the idea so Alice was trying to break the news gently.

After a fond farewell to the Bedggoods and their happy home, we drove east and north to the Muskoka region. Our destination was a few miles from Port Carling to visit with Max and Aileen Braithwaite, who had sensibly given up any thought of making a home in the Magdalen Islands. Instead, they had winterized their cottage on the shore of Brandy Lake.

The day we arrived Max had received a copy of a paperback edition of his newest novel, *A Privilege and a Pleasure*. The cover was illustrated with a picture of a semi-nude woman—more typical of the spicy romance novels sold in racks at neighbourhood drugstores and supermarkets.

That blatantly sexy cover on a novel by a serious Canadian writer—even a novel that did revolve around an illicit love affair—was causing an uproar. Several radio broadcasters and newspaper reporters had already phoned

Max to ask what he was going to do about the lurid cover. Didn't he consider it an insult? Should the book be banned, someone wanted to know?

Max told them all that he thought the drawing of the scantily clad woman was beautiful. If his publishers had decided it was the appropriate cover, it was quite all right with him. Max knew, as we did, that controversy helps to sell a book. He was in a rare good mood that evening. Luckily Farley had brought along a bottle of champagne. We had not mentioned it beforehand but that day was my birthday, so we had a joint celebration of Max's sexy book cover and my forty-two years of life.

A couple of days later we drove south to Lakefield, the small town near Peterborough where Margaret Laurence had recently bought a home. Margaret, by then in her late forties, had finally found "a place to roost" after a peripatetic life that had taken her to Africa, England, and several places in Canada. For ten years she had owned a house in England that she had imagined would be her permanent home, but in the end her roots had brought her back to Canada. Long divorced from Jack Laurence, she was now living alone in a solid brick house on Regent Street in downtown Lakefield.

Being the warm, welcoming person that she was, she attracted a steady stream of visitors: old friends, new friends, and her grown son and daughter. When we arrived we found novelist Marian Engel there. Marian was on the verge of breaking up with her husband, Howard Engel, and was looking for moral support from Margaret and possibly a shoulder to cry on.

I was sorry to hear about yet another marital casualty in the writing community. The few times I had met Howard I had found him an engaging fellow and I couldn't imagine what had gone wrong with the marriage. They had two children—twins, a boy and a girl aged ten, who were staying with their father while Marian tried to "sort out her priorities."

Marian had arrived by bus from Toronto. Neither she nor Margaret had ever learned to drive a car, which was why, Margaret told us, she had chosen this house in the centre of a small town, so that she could walk to various stores, to the post office, and to the bus station.

Marian had recently been commissioned to write a book about Canada's best-known islands. This was to be a collaboration with a photographer to produce a coffee-table book for the Christmas trade. The Magdalens were

Farley with Margaret Laurence and Marian Engel, Lakefield, Ontario, 1975

on her list of places to visit, so she asked us if she could come and see us in the summer and learn more about the islands. We were glad to help.

Margaret was then writer-in-residence at Trent University in Peterborough. Her celebrated masterpiece, *The Diviners*, had been published only a year earlier and she was Canada's most popular and successful novelist, having published five major novels over the previous ten years. She wasn't doing much serious writing that winter. Her involvement with the university was consuming most of her time and energy, and she was so uneasy about getting up in front of a group of students to give a talk that she literally trembled before, and during, her time at the podium.

"A good belt of scotch would help," Farley suggested.

"Absolutely not," she protested. "Afterwards, by all means. But not before."

Margaret had a fondness for scotch whisky, but was too conscientious to rely on it for courage. However, at home her self-imposed restraint often vanished.

That night Margaret, Marian, and Farley did some serious drinking and some serious talking about, inevitably, the writing life. Marian was at work on a novel about a woman living in northern Ontario who had fallen in love with a bear. It was not the sort of love one might feel for a pet but a genuine sexual longing for one particular bear who hung around her fictional character's cabin. This struck me as an improbable tale, knowing the little I did about the unpredictable and sometimes unfriendly behaviour of bears. Marian's main concern was how she was going to find time to finish the manuscript if, and when, she left her husband, because she would then have to find some sort of steady work. She was hoping to get a position as writer-in-residence at some university to support herself and her two children.

As the evening wore on, Margaret became morose about her writing. She lamented that she didn't have another novel in her. She felt she had written her last. The three of us tried to reassure her that this was a temporary writer's block, and that all writers went through dry spells; but she remained convinced she had no literary future.

As it turned out, she was right. Over the next dozen years, before her death in 1987, she wrote only a minor memoir and three short children's books. There were no more Staceys or Rachels or Morags, those gutsy women who had infused so much life into her major works.

Marian and Margaret complained that writing books was such a solitary vocation. And indeed it is. Farley acknowledged that he was luckier than these two women because he had a wife. At the end of his long day at the typewriter he could emerge from his labours and have lunch or supper with me and I would sympathize when his work was not going well or rejoice when it did.

I went to bed around midnight but the others sat around talking until 3:00 a.m. Farley was not feeling particularly bright next morning when he drove Marian to the bus station, then returned to have breakfast with Margaret before he and I set off for Port Hope.

On our return home Farley was greeted with the news that Coles Bookstore in Toronto was selling remaindered American editions of two of his current books at giveaway prices. He would not receive any royalty payments on these sales. Selling remaindered US editions of Canadian books in Canada was unfair and unprincipled, but there was no legislation to protect Canadian writers or publishers from this kind of exploitation.

Jack McClelland was furious that books by two of his best-selling authors—Pierre Berton and Farley Mowat—were being sold at less than half the price of the Canadian editions. He planned a protest in front of the offending bookstore and wanted Farley and Pierre to take part.

Before this issue could be resolved Farley had another hassle: this time with the Department of Revenue. Best-selling authors had often been the targets of income-tax inspectors. I suspect the tax people had the idea that these authors were rolling in money—a concept originating in the United States, where prominent writers were sometimes paid astronomical sums for best-sellers and for movie rights to their books. A popular novel in the USA might sell a million copies and indeed make its author wealthy. A similar book in Canada would be counted a runaway best-seller if it sold twenty thousand copies. With a royalty of ten, or even fifteen per cent, on a list price of ten dollars (the average sale price in 1975) for a book that had taken one or two or more years to produce, even the most successful Canadian authors could hardly be considered filthy rich.

Back in 1971 Farley had begun giving his manuscripts, letters, and research papers to the archives of McMaster University in Hamilton. These donations were evaluated by a federal archivist and Farley received a tax credit for them. Now the Department of Revenue demanded Farley prove this was not equivalent to income. It was one more irritation for him to have to search through four years of receipts and statements in order to appease some number-cruncher from the government.

The last straw was David Mowat. During our absence he had quit his job and disappeared from his boarding house. His landlady had no idea where he had gone; nor did his employer, who hadn't seen him for a week. Fran Mowat had not heard from him either.

Farley and I both felt utterly defeated by David's behaviour. He wasn't aggressive or belligerent or rude. He simply wandered away. We could never count on him to be where he said he would be, to stay in one place, or to tell us where he planned to go or where he had been. However much we, or Fran, or his various teachers had tried to make a responsible citizen out of David, it hadn't worked.

Farley shrugged in exasperation. "He's almost nineteen. Old enough to vote or join the army—not that he would do either. There is nothing more you or I or Fran can do. He's going to live his life his way, no matter what. It's time to let go."

Eventually David phoned to say he had found a place to stay in Orangeville. Did he have a job? I asked. He thought a friend of his might have something lined up, but he didn't say what. Did he want any of the clothes he had left behind in his room? No, he didn't. Could we please have his phone number? Sure, as soon as he got a phone. What about his address? He was moving to a new place next week. He'd be sure to let us know. He never did.

At this time Farley's doctor diagnosed high blood pressure, which wasn't surprising. The doctor prescribed some pills and mentioned that a holiday might be a good idea.

"Let's go east," Farley said the next morning.

"Where?"

"The Maggies. We have a perfectly good house sitting there empty."

"But it's only the first of March. It's midwinter out there. The Gulf is full of ice. There's no ferry," I countered.

"We can fly. We'll drive to Charlottetown and fly over. The airport is open year-round. I just bloody well want to get away from . . . everything."

On second thought it wasn't such a crazy idea. I wanted to get away too. The Magdalen Islands in winter would certainly be a retreat. We could put distance between us and a load of hassles and disappointments. We could get back to our writing. Within a week we had cancelled commitments, postponed appointments, made an arrangement with a neighbour to check our house, got the car serviced, and bought a folding dog kennel for Edward so he could fly with us to those ice-shrouded islands.

The gods must have wanted us to make the journey. We drove from Port Hope to Charlottetown in two days on the heels of a storm that had passed through, leaving all of eastern Canada deep in dazzling white snow under blue skies. The flight out to the islands in the little Dart Herald departed right on time and we got there without a hitch.

Our friends the Warrens, who had been there all winter, were delighted that we were coming back so soon. They had turned on the heat and the running water in our house. They met us at the airport and drove us back to Grande Entrée.

The islands, deep in snow and encircled by an ocean of drifting ice, turned out to be even more captivating in winter than in summer. There

Edward on top of a snowbank, the Magdalen Islands, 1975

were no tourists tramping across our property. The local people were all too busy with the seal hunt or with preparations for the start of the lobster season on the first of May to bother with us.

We stayed for two months. Storms came and went, leaving us with blinding spring sunlight on mounds of melting snow. We both wrote for several hours a day. For recreation we took long walks on ice-encrusted beaches. We had some get-togethers with Arnold and Vi, and with a few local friends, like Father Landry. In April the Warrens left for a month-long trip to Ontario, leaving their Labrador dog, Prince, with us. There were times after their departure when I felt lonesome but the peace and beauty of the place, and our orderly days, were exactly what we needed.

Because the previous months had been so full of interruptions Farley had not had time to concentrate on writing a new book. Jack McClelland had suggested an anthology of Farley's best short fiction in order to have a Farley Mowat title on the fall list for 1975, so Farley spent the rest of the winter editing a collection of his short stories. Most of them had been published in various magazines over the previous twenty years.

Peter Davison, at Atlantic Monthly Press in Boston, did not agree with Jack's endeavour to have a new Mowat book published every second year, at least. He believed Farley should publish fewer, but better, books. In his opinion producing a book a year left too little time for reflection. However, Peter apparently did not grasp one significant difference between writing in Canada and writing in the United States. A best-selling book in the States, with its much larger market, could support its author for several years and allow the luxury of time to ponder the next book, whereas in Canada most authors and their publishers, if they were to survive in our much smaller market, had to publish much more frequently.

Farley selected eleven of his short stories, all of them set in the far north. Searching for a title for this book was not as difficult as usual. The title of one of the stories suited the nature of the book. It would be called *The Snow Walker*.

It was still cold in early May when we left the Magdalens. I would have liked to have stayed and observed the slow, brightening spring gradually turn into summer, but Farley had arranged to take his son Sandy on a trip to Scotland. So we flew back to Charlottetown, picked up our Volvo, and drove home to Port Hope.

A week later Farley and Sandy left Toronto on a flight to Glasgow, where they rented a car and set out on the long drive north to Caithness at the northern tip of Scotland. Their objective was Canisbay parish, from which their ancestor John Mowat had sailed to Upper Canada in 1812 as a sergeant with the British Army defending Upper and Lower Canada from invasion by the United States, a battle in which Farley was still engaged.

Sergeant John saw the possibilities in Upper Canada and after the war sent for his bride and they settled in Kingston. He could hardly have imagined that more than a century and a half later his great-great-grandson and his great-great-great-grandson would be flying back to visit the humble croft where he had been born and raised.

Chapter Twenty-nine

By the beginning of July we were all back in the Magdalens, including Sandy Mowat, who stayed most of the summer. During the winter Arnold and Vi had indulged in their true passion—flying—and had bought a second-hand (or maybe tenth-hand) two-seater airplane. They planned to use it for short flights around the islands and occasional journeys to PEI or Cape Breton. I had to admire their pluck and I wished them well—as long as they didn't expect me to join them up in the sky in their tiny aircraft. To me their plane looked like the one I had seen in photos of Amelia Earhart as she embarked on her round-the-world flight, from which she disappeared in 1937.

In midsummer Joan Richards, by then seven months pregnant with her third child, packed up her belongings and their two little daughters and went to stay with her parents in Charlottetown. There had been some sort of row—apparently with Stuart's mother and some neighbours—and Joan was angry because Stuart had failed to take her side. I missed Joan very much. However, we did see lonesome Stuart more often than usual.

One day Stuart suggested he and Farley should go camping together. He owned a tent and camping gear and he was familiar with Dune du Sud—a ten-mile stretch of sandy beaches that could only be reached by boat, a place his father had taken the family for picnics when he was a child. No one lived anywhere nearby; the adjacent lagoon was home to dozens of grey seals, and the sky and the shores were full of marine birds. Farley was agreeable, so the two men set off in our motor boat one warm August morning.

I was glad to have a couple of days to myself to get back to the book I was ever so slowly writing. But first there was a mountain of laundry to do. My spin-dry washing machine was soon chugging diligently away. As always, I blessed the person who had invented this trusty little machine that had liberated me from the wringer-washer. It made quite a racket when it was spinning the moisture out of the clothes, but that was a small price to pay.

Because of the noise I did not hear the approach of a motor vehicle until it was roaring through our back yard, barely missing the kitchen porch. It was a four-wheel-drive Bronco and it had come, not from our side road, but from the top of our hill, having been driven across the beach in front of the Warrens' house then upward around the cape. When the driver reached the top of our hill, where there was a tangle of trees, he realized the only way out was either to retrace his route back around the cape or else drive downhill through our field and yard to reach our driveway and then the road.

I dashed outside in time to see the Bronco screech to a stop in front of our gate, which was wired shut. A passenger was trying to get the gate open when Arnold and Vi arrived on the scene, panting, with me following close behind.

Out of breath and furious, I glared at the driver. He and his passengers—another young man and three teenaged girls—stared back at us insolently.

"You could have killed our dog!" I shouted angrily. And it was true. Edward had been in the house with me, although normally he would have been lying on the grass outside watching the driveway as he waited for Farley to return. He would not have seen the vehicle approaching from behind and even if the driver had seen the dog, he was travelling at such a speed he would not have been able to stop in time.

The driver gave me a black look. He couldn't have cared less about our dog, or our property.

"Were you born 'ere?" he asked defiantly. He was playing his trump card.

At this point Arnold stepped up to the driver's open window and, with the voice of authority he had acquired in the air force, demanded to see the young man's driver's licence.

Taken aback, the fellow hauled out his wallet. His licence showed he was twenty years old and lived in Ste Foy, a suburb of Quebec City. He and his friends were the worst kind of tourists, the kids from the cities who treated the place as if it was their personal sandbox.

Arnold shoved the wallet back at him.

"You're trespassing on private land. Get out of here and don't come back!"

Vi opened the gate. Wheels spun in the gravel. The driver turned sharply and the Bronco sped up the road and was gone.

"Damned four-wheel drives," Arnold muttered into the cloud of dust. "Damned barbarians."

"Good thing you saw them roar up to our hill," I gasped. "I had the washing machine going so I didn't hear them until they were outside the back door. It was sheer good luck Edward was indoors."

"Idiots! They could have gone over the cliff and ended up in the ocean," Vi added.

Indeed, they easily could have. In many places the cliff edge was dangerously undercut—strong enough to support the weight of a person but not a motor vehicle. They could have tumbled down the height of a four-storey building into the surf below. At that moment I was so furious at them I wouldn't have cared if they had.

"Claire, come over and have supper with us," invited Vi, who could see how disturbed I was. I felt as if I had been assaulted in my own little sanctuary. The tire tracks the Bronco had gouged down the hill and across our lawn would remain there for a year or two to remind me of this violation—and the nasty touch of chauvinism that had accompanied it.

Farley and Stuart returned home the next afternoon, a day early.

"I didn't expect to see you two so soon. How was your camping trip?"

"Hmm..." Farley began. "Dune du Sud's a lovely place all right and we had great weather but...we sure in hell weren't alone there."

"Surely it wasn't crowded?" I asked, incredulous.

"Not exactly," Stuart explained apologetically. "It's just that the four-wheel drives have discovered they can get to it. They were roaring up and down like it was a drag strip. It's pathetic. That place used to be so peaceful."

"So much for the nests of the piping plover," Farley added angrily.

I made a pot of tea for the three of us, then told them my sorry tale. It didn't improve Farley's mood. He resolved to put some booby traps out along the headlands: ditches, piles of logs, anything he could devise that would impede vehicles and their rampaging drivers. I told him Arnold was thinking of doing the same thing.

"But nothing can be done to keep those bastards off the dunes and the beaches," said Stuart.

"We could string wire across their paths. We did that when I was in the army in Italy, patrolling behind the German lines."

"Attached to what? No trees out there," Stuart noted.

"Come on guys," I cautioned. "We don't need any more warfare around here. We can't take charge of all the shoreline on the islands. Close to home is what matters."

We stayed close to home for the rest of the summer, making no further attempts at camping on Dune du Sud or anywhere else.

Marian Engel arrived at the end of August to continue research for her book about Canadian islands. She phoned to tell us she and her two children were staying in a rooming house in Grindstone, surely the least appealing place anyone could find on the Magdalens. Marian, who didn't drive, wanted to know how they could get to Grande Entrée to visit us. Farley suggested they hitchhike, which was still a safe, reliable way to get around locally. On their first try they were picked up in a matter of minutes by a French-speaking Madelinôt, who drove them right to our front gate. Madelinôts would not leave a mother and two children stranded on the side of the road.

Marian, who was the same age as I was—forty-two—had a girlish, round face, dishevelled brown hair, and a somewhat chunky figure. She was particularly attached to a hand-knit, Irish fisherman's sweater and her well-worn jeans. I don't recall seeing her dressed in anything else, wherever I happened to meet her after that.

The day was sunny and breezy and the islands were at their pristine best, so we suggested that Marian and the ten-year-old twins, William and Charlotte, join us for a stroll around the capes. It was an enchanting walk and we stopped frequently to peer down from the cliffs at the glittering sea boiling in and out of the water-worn grottoes far below us. Further along the path there was a blowhole the size of a dishpan where the pounding ocean had gradually penetrated the sandstone. When a wave rolled in beneath us it sent a column of spray up through the hole. It looked like a miniature geyser and the kids were fascinated by it.

Having spent a gruelling summer of travel, coupled with the depressing details surrounding the demise of her marriage, Marian began to visibly relax. Here were the ocean, the cliffs, the birds, and the kids having fun.

What's more, she could enjoy it in the company of newfound friends—us. As we completed the circular route and were passing the Warrens' house we saw Vi out digging carrots in her vegetable garden.

"Come on over, you and Arnold. We'll have some lemonade. Or whatever," I called.

We gathered in the circle of garden chairs behind our house. Marian drank beer straight from the bottle, a hearty chug-a-lug that soon led to a second beer, which unleashed lamentations. Now that she no longer lived with her husband she was constantly broke. But just as bad, she complained, was the lack of fucking in her life. She used the word right in front of her children, which I could see was a shock to Arnold and Vi, as indeed it was to me. In fact, she sprinkled the F-word through her conversation as freely as I might have used the word "damn." I reminded myself that times change and so do expletives. Marian's kids seemed quite accustomed to their mother's vocabulary.

Marian and the twins stayed for supper, as did Arnold and Vi. I served my standby meal for unexpected company—spaghetti with Farley's homemade sauce. Vi brought over a banana nut loaf for dessert. We drank several bottles of Arnold's homemade wine. The merriment lasted for hours. Then we had to face the problem of how to get Marian and the twins back to their rooming house in Grindstone. None of us was in any shape to drive them. In the end Marian slept in one of our two spare bedrooms and William in the other. Charlotte stayed over at the Warrens'.

The Engel family didn't want to spend the rest of the week in Grindstone so we phoned Rhoda Turner to ask if anyone was renting her cottage. No one was so we made the decision for Marian that she move to Old Harry for the remainder of her Magdalen visit.

We saw them often after that, fetching them to our place so they could join us for swims and meals. The day before they were to leave we organized a picnic for them out on uninhabited Seal Island—even though we knew we would likely get a nasty phone call afterwards from Ethel Kincaid, who, we had discovered, was the unidentified caller who claimed she owned the island.

The children loved Seal Island and busied themselves digging for buried treasure, which was the theme of a book they had recently read.

Farley encouraged their fantasy and joined them in their pursuit. Lacking shovels, they were all using the large clam shells that littered the shorelines.

Marian and I sat idly on the shore. She drank beer from the bottle while I sipped red wine from a plastic cup. Marian was in a wistful mood. Summer was over and her research for the Canadian islands book was almost complete.

"I'll tell you something," she confided sadly. "There are a lot of women out there who've left their marriages. And now they wish they had the guy back."

I didn't know what to reply. Did she want Howard back? I didn't like to ask. I knew very well that having a husband made a lot of things easier. The list of advantages was long, yet I wasn't about to mention any of this to Marian, who had recently made some wrenching decisions about her life.

"But," she sighed with resignation, "when it's over, it's over." She downed the rest of a beer.

So many marriages had broken down over the previous few years. There were, of course, valid reasons why unhappy, destructive marriages should end, but it seemed to me, in quite a few cases, that feminist dogma was the driving force behind the break-up rather than some alleged incompatibility. "Who needs a man around the house?" was the unspoken creed of some women who set out to prove they could do the same sort of work that most men did and, apart from their biological role in human reproduction, men were irrelevant and not worth the bother of sharing your life with. But I wasn't about to raise this issue with Marian as she sat there thinking about which fork in the road her life, her kids, and her writing career were about to take.

"Hey, come and see what we've found!" Farley called.

We walked over and found him holding the skull of a young walrus. William was ecstatic. This wasn't a chest of gold doubloons, but a skeleton of any kind was a good second best, especially a walrus.

The two children continued digging energetically in the sandy soil, unearthing bits of bone and ancient, yellow teeth.

These islands had swarmed with walrus at one time, Farley told them. When Jacques Cartier sailed here in 1534 the beaches were loaded with more walrus than could be counted. Yet by the end of the nineteenth century they were extinct in the entire Gulf of St. Lawrence.

"What happened to them?" Marian asked.

"They were slaughtered—by the Basques, the Portuguese, the French, the British—by us, the greedy human race. Walrus ivory was a precious commodity, as were the hides and the oil. So they killed every last walrus they could find. The only walrus to survive now live in the Arctic, their last refuge."

"How awful," I thought. In my mind's eye I could picture these great stretches of beach fringed by thousands of rotund walrus lolling in the surf. And now they were long gone.

"Look, we found another one!" called Charlotte. This second, sand-covered skull even had a few small teeth in it.

Farley inspected it. "Hard to figure why they would be buried here," he pondered. "These are very young animals, too young to have tusks. It wouldn't have been worthwhile to kill them."

"Maybe they died of starvation when their mothers were killed," I speculated. "Their dead bodies would have become putrid so somebody wanted to get rid of them."

"It's possible," Farley agreed. "Anyway, we've got a unique souvenir of our day here, something to remind us of a time when the Maggies were home to a nation of walrus, and very few people."

Marian balked at the idea of her kids taking the crumbling skulls back to Toronto in their luggage so the children settled for a fistful of teeth.

"I'll bet Ethel didn't know she had a treasure trove of walrus bones on 'her' island," I said as we were preparing to leave.

"I doubt she'd consider a pile of old bones a treasure," Farley replied. "Maybe she's like the kids. Maybe she believes there's gold buried in the sand. Could be the reason she gets so possessive whenever she sees anyone out here."

Marian and her twins departed at the end of a week, suntanned, relaxed, and somewhat enlightened about the nature of these enigmatic islands. Farley and I returned to a near-normal existence, including our writing routine.

The two walrus skulls, which now sat on our mantelpiece, had started Farley thinking about all the other creatures that had once existed in great numbers in Atlantic Canada: creatures like the cod fish that had been so abundant in John Cabot's time that his crew could lower a basket over the side of their ship and haul it up full of fish. Farley knew that white bears, now known as polar bears, had also lived along all the shores of Newfoundland, although only occasional stragglers were seen there now. Then there had been the great auk, a flightless, penguin-like bird once common along the Atlantic coast and long since totally extinct. Farley began to wonder about them and about all the other beings whose world this had been before Europeans descended on it.

Although he was then working on a book about the years he spent as a Canadian soldier in Europe during the Second World War, the history of natural life in the Gulf of St. Lawrence intrigued him more and more. Eventually his curiosity would lead him to a full-scale investigation, and then to writing a book about his discoveries. But it would take him five years to research and then another five to write *Sea of Slaughter*. Published in 1984, it is a chilling account of what rapacious human beings have done to life on the Atlantic seaboard over the past four centuries.

The Warrens were driving to Ontario for a month in early October. I jumped at the chance to go with them, to get away from this place where, no matter what I did, I felt I would never be accepted. Accidents of history had defined me as an *Anglais* in this place and, worse, an *Anglais* who hadn't been born here. It sat heavily on me, yet so lightly on Farley. He intended to remain in the Magdalens for many more weeks—an uninterrupted time to finish writing his war memoir, which would be called *And No Birds Sang*. I had writing to do as well but I believed I could do it less stressfully in our home in Port Hope.

The Warrens and I left the islands on board a new car ferry that had recently replaced the ill-named *Manic*. This ferry was the larger *Lucy Maud Montgomery*, which had originally been in service crossing the Northumberland Strait linking PEI and New Brunswick. Farley speculated that she was the only vessel in Canada ever to be named after a Canadian author.

I was not happy that fall. Nor was Farley because once I had left he found the Magdalens a lonely place. We sent a lot of anguished letters to one another, partly because we both expressed ourselves well in letters and partly because long-distance telephone calls to the islands were often static-ridden and barely audible. I despaired that we would ever resolve the problem of where we were going to live together happily. Farley hated "city" life. Even Port Hope, with only nine thousand people at that time, was, to him, urban and crowded. But by then I knew I could never live a fulfilling life on the Magdalen Islands, however beautiful they were.

One October day I heard on the radio news that Margaret Trudeau had given birth to the Trudeaus' third son. He was to be called Michel. Lucky devils, I thought, with their perfect little family. I wondered if they had yet built their dream home on the land Pierre owned in the Laurentians.

It was the middle of November before Farley finally returned to Port Hope, and it was the first of December before the two of us set off on one of those long, wearisome, cross-Canada book tours, during which Farley would be promoting his short-story collection, *The Snow Walker*. The book was selling well with good reviews and it was included on all the best-seller lists. Farley wanted me to join him for most of the tour and so I did because we had just spent six weeks apart. As well, the book's success had put him in an optimistic mood for the first time in many months.

December is not considered the best month to promote a book. Book buyers have usually made up their minds by November as to which gift books they will buy. December is more about parties and food and Christmas decorations than it is about book reviews and author interviews. But the publishers had decided better late than never, so off we shuttled between Montreal in the east and Victoria in the west.

As if on cue it snowed in every single city we visited. This would hardly have been a surprise in, say, Ottawa, Winnipeg, or Edmonton; but even balmy British Columbia was deluged with snow the day after we arrived, bringing the city of Vancouver to a standstill. One memory that stands out was the odd sight, in Victoria, of the crew of a television station rushing to the door to stare at the unfamiliar sight of snow falling gently on the street outside.

For us two snow walkers it all seemed singularly appropriate.

Chapter Thirty

EARLY IN 1976 WE BOUGHT Farley's mother's house. She had turned eighty that year and it was becoming too much for her to cope with the complexities of running her own home, especially a very old one that needed so many repairs. In the spring we helped move her into a seniors' apartment complex. After that we arranged to have renovations done to the King Street house during the summer when we would be away. In the fall we would list our John Street house for sale and make our move into Helen's former home.

The move made life easier for Helen and, by selling the house to us, she would still be able to return and visit her former home from time to time. It also partly solved our dilemma. In moving to King Street we would be on a quieter, tree-lined residential street and Farley would not feel as hemmed in as he had on John Street, in the centre of the business district. I hoped he would find it easier to feel at home in Port Hope, at least in the winter.

But one question remained: where were we going to spend our summers for the foreseeable future? I could not picture us growing old in the Magdalen Islands. Even the thought of spending the coming summer there made my heart sink. Seven years earlier we had gone there full of high expectations but now I felt utterly disillusioned. It had been like falling in love with a strikingly beautiful person only to find, as time wore on, that he or she was neurotic, insecure, and given to bouts of ill will and heavy drinking. Inevitably the love affair reaches a bitter end.

Chip Climo, the candle-maker, had come back into our lives briefly while he was visiting Ontario. His marriage to Lindee had ended a year earlier and by then he was living on Cape Breton Island with Sybil, the new lady in his life. Sybil knew a real estate agent in Port Hawkesbury and when we were telling Chip about our difficulties in the Magdalen Islands he suggested Sybil's friend might be able to help us find the sort of place we wanted.

Claire and Farley in front of their King Street house, Port Hope, Ontario

"Let's take a look," Farley said to me. "What have we got to lose?"

A couple of weeks later we contacted Jim Marchand, the real estate salesman, and told him what we were hoping to find.

"We want a fairly large chunk of land," Farley said, "something with a view and a house site. We'll get in a contractor to build a house exactly suited to our needs."

With Jim as our guide we set off to look for the ideal property. Once again I found it bewildering to be in unfamiliar territory looking over assorted fields, forests, and, in one case, a steep hill where the wind nearly knocked me off my feet. I couldn't picture myself in some yet-to-be-built house in any of these unaccustomed locations.

"There's one other place I'd like you to see," said Jim. "It does have a house on it already but it's a great piece of land—on the ocean and very private."

He drove along Highway 4 and, somewhere east of Louisdale, turned off on a gravel road that ran beside an arm of the sea. We could see a house in the distance—tall and white, situated high on a grassy hill.

I think Farley made up his mind before we even reached the place, which turned out to be a peninsula encompassing about one hundred and fifty acres of spruce forest and bog, including a dozen acres of cleared land that had once been pasture. Whichever way we looked we could see the ocean. The property was called "The Brickery" because the French had actually made bricks there in the early 1700s for the construction of the Fortress of Louisbourg, fifty miles to the northeast.

The frame farmhouse was about a hundred years old and needed repairs but it was charming and I could see its possibilities. The middle-aged couple who owned it had recently returned to Cape Breton, along with their teenaged daughter, after twenty-eight years in Toronto. Herman Morrison had been born and raised in that house but had left at the age of nineteen to join the air force. Later he and his wife had settled in Toronto but through all those years he had dreamed of coming back to Brick Point.

Unfortunately, his English-born war bride, Margaret, had not shared that dream. A city woman in both England and Canada, she preferred a modern house in close company with neighbours. This old and isolated house was certainly not that. Margaret was ill at ease with the sound of the wind rattling the windowpanes at night. She especially disliked the narrow, gravel road full of ruts and dust in summer or deep puddles and slush in winter. As a result the house and property were now for sale.

It didn't take us long to make an offer and within days we owned the place. The Morrisons would remain there as our tenants until next year, giving them time to find a new home and giving us time to arrange the sale of our beautiful, but beleaguered, home in the Magdalen Islands.

I didn't relish the prospect of telling Arnold and Vi that we had once again bought another place and this time we really were going to leave the islands. I worried that they would find it lonely there after we had left.

"Look, don't feel you're deserting us," Vi reassured me when we broke the news. "We made our own decision to live here. It's been great. We'll be okay."

Vi was a trooper. I know she was trying to put the best possible face on our impending departure but I still felt we were letting them down, especially when we learned that Stuart and Joan Richards were also planning to leave.

Something else added to my unease in our last months at Grande Entrée. Morris McQuaid died of cancer. Farley believed Morris had really died from a broken heart after the cunning entrepreneur from Cap-aux-Meules had effectively robbed him of the boat that had been his masterpiece, and after Norma, having cleverly persuaded Morris to sell her the schoolhouse, had moved into it along with her French-speaking boyfriend.

Morris's death brought an end to the McQuaid saga. Rose was sent back to the Douglas Hospital in Montreal. Morris's mother, Elva, was ninety years old and frail, and she went to live with a daughter in Grindstone. The McQuaid house, directly across from the Warrens, stood forlorn and empty.

So would ours stand empty after September, unless we could find a buyer, or at least a tenant, for the winter.

We were going to greatly miss the Warrens and Stuart and Joan Richards. The six of us had shared so much together. But there had probably never been any real possibility that any of us could have stayed peaceably on these islands for very long.

The remainder of the summer of 1976 was bittersweet. The beaches and the surf were as inviting as ever and on sunny days when all was well I sometimes asked myself why we had decided to leave. One final incident made it easier for me to live with our decision.

The short, gravel road on which we lived had been given an official name on a highway sign that year: Chemin Anglais. All of us along the road did speak English with the exception of Raoul, Norma's boyfriend. Yet to me that sign set us apart from the larger community, almost as if we were a ghetto or an Indian reserve. Then we discovered the municipality planned to pave our road, thereby making it all the faster for yahoos to speed down to the beach at the foot of the Warrens' property, where they could sit in their cars drinking beer, throw the empty bottles at rocks, piss in the sand, or practise their marksmanship on passing terns and gulls.

There were only five households along the road and none of us wanted the road paved. Arnold and Farley attended a meeting of the Grande Entrée Council to say we all preferred a gravel road and to point out that the council could save money by leaving Chemin Anglais the way it was.

A couple of days later Arnold answered his phone to an anonymous male caller. "Eef you do not stay out of des affairs of Grande Entrée we will burn your 'ouse to de snow. An' tell Meester Mowat de same."

Perhaps it was merely because we were resisting pavement—the holy grail of rural Canada—rather than the fact we were Anglais; but whichever way the threat was interpreted, the effect was equally disturbing.

In August I picked my final batch of wild strawberries and put up a dozen bottles of the world's most delicious strawberry jam. I always gave one to Angus for Christmas for he much appreciated the intense flavour of the jam and my painstaking effort at picking the tiny berries. The rest Farley and I would eat ourselves, remembering the good and bad times, and how abundantly the strawberries grew on the grassy hill in the place we had once called home.

Chapter Thirty-one

IN THE SPRING OF 1977 the Trudeaus' marriage came to an end. There had been rumours of trouble between Pierre and Margaret for a couple of years but I had dismissed these as malicious gossip. That marriage, I had so wanted to believe, was made in Heaven. Perhaps it had been at the outset— something like our initial infatuation with the Magdalen Islands. In both cases the honeymoon didn't last.

In March photographs of Margaret appeared in the newspapers and on the cover of *Maclean's* magazine: a cigarette in her hand and a defiant smile on her lovely face as she stood alongside Mick Jagger of the Rolling Stones. She had been hanging out at a rock concert in Toronto while her husband and three small children remained in Ottawa. I didn't like to think about their reactions or why she would indulge herself in such a blatant demonstration of indifference to what the public might think of her. I knew what my reaction was: one more shattered illusion. That year I gave up believing in fairy tales.

During the winter Angus Mowat was diagnosed with lung cancer. Radiation treatment seemed to have brought it under control and for a time he was not considered to be in any immediate danger. We visited him frequently at Northport and found him cheerful and active and looking forward to sailing in the summer in his lovingly restored boat. Barbara, feeling vulnerable, stopped taking swipes at us and, for a change, seemed friendly and uncritical.

We did not leave for the Maritimes until July and when we did it was towing our Cygnet trailer, which had been on loan to the Schreyers for three years. It came back into our lives after Farley and Sandy Mowat and Max Braithwaite drove out to Manitoba to retrieve it. Now Farley and I were towing it to our new home, The Brickery, in Richmond County, Cape Breton Island.

The Morrisons had meantime found themselves a modern house on Highway 4 and had moved out, leaving us with a large, very empty house.

Sandy Mowat, Farley Mowat and Angus Mowat, Northport, Ontario, 1975

The prospect of renting a truck and driving out to the Magdalens to collect our furniture was dismaying because in midsummer the line-up for the ferry between Souris and the Magdalens could be three days long. We decided to wait until fall to make that journey.

Meanwhile our little caravan would provide us with a place to sleep, a tiny kitchen, and a cozy haven to sit out rainstorms. The empty house provided us with a bathroom, a kitchen sink, and a telephone.

It was fun living so minimally. Neither of us was attempting any serious writing that summer so we had lots of time to explore our new property with its thick forest, a mile of stony beaches and even its own little offshore island. We also had time to get acquainted with some of our neighbours, notably three generations of the Touesnard family, who lived along the winding Grand Gully Road. Most of the people in our community were of Acadian descent, essentially the same ethnicity as the French-speaking people of the Magdalens. But here there was a major difference: they only spoke

French at home among themselves, a private language they did not expect strangers to use. To us, and to the world around them, they spoke English.

Everywhere we went we encountered friendly, welcoming people. At the end of July we were invited to the wedding of Ervin Touesnard and Janice Stone—even though they had only known us for three weeks. I took this as a good omen.

In September we finally headed back to the Magdalens to pick up our household furnishings. We had arranged with the newlyweds, Ervin and Janice, that once we had finished the packing there we would phone them and they would drive over with a rented truck. Like a lot of Maritimers, they were curious to see these faraway islands.

Vi and Arnold welcomed us back to Grande Entrée with hospitality and help. We learned from them that our home had been broken into again, this time by some young campers from Montreal who, evidently realizing from books, posters, and photos that they were in the home of Farley Mowat, left him a note thanking him for the use of the place and apologizing for having broken a window to get in. They had also used the toilet but, with the water turned off, it wouldn't flush. At least they were more courteous than the local break-and-enter squad. Vi had cleaned up the mess in the bathroom and Arnold had nailed a board over the broken window. At that point I no longer cared who had been in the house. We were only there to pack up and leave.

Two days later Vi came knocking on our door at 6:00 a.m. We had given the Warrens' phone number to Farley's aunt, Fran Thomson (who was by then also his secretary) in case anyone needed to reach us. Vi told us Farley's brother, John, had called to say that Angus had died during the night and his funeral was to be held tomorrow.

We had to make some very fast arrangements. There was a scheduled flight from the Magdalens to Charlottetown at eight every morning. Could they find space for us? After that could we get seats on a flight from Charlottetown to Montreal? And after that a flight to Toronto? Could John Mowat meet us at the airport?

"You two get dressed," said Vi briskly. "I'll get things moving."

She hurried back to her phone and half an hour later returned to report, "You're on, all the way to Toronto. Arnold's got breakfast ready. I'll drive you to the airport."

John Mowat met us at Toronto airport and drove us to Angus and Barbara's house at Northport, two hours away. Though John was deeply shaken by Angus's death, he didn't say much until we were well on our way.

"It was pneumonia that killed him. She must have known he was going."

Barbara seemed surprised and not the least bit pleased to see us. Against the odds, we had managed to get there in time for Angus's funeral, which she had clearly intended would take place before we could arrive. We discovered there was to be no service of any kind. The undertaker would simply drive the coffin to a small cemetery a few miles down the road from Northport, where it would be lowered into the grave in the presence of a handful of neighbours. Angus Mowat was to be buried with as scant a ceremony as would attend the funeral of a dog.

We stayed at the Northport house only long enough to have a polite cup of tea and after that Farley, John, and I drove to Picton to find a motel and a restaurant. We also went to the funeral home to see if we could arrange to augment this meagre burial that was to take place just thirty-six hours after Angus's death.

The undertaker listened patiently as Farley outlined his father's life and how he deserved a better send-off than the one Barbara had arranged. Angus was a war veteran and as such should at least be given a last salute by a colour party—but the Hastings and Prince Edward Regiment, to which he had belonged, had not even been notified of his death.

My most lasting memory of Angus was how he had done everything with a flourish. I remembered how he always wore his kilt when there were guests for dinner, the silver buckle on his belt freshly shined for the occasion. We could not imagine that this mean little funeral would be what he would have wanted. Barbara, for whatever reasons of her own, had arranged to bury this man who loved ceremony as unceremoniously as possible.

"I am sorry. Those are the family's wishes," the undertaker said apologetically. "I cannot alter them." No doubt he had been through this sort of thing before. One member of a family makes funeral arrangements that the others don't like. This man must have known Barbara wasn't going to change her plan.

Late that night, after many phone calls, Farley managed to contact the commanding officer of the Hastings and Prince Edward Regiment. He was sympathetic and shared our concern, but there was no time to assemble a colour party unless the funeral could be postponed for another day. He would, however, do his best to find a piper.

He was as good as his word. The next day the skirl of the bagpipes contributed to our overwhelming sense of loss as six men carried the coffin from the hearse to the grave. By then Sandy Mowat had joined us. So had Mary Mowat and her husband, as well as three or four of Angus's other relatives. The poet Al Purdy and his wife, Yurith, who lived nearby were also present. Farley asked Al to say a few words in memory of Angus. Al did so—but I believe he was as ill at ease as the rest of us were, witnessing this drab farewell to such a vibrant man.

No doubt there are other funerals like this one where family members who can barely tolerate one another end up standing side by side around the grave; but this was the first time I had experienced such an occasion. It made me uncomfortable as well as sad. A funeral for someone at the end of a long life should have an element of gladness in it, some joy at having known that person and being there to celebrate that life. I was not glad in my heart that day.

Farley, with a masculine reaction to this pauper's funeral for his father, was even more sorrowful than I was. But he was also angry—angry that Barbara, for her own convoluted reasons, had organized this hasty departure, and even angrier that she had generated so much conflict in our family and that Angus had simply stepped aside and let her do it.

John drove us back to our Port Hope house, where Farley and I remained for a few downcast days. One evening we invited Farley's mother to join us for supper and an evening by the fire. Helen, as ever, wanted to talk about Angus and about the life they had shared long ago.

It turned out to be one of the uncanniest evenings I can remember. The wind was roaring as a late-September gale swept over us. We had just settled down in front of the fire when the power failed and the lights went out. I retrieved some candles from the dining room buffet, stuck them in a candelabra, and walked slowly back into the dark living room, looking, I suspect, something like a character in an old British film about Jane Eyre.

A few minutes later a sudden harsh gust of wind brought down a branch from the giant gingko tree next door and it struck our window with a heavy thud and cracked a pane of glass. All through that evening the wind continued to moan while we sat in the semi-darkness remembering Angus.

That spooky evening somehow seemed a more fitting farewell to this man we had loved than his funeral had been. It was as if he personally had caused the electricity to fail, the wind to howl, and the tree branch to crack the window.

We had to get quickly back to the Maritimes, where we now owned two houses—one we were moving out of and another we were moving into. We had left one of our dogs, Lily, in a kennel in Cape Breton because she was in heat. Our other dog, Edward, was staying with the Warrens in the Magdalens. That fall I hardly knew where I lived.

It was something of a relief to return to the Magdalens, where the bitter taste of losing Angus wasn't so acute. On our first afternoon I took Edward to the beach for a long walk. It was early October by then and the day was cool and breezy. There wasn't another soul on the beach. In a burst of pent-up energy I started to run along the cold, hard sand with the dog at my heels. And then inexplicably I started to scream. "God!" I cried, "I'll never see that woman again! Never! Ever!" I hollered over and over until I ran out of breath. Never again would I have to put up with Barbara's cunning nastiness. Finally she was out of my life.

The next morning I knew I was ill. My throat was sore. My nose was running. I felt hot and miserable. The turmoil and the exhaustion of the past weeks had caught up with me. There was nothing for it but to take to my bed until I was well enough to tackle the final packing and closing of this house.

I felt isolated from the world. We had already removed our radio, and cancelled the telephone and the mail delivery. Our books were packed in boxes. Our first-aid kit was also packed away somewhere and I couldn't find a thermometer to check how high my temperature was. As well, we had cleared everything out of our freezer the previous fall so the usual supply of casseroles and other food I kept for emergencies wasn't there any more.

Farley wasn't feeling very well either but with Vi and Arnold's help we managed. Vi brought us groceries and our few phone messages and, from the radio news, told us what was going on in the world. Arnold always baked his own bread and made his own wine, and he supplied us with both. Then there were the potatoes. When we had left a year earlier we had urged Stuart Richards to use our garden in the spring. It was a plot of rich earth Farley had built up over several years and he hated to think of it going to waste. Stuart had planted one crop only: potatoes; and he had left hundreds of them still in the ground. We had crated our garden tools but Farley managed to dig a few potatoes every day using a large kitchen spoon.

For a week I lay in bed coughing and feeling rotten, until I was finally able to be up—just as Farley succumbed to the same virus. I took over, digging our daily potatoes and putting together simple meals from the dwindling supply of canned goods still in the house. Edward and I took a walk each day as the gales of October spurred the ocean to ever-greater frenzy. I did not scream and yell any more. Some sort of peace had settled on me.

Our house was eerily quiet, except for the fits of coughing that plagued us both. During my week in bed I had worked my way through a long book that I found at the top of one of the cartons. I had always intended to read it but had never found the time. It was *Black Lamb and Grey Falcon* by Rebecca West, a thousand-page epic from the 1930s recounting the author's extensive travels in the Balkans. It was the sort of book that Angus Mowat would have approved of, something published forty years earlier that had stood the test of time. I felt sad that I couldn't tell him that I was reading it.

Vi came over one day to tell Farley that someone had phoned from Winnipeg and asked him to call back. There was a provincial election in Manitoba that October and it looked as if Ed Schreyer's New Democrats might lose. The campaign manager wanted Farley to come to Manitoba right away and lend a hand, as he had done during the election of 1973.

He was too sick to go. We wondered, in fact, if and when we were going to be able to complete our move to Cape Breton. By late October the Magdalen ferry service became intermittent as the Gulf of St. Lawrence grew more and more stormy. It would be possible to get a rented truck over to the islands from Nova Scotia, but we could then be stranded for a week waiting for favourable weather in order to leave. We decided to abandon the attempt and phoned our friend Ervin Touesnard in Cape Breton to tell him not to come.

When we finally felt well enough to travel we loaded our Volvo wagon to the hilt and departed. We managed to get in a table (upside down), a couple of collapsible chairs, two typewriters, some saucepans, a set of sheets and towels, a small carpet, and a few assorted treasures like the walrus skulls.

There was a lull between the storms so the ferry was able to sail to Souris. From there we drove across Canada's smallest province to the next car ferry—from Wood Island, PEI, to Pictou, Nova Scotia—and finally made a highway journey to the Canso Causeway and eventually to our new home in Cape Breton Island.

A second phone call had come from Ed Schreyer's office just before we left. The New Democrats had lost the Manitoba election and Ed was no longer premier. Somehow it didn't surprise me. For a lot of us this had been a season of losses, a time of endings.

But endings lead to beginnings. There were tears the morning we drove away from that house in Grande Entrée I had loved and nurtured. We had given it our best but there is a time to cut your losses. We were moving on.

Epilogue

ARNOLD AND VI WARREN continued to live at Grande Entrée for another three years, then returned to Ontario to settle in the village of Colborne.

Joan and Stuart Richards moved to New Carlisle on the Gaspé coast, where Stuart became the regional director of adult education and Joan became an activist with the Alliance Quebec, an advocacy organization that works to protect the rights of the English-speaking minority in Quebec.

A year after his defeat in Manitoba Ed Schreyer was named Governor General of Canada. The appointment surprised everyone, including him. Once the family moved to Ottawa we saw them a good deal more often than we had when they lived in Winnipeg.

Pierre Trudeau carried on as a single parent of three boys. He lost the election of 1979 but regained power in 1980, and finally retired as prime minister in 1984. Margaret Trudeau married a second time and bore two more children.

Marian Engel completed her book *The Islands of Canada* and also finished her novel *Bear*, which won the Governor General's Award for Fiction in 1976. Marian wrote seven novels altogether before her untimely death from cancer in 1985, when she was only fifty-one.

Home Rule was established in Greenland in 1979, a lot sooner than the former governor would have liked. All place names that had originally been Danish were changed to Inuktitut names. Even the country itself is now named Kalaallit Nunaat, although the rest of the world continues to refer to it as Greenland.

We never did see Barbara Hutchinson again. Barbara died in 1993 from an asthma attack at the age of sixty-six.

The book over which I had laboured for so long, and whose merits I had doubted, was published in 1983. *The Outport People* sold very well and got some great reviews.

And the house at The Brickery? We're still there and more in love with it, and Cape Breton, every year. But that is another story.

My thanks to Mary Talbot, for her careful scrutiny of everything I write; to Meg Taylor, for her finely honed editorial skills; to Anna Porter, who waited patiently for this book to be finished; to Robin Long, who provided me with a place to work. A special thank you to Farley, who shared these adventures, and to the good people of Old Harry, Grande Entrée, and Leslie/Grosse Île.

AUTHOR'S NOTE

The names of some of the people in this story have been changes to protect their identity.